THE ULTIMATE
CLASSIC CAR
BOOK

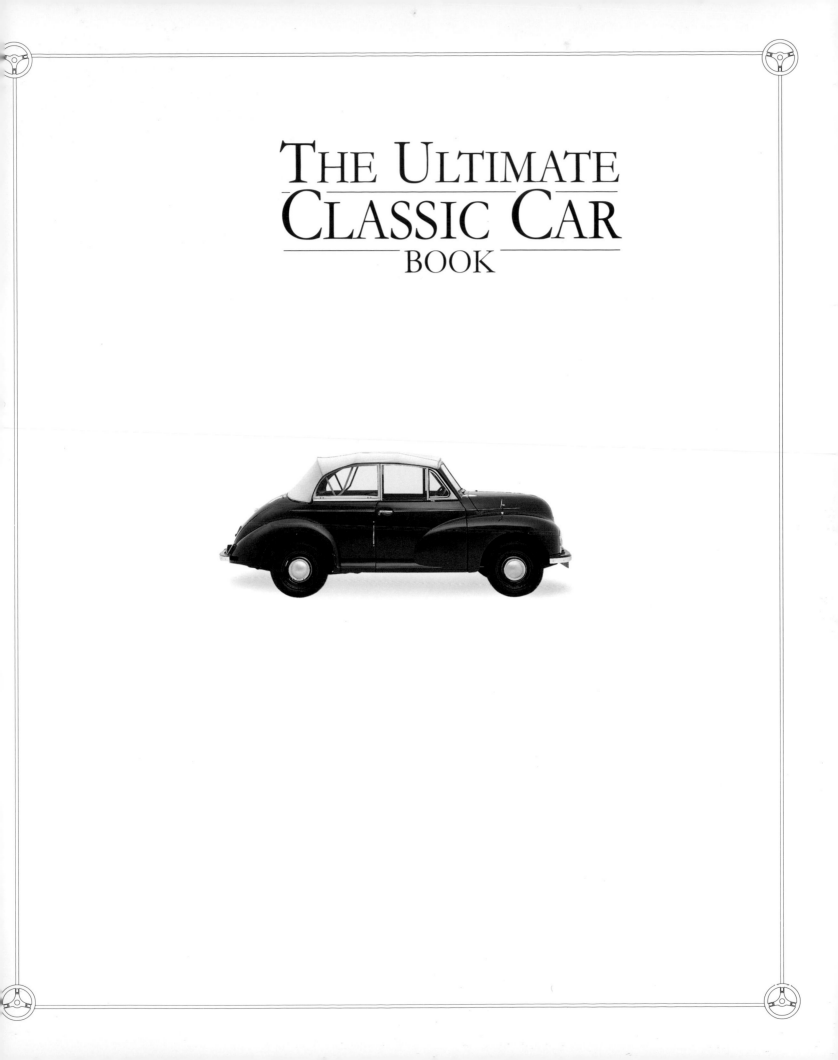

THE ULTIMATE CLASSIC CAR
BOOK

Quentin Willson
with David Selby

DORLING KINDERSLEY
LONDON • NEW YORK • SYDNEY • MOSCOW

A DORLING KINDERSLEY BOOK

www.dk.com

PROJECT EDITOR
PHIL HUNT

ART EDITOR
KEVIN RYAN

DESIGNERS
WENDY BARTLET, LUISE ROBERTS

MANAGING EDITOR
KRYSTYNA MAYER

MANAGING ART EDITOR
DEREK COOMBES

DTP DESIGNER
CRESSIDA JOYCE

PRODUCTION CONTROLLER
ADRIAN GATHERCOLE

PHOTOGRAPHY
ANDY CRAWFORD, MATTHEW WARD

•

First published in Great Britain in 1995
by Dorling Kindersley Limited,
9 Henrietta Street, London WC2E 8PS

A CIP catalogue record for this book is available
from the British Library

ISBN 0-7513-1832-9
Colour reproduced by Colourscan, Singapore
Printed and bound by
C & C Offset Printing Co., Ltd, Hong Kong

•

NOTE ON SPECIFICATION BOXES
Every effort has been made to ensure that the information
supplied in the specification boxes is accurate. As a rule,
engine capacity is measured in cubic inches (cid) for American cars
and cubic centimetres (cc) for all other cars.
A.F.C. is an abbreviation for average fuel consumption.

CONTENTS

AUTHOR'S FOREWORD   7

INTRODUCTION

THE CLASSIC CAR GALLERY

AUTHOR'S FOREWORD

Between these pages you'll find ninety of what are loosely termed classic cars – a catholic collection of some of the most fascinating motoring confections spanning four decades. There's no particular order or hierarchy, no attempt at a definitive roll of honour. This is a selection of curious cars, products of another age that remind us of the way we were. The biggest problem I've had in compiling this book is deciding which cars should go in and which shouldn't. Not an easy job. Only a fool would argue that a Facel Vega HK500 is a better car than a Mk II Jaguar. It isn't. But the Facel, with its gloriously eccentric Gallic styling, is the more interesting of the two. And that's why it's here and the Jag isn't. Degas once said that people should be full of those charming little idiosyncrasies without which there is no life. I think it's the same with cars. We prefer them to be interesting, diverting, beguiling even. Classic cars didn't exist before we invented them – a knee-jerk reaction to all that soulless modern metal that looks like it's been carved from a solid block of tungsten. In today's car, efficiency has supplanted aesthetics and technology has displaced charm. Our affair with old cars is purely emotional, fiercely partisan, terminally subjective and completely without logic or order. And that's why nobody can define exactly what a classic car is. We've been trying for twenty years and still no-one's even come close. The best I can do is to say that a classic car makes you smile when you look at it, grin when you drive it and feel warm approval for the era it evokes. Old cars are thundering good fun.

Quentin Willson

Why Classic?

CLASSIC CARS are simply nostalgia triggers. They're a reminder of how we used to be. Of all the material symbols in society that define our worth and position the motor car is the most powerful. It's tangible, mobile and a currency everybody understands. Many of us have an uneasiness with modernity that makes us retrospective creatures. We're drawn back to those decades of change and excitement – hence our love affair with all things of the Fifties and Sixties. From tall, round-shouldered Frigidaires, neon diner signs, and flamboyant Wurlitzer jukeboxes to sunglasses, clothes and music, they all appeal to us as talismans of what we remember as golden years.

VEHICLES FOR NOSTALGIA
Classic cars like this AC Ace are not simply quaint mechanical objects, but social monuments that remind us of the way we were.

surely a need to recreate fond memories. We grew up with old cars, went on holiday in them, were ferried to and from school, saw them in movies and on TV and idolized our role models who drove them. They're as much a part of our consciousness as Elvis Presley, mini skirts, Kennedy, Lee Harvey Oswald, Korea, Vietnam, Woodstock and Jimi Hendrix. It's not surprising that Sixties classics are proving the most popular of all. We take one look at an Edsel or a Chevy Impala and realize that the world will never be the same again. Apart from being able to drive them every day (and keep up with modern traffic) they were the cars many of us promised ourselves as children, nose stuck to the showroom window thinking "some day, some way".

Part of our Past

And what better transport of delight than the period motor car? The act of buying an old car demonstrates a subliminal desire to revisit our youth. We may say we've bought a beautiful inanimate object in need of restoration, rejuvenation and preservation, but one of the prime motivations is

Decades of Change

And we're doing it again with the Eighties, another decade of upheaval. Already cars like the Mk I Golf GTi, Saab Turbo, Audi Quattro, Jaguar XJS and Lancia Delta Integrale are being hailed as emergent classics. We feel the growing urge to cherish them as social sculptures, monuments to a faded lifestyle. Previous generations initiated the preservation of buildings, music, paintings and literature. As New-Age technological sophisticates, we are now choosing to cherish fine examples of the man-made objects which have become such a dominant feature of our twentieth century past – the motor car. Perhaps this love affair is all about a need for simplicity, a suppression of reality. Modern life can be unromantic and modern motor cars are mostly clinical, complex things. Who with a soul could not be moved by the wholesome innocence of an MGA or a Frogeye

POST-WAR STYLING
Cars like the flamboyant Edsel are empirical proof that post-war America really was like Hollywood told us. Their baroque styling shows everything that was right, or indeed wrong, with the swansong years of the most powerful nation on earth.

Sprite? With their quaint buttons and switches, dainty gauges, spoked wheels and hectic styling, they exude an eccentric charm which has no modern day equivalent.

THE RETRO LOOK
The modern Mazda MX-5 is a lookalike 1960s Lotus Elan that trades heavily on our fascination for retro styling.

And if you want to know exactly how deeply classic cars have penetrated the suburban psyche, look at a new movement evolving from the car designer's drawing board. For years car manufacturers thought we wanted the last word in sanitized efficiency. They tried to banish every sensation of noise and movement, sought to purge the motor car of every tremor and vibration. Yet our worship of yesterday's technology, the fact that we actually like an engine note that sounds like someone tearing sheets, that we want our instruments to look like instruments and not LCD computer readouts means that really, if we're honest, we don't want perfection. We want our cars to have personality. When Mazda designed their MX-5 sports car they spent months trying to reproduce the authentic rasping exhaust note of a Sixties sports car. They wanted to recreate the past with modern engineering.

Consumer Durables

Already there's a detectable movement away from the efficiency and order of modern metal. Most people, if they had the choice, would really prefer something more separate. Our punishment for buying all those blameless, zero-defect cars is a plague of bland models with all the passion of a dishwasher. Our obsession with control has made cars look and feel like consumer durables, labour-saving devices to be parked a short step away from the microwave. Mass-produced for mass appeal, they lack sexuality, emotion and excitement. But some car manufacturers have

recognized the fashion for old cars for what it is – a consumer's *cri de coeur*. They've realized that so much retrospective admiration has a point – people prefer cars to look like cars. Jaguar have made their new models look so much like their old ones, because they know that the Sir William Lyons tradition of swooping curves and chromium grins is actually what people want, and to lose that stylistic bloodline would turn their products into pale facsimiles.

The retro look, they say, is back. Witness the latest crop of sports cars with cowelled headlamps, rakish lines, white dials and badges in flowing chromium script. Bristling with antique styling cues, they're all part of a new wave of cars deliberately sculpted to tap into the vogue for nostalgia. And the classic effect has even touched the odd mainstream motor. Major manufacturers are considering it necessary to add the occasional flourish of old world dignity with wood and hide interiors and chrome radiator grilles. For all its self-indulgent enthusiasm, the old car movement has had a greater effect than you might think and has influenced the way multinational car makers style their products. It's taken a couple of decades, but now the motor mandarins have got the message. If a large body of people, faced with buying a shiny new saloon or an elderly Austin-Healey, choose the Healey, then it means that classic cars are here to stay.

CLASSIC GLAMOUR
Jaguar boss Sir William Lyons hands over an XK120 to Clark Gable. With period visions like this dripping with Fifties' glamour, how could classic cars fail to capture the popular imagination?

The Classic Car Phenomenon

THIRTY YEARS AGO, the classic car hadn't been invented. There were "old cars", which were the province of the lunatic fringe, fêted and lionized by blokes with twigs in their beards and oil under their fingernails. Before this, during the Fifties, vintage and veteran cars had been quietly preened and polished by an insular group of car buffs. In England, clubs like the Vintage Sports Car Club and the Historic Sports Car Club laid down the ground rules. Pre-1919 cars were Edwardian, pre-1931 Vintage and a handful of models produced up to the beginning of the Second World War were loosely named Post-Vintage Thoroughbreds. The icons then were machines like the Bugatti Type 35, Eight Litre Bentley, Duesenberg, Auburn and Hispano Suiza. These were the Chippendales and Sheratons of an arcane catalogue of motorized antiques.

Sixties Sports Cars

Then came the Sixties, when Britain invaded the rest of the world with a new secret weapon – the sports car. These were the heady days of the E-Type, MGB, Austin-Healey and Triumph TR. Roads without speed limits opened up a whole new fantasy world of power, sexuality and image. Mass production brought catwalk looks and hard-charging performance to the ordinary motorist. America came

VETERAN VERSUS CLASSIC
Veteran and vintage cars have never had the mass appeal of Fifties' and Sixties' boomer classics. These dignified Edwardians are expensive, need constant tinkering, and can be a liability in modern traffic. More importantly, they are too old to be part of most people's childhood memories and are just museum pieces.

EYE OF THE BEHOLDER
This 1935 Lagonda Rapide might look a million dollars, but most old car fanciers get more excited over a '60s Jaguar E-Type.

OSU 887

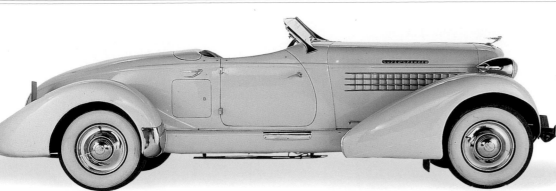

up with the "muscle car" – Mustangs, Corvettes, Chargers, 'Cudas and Firebirds. It was motoring's most exciting decade, when a generation let its motoring imagination run riot. But one day the humourless legislators slapped on mandatory speed restrictions, asphyxiating engine power outputs with sweeping emission regulations. The motor car, they insisted, was getting too big for its boots.

Seventies Kitsch

Their legacy was the motor-history of the Seventies, a decade of kitsch that spawned machines like the gawky Triumph TR7, the rubber-bumpered MGB, the emasculated Mustangs, the pot-bellied V12 E-Type, the truncated Cadillac Seville and the unlovely Rolls-Royce Camargue. Mainstream cars were even worse. Who will ever forget the Austin Allegro,

Morris Marina, Vauxhall Ventora, Chrysler 180, Peugeot 604, Datsun Skyline, Volkswagen K70 or AMC Pacer? Truly awful cars painted in violent hues, laden with safety devices and strangled by emission pipery. In desperation, enthusiasts looked backward and found that there was a cornucopia of interesting secondhand motors that could be bought for a fraction of the price of new ones. XK Jaguars, MG TFs, Aston Martins and Sixties' Maseratis and Ferraris could be bought for the price of a two-year-old Ford. £3,000 was all it took to buy a Ferrari Lusso, £3,500 bought a Dino 246, and forking out £5,000 meant you drove home a genuine AC Cobra.

Cars with Attitude

In October 1973, a British magazine appeared called *Classic Cars*, its alliterative title coining a badly needed generic term. From then on these old cars with attitude became affectionately known as classics, giving a new name to a hobby that in just ten years would mushroom into a multibillion pound industry. By 1982, interest in old cars had increased dramatically and the price of an E-Type had risen from £1,000 to around £5,000, Dinos sold for £10,000, and Ferrari Lusso adverts were followed by the ominous phrase – Price on Application. Classic cars had become fashion accessories.

SIXTIES CLASSIC
This Ferrari Lusso is the most admired car on the page because it's neat, modern-looking, easy to drive, and summons up the glamorous Sixties.

ANOTHER WORLD

This 1933 Duesenberg SJ Speedster is serious collector's stuff and so far removed from most people's sphere of reference that it has assumed the status, not to mention the price tag, of fine art. Cars like this have become the province of the very well-heeled — mothballed in heated motor houses or exhibited as rarefied automotive antiques.

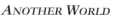

MAGAZINE COVERAGE

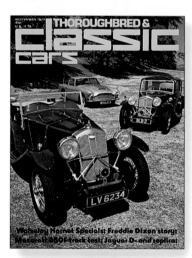

Classic Cars, *the magazine that really started it all, first appeared in October, 1973, and kick-started a motoring revolution — giving voice to a growing disenchantment with modern motors.*

ENGLISH TOURER

This 1934 Bentley 3-litre may be the quintessential pre-war English touring car, but, given the choice of a weekend with the Bentley or the Ferrari Testarossa, which would you choose?

Greatness was suddenly thrust upon old cars. Demand for classics was so huge that values exploded. The real price rises began in '83 when Ronald Reagan gave the American public tax cuts. Within months, Americans came to the UK, lavishing their new found affluence on "collectable" cars, accelerating an unbelievable price spiral in the process. In England interest rates had fallen, house values soared, and corporate profits were up. The taxman hadn't even dreamt about taxing the capital gain on classic cars, so opportunist speculators moved in. The smart money poured out of the world's stock markets into "investment cars", graphs of appreciation were plotted, and syndicates laid down old motors like fine wine.

1984 saw the first of many banner headlines proclaiming the highest price ever paid for a classic. Sotheby's sold the ex-Woolf Bernato "Blue

FERRARI TESTAROSSA
The Testarossa is exciting because it comes from an exciting decade – the 1980s. Many of the world's most admired classics reflect times of social change and upheaval.

Train" Speed Six Bentley for a jaw-dropping £246,000 – awesome at the time but a fraction of the amounts that were to be bandied about in the next four years. Dealers, some of whom had quietly become large and very profitable corporations, crammed the pages of the classic car press with "gilt-edged investments" and "appreciating assets". Restoration firms and parts suppliers flourished, owners clubs grew, and historic racing boomed. Messing about with old cars had become big business.

Market Mayhem

By 1986 things started to go berserk. Prices went up by the month, propelled by a seemingly insatiable demand tearing away at a dwindling supply. Auction records were made and broken in the same month. An American Duesenberg sold for the magic US$1 million, becoming the new highest amount paid for a motor car at auction. Within eight months a Bugatti Royale sold for US$6.5 million, changing hands again only three months later for a staggering US$8.1 million. The press fanned the flames with more hype and headlines, and in 1987 the sale of a Bugatti Royale Kellner took the market's breath away by selling at Christie's for an absurd £5.5 million. With the vintage greats out of reach for all but multimillionaires, other lesser cars were suddenly catapulted to stardom. Investors cast round for other sources of capital gain, and word spread that Ferraris had what it took, so up went their value. The Daytona that might have sold for £4,000 in 1973 had an asking price of £190,000 by 1988. GTOs and 250 Testarossas hit the million mark

and rumours were rife of a 330 P4 selling privately for over £5 million. Even the modern Ferrari Testarossa – a brand new car with a list price of £90,000 – was being advertised at £200,000. Then the value of Aston Martins exploded with DB5s and DB6s soaring from £12,000 in '87 to a peak of £70,000 by '89. The domino effect dragged up Maserati values, which in turn invigorated E-Type prices, and so it went on. By the peak in 1989, the once £1,000 3.8 E-Type was homing in on £40,000.

As the supply of cheap classics in the UK evaporated, the classic car trade turned to America, South Africa and New Zealand as a rich vein of rust-free Sixties sports cars. Thousands of left-hand drive MGs, TRs and Jaguars filtered onto the world's markets – some of them not so rust-free. The small ads were crammed with cars advertised by owners and dealers out to turn a profit. Classic car auctions were held every week and more and more classic car magazines lined the newsstands. But suddenly the market started to creak. In 1989, there was a worldwide recession. Interest rates rose and borrowing money became expensive. There was a retail slowdown, cash was tight and the old car market spluttered and stopped. Demand died almost overnight and cars weren't selling.

BUGATTI LEGEND
Bugatti is still one of the world's most evocative and romantic car badges, but unfortunately accessible only to the privileged few.

CAR AUCTIONS
The first classic car auctions, like this one held in England by Sotheby's in 1982, were rather charming, ingenuous affairs. These days, old car sales are hi-tech, with satellite link-ups, multinational bidders, and glossy four-colour magazines.

Prices fell, slowly at first, but by 1990 grass roots enthusiasts who had jumped on the bandwagon too late unloaded their cars in desperation to the highest bidder. Distress sales were common and prices hit the floor. The value of an Aston Martin DB6 that had pole-vaulted to £70,000 plunged to £25,000. The £40,000 E-Type Roadster swallow-dived to £20,000, and the Ferrari F40 that was hyped to nearly a million in '88 languished unsold with a price tag of £200,000.

In the late Eighties speculators jammed Jaguar's phone lines, desperate to put down

deposits on the new XJ220 at a whopping £415,000. They were sure it would double in value overnight, that it was the king of classics. They couldn't have been more wrong. When they took delivery – and many tried not to – it was too late. The market had crashed like a milk bottle falling on a stone doorstep. XJ220s wouldn't even return their list price, let alone make a profit. One desperate owner put a delivery mileage example through an English auction house only to watch it struggle to make £150,000 – net loss £265,000. For a while classic cars had fired the world's imagination as recreational money-spinners. Prices had been inflated by market stimulation and, if we're honest, by pure greed. Owners of classics had seen similar cars advertised at madder and madder money and priced theirs accordingly. The less scrupulous auctioneers had invented non-existent high bids to further boost values and dealers had done what they always do – slapped a couple of thousand more on the screen.

The Emperor's New Clothes

Was it all just sound and fury signifying nothing, a momentary derangement of the mass imagination, or were classic cars really "investments" that would have gone on increasing in value but for a badly timed recession? Certainly there was an awful lot of schlock talked with naive enthusiasm and dubious authority, and here the classic press must shoulder some of the blame for deifying old cars indiscriminately. What started as an innocent and enthusiastic hobby went totally out of control. No enthusiast would deny that a Ferrari Daytona is worthy of

JAGUAR E-TYPE
The most romantic E-Type, the 3.8 Roadster, is probably one of the most lusted-after classics of all. Its appeal functions on many levels, but primarily as a direct link to the swinging Sixties. Most of today's E-Type buyers vividly remember its launch day in March, 1961, just as they recall the day JFK was assassinated.

preservation, but a Datsun Bluebird ? Surely not. Towards the end of the boom the earnest amateurs and dilettante buyers arrived and proceeded to hail some of the most appalling pieces of scrap ever to disgrace tarmac as desirable properties. Cars that should have been allowed to go the way of all flesh were often just cosmetically resurrected and unloaded on fond fools as collectors' items.

A Good Return?

As for the notion that an old car is a "good investment", there must be scores of old car buyers who now rue the day that they were taken in by the idea. Some cars have indeed appreciated above the rate of inflation and shown their owners handsome gains. But they're usually the rare, very expensive and highly desirable models rather than the less substantial mass-produced machines, which represent the bulk of the market. You could have bought a Jaguar 3.8 E-Type for £1,000 back in 1970. Today that car, in superlative condition, is worth around £23,000.

A thumping profit you might say – but don't forget inflation. Remember that £1,000 had quite a bit of purchasing power in 1970, and then consider that you'd have to add the cost of storing, insuring and keeping the thing immaculate for 25 years, and that's only if it never turned a wheel. Enjoy your investment and drive it about and you'll have to throw in petrol, oil, tyres, body restoration, servicing and more, by which time your paper profit turns into an actual loss. Shrewd and strict accounting says that you'd have been better sticking your money on deposit for 25 years and forgetting all about the Jag.

It is a sad but inescapable fact of life that to popularize is to debase. The concept of the classic car was adulterated beyond recognition by avarice, ignorance and misrepresentation. Profit overtook pleasure, misty-eyed idealists were duped into handing over handsome amounts for indifferent cars and, as with all mass markets, the lure of easy money attracted the less than upright. Chassis numbers were doctored, provenance was falsified and authenticity manufactured. Too many people jumped on the boat and it began to take on water. Glossy adverts appeared from Finance Companies, Banks, Insurers, Auctioneers and Car Brokers, all hungry for a piece of the action. They spoilt an innocent pastime by creating a bull market that wasn't mature enough to support itself.

The Wheel Turns Full Circle

Those knowledgeable car buffs who stood back and shook their heads now breathe a deep sigh of relief. The market mayhem is over and the bulk of old cars are no longer being talked of as investments or designer accessories. The cautious and learned enthusiast, who drew the world's attention to classic cars in the first place, has supplanted the opportunist speculator and now represents the only market force. Prices are down to affordable levels and cars are once more being bought for enjoyment. The classic car boom was undoubtedly a bad thing for everybody, but out of it has come some good. Many cars were lavishly restored and saved for posterity, we've all learnt a lasting lesson and the huge losses suffered must serve as an awful warning that such anarchy should never happen again.

THOSE WERE THE DAYS
Fifties' and Sixties' sports cars radiate nostalgic messages. This Triumph TR2 sales brochure evokes laurel wreaths, chequered flags, and bravado – a glamorous, innocent world when men were men, cars were cars, and the girl in the passenger seat always wore a headscarf and pearls.

How to Buy a Classic Car

ONLY A BRAVE MAN says he can accurately and honestly value a classic car. The old car market got the jitters because there was no established, thorough guide to the delicate business of accurate valuation. The pricing structure that exists is based on opinion and exaggeration. Traditional methods of collating historical auction prices along with publicly advertised prices all too often ignore the vital factor of condition. It isn't enough to take an auction figure and accept that price as a benchmark for similar models. And you can't base values on advertised prices where descriptions of condition are imprecise and prices optimistic. The classic car in question will have been subjected to many years of wear and deterioration. Age alone doesn't give it any value – it's the condition in which it has survived the ravages of time that really matters. So no two cars can ever be assumed to be in the same condition and command the same price.

Buyer Beware

All used cars are by definition flawed and defy accurate valuation. Modern cars are priced with the help of data from daily auctions, leasing companies, franchised dealers, used car dealers and fleet operators. Even with so much regular information available, values of modern cars are still unpredictable. So what hope for classic car values? The used car is a unique product – only a third is actually visible. The rest lies behind a

cosmetic skin, hidden from view unless dismantled. This is why documentation like service history, number of previous owners and accuracy of mileage are vital to help make an informed guess about a car's previous existence. With old cars the job is ten times more difficult. Most classics have had many owners, many resprays and covered hundreds of thousands of miles. Buyers have been conditioned to accept that documentation is not always necessary or available because it's been lost or obscured in the mists of time. Without documentary help you're left to judge a car's mechanical and bodily state by eye. Unless you're highly experienced or psychic, expensive mistakes can be made.

Only recently have old cars caught the public's imagination so the market is young and foolish. Demand propelled by emotion accelerated values, ignoring more down-to-earth considerations. The desire to own, at any price, sometimes obscures reason. Buyers entered the market without questioning the intrinsic value and condition of the cars they were buying. Only now has it become clear that the prices they paid were based, in most cases, on nothing more than hot air.

For enthusiasts to buy and enjoy old cars, the pivot on which the market hinges, they must be affordable and realistically priced. The market is heavy with bad cars dressed up as good, whether restored at exorbitant cost or not, which places a considerable premium on well kept, genuine and properly documented examples.

Classic Caveats

Honest, well maintained and unrestored cars are worth more than recent restorations. And don't ignore mileage or take it on trust. Find a car that has documentary evidence. Ignore statements like "mileage believed genuine". Make sure mileage is warranted in writing. Recognize the value of previous servicing bills and invoices. Choose a

CHASSIS CHECK
This DeLorean chassis plate can help establish the exact date of manufacture and the name of the first owner. Avoid cars with missing chassis plates.

classic with a history file. Remember that originality is all. Value carefully cars with colour changes, non-standard plastic instead of leather or replacement engines. Watch out for chassis and engine numbers that don't match, and go for a car with as few owners as possible.

Be fussy about detail. Don't tolerate anything that looks like it's just been tarted up. While you may not be bothered about originality and provenance, the next man who buys your car almost certainly will. Don't assume all classic car sellers and dealers are nice people. Rough cars and rough people sometimes go together, classic or not. If you're in any doubt about mechanical and bodily condition, have your potential purchase inspected by a qualified independent examiner.

The Desirability Factor

Old car values rely on desirability, which depends on their image and how much nostalgia they evoke. Some cars, even though identical in body shape, can be miles apart in value. A 1968 Jaguar 240 is the least valuable and desirable Jaguar Mk II. Why? The 240 has the smallest engine of the range and cheaper trim. 240s had slimline bumpers and plastic upholstery, which aren't as nostalgic as the broad-bladed bumpers and hide seats of the pre-'67 models.

Why is a 2 + 2 E-Type worth considerably less than a Series I 3.8 F.? The 2 + 2 was designed as a four-seater and looks ungainly with a higher roof line and steeper screen. It's slower too. The earliest 3.8s are romantic because they were the lightest, fastest and purest E-Types of them all, so they're the most sought after. The same is true of Series II E-Types. These had

PANHARD PL17
Garish mock tiger skin door-inserts might offend the untrained eye, but they are completely original and exactly the way they left the factory – making this PL17 a prince among Panhards. Unusual period weirdness is highly desirable.

CLASSIC WITHIN A CLASSIC
Not just every Jaguar Mk II is worth a mint. This one, a 240, might have wire wheels, but it also has slimline bumpers and plastic upholstery. Pre-67 Mk IIs had much more nostalgic broad-bladed bumpers and leather trim, and are worth more. The market prefers its old cars as traditional as possible.

open headlamps and bulky rear light clusters spoiling the smooth lines. Sounds silly – it's still an E-Type – but a mint Series II will always be worth less than a mint Series I. Why is a Frogeye Sprite worth more than a Mk II Sprite? Even though the later car has more creature comforts, is faster and has a boot that opens, the Frogeye is the most loved. Nostalgia wins again. The Frogeye looks cheeky and is the oldest and purest Sprite, so it's become a cult car.

And so it goes on, illogically and irrationally. And it's not always age that's the deciding factor either. The last of the Jensen Interceptors, the Series III, is worth more than the first Series I models simply because the later car is faster, better built and more refined. Unless you know which models have a fashionable image and high market profile, you can easily overvalue a car. Some cars have added value because of special coachbuilt or limited edition bodywork. A Harrington Sunbeam Alpine is worth 30 per cent more than a standard Alpine because of rarity. Rolls-Royce and Bentleys are another example. Hand-built and specialist coachwork conversions such as Hooper, James Young and Mulliner Park Ward are more coveted and therefore more valuable than standard steel cars.

WHY SO SPECIAL?
This early MGB is the most valuable of the marque because it has pressed disc wheels, rare pull door handles, and is finished in unusual but original Iris Blue.

Factory listed options can enhance an old car's value, whereas non-original after-market accessories can actually detract from the value. Power-assisted steering on Bentley S-Series and Rolls-Royce Silver Clouds is considered essential to their value. Cars without should be penalized by as much as 20 per cent. An automatic gearbox on an MGB or a Sunbeam Alpine, although a factory option, reduces the car's value because it spoils the sporting character and performance. Wire wheels are a period accessory and highly sought after. On an MGC they're essential, even though an option. On a 1970s Mercedes 350 SL, leather interior and air conditioning will boost the car's value by 30 per cent. But things like modern wing mirrors, spotlamps, glass sunroofs and non-standard alloy wheels ruin a car's originality and its period attraction.

Classic Car Auctions

Over the last few years the classic car auction has dominated the old car market as the most convenient way of buying a classic. Auctions, whether for old or modern cars, are dangerous places. You can't drive the car, have it inspected on ramps, or speak to the seller. Sometimes you can't even hear the engine running. So the risk of buying something which is not what it seems is huge. Many believe that the classic car auction is the best place to buy old cars – in fact it's the worst.

CAUTION REQUIRED
Classic car auctions are dangerous and expensive places where you cannot inspect or test-drive properly. Emotion and money make unhappy bedfellows and it's easy to get carried away in the heat of the moment.

Buying anything in a competitive and emotional environment without the time or opportunity to make a balanced decision is courting disaster. Add to this dubious practices like unrealistic reserves, invented bids, and a system which conceals the seller from the buyer and you begin to question the popularity of auctions. Often it's far wiser and cheaper to buy privately or from a dealer, where you have the leisure to ask questions, make a thorough inspection and drive the car at operating temperature. It's no coincidence that some of the highest prices achieved for classic cars have been at auction. The most important thing to remember is that unless the car is sold with a warranty, which is rarely the case, your rights at auction are few.

The Bottom Line

Buying a classic requires a steady hand. Reason, not emotion, must be your constant companion. Go at it blind, giddy with dewy-eyed sentimentality, and you'll rue the day you ever went near an old car. Practise a little temporary detachment, negotiate ruthlessly, and you'll buy a winner. And there's no better feeling than being a successful player in that sepia-tinted fantasy we call classic cars. They're a unique, innocent, and disarming form of amusement, fashionable, separate, and involving. Old cars have class.

Classic Car
GALLERY

·

Here are ninety of the world's most beguiling old motors. From the quaint and charming to the stridently flamboyant, they're just a small foretaste of the magic called classic cars.

AC *Ace-Bristol*

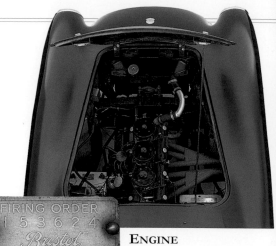

AGONISINGLY PRETTY, the AC Ace catapulted the homespun Thames Ditton company into the motoring limelight, instantly earning it a reputation as makers of svelte sports cars for the tweedy English middle classes. Timelessly elegant, swift, poised, and mechanically uncomplicated, the Ace went on to form the platform for the legendary AC Cobra *(see pages 22–23)*. Clothed in a light alloy body and powered by a choice of AC's own delicate UMB 2.0 unit, the hardier 2.0 Bristol 100D2 engine, or the lusty 2.6 Ford Zephyr power plant, the Ace drove as well as it looked.

Its shape has guaranteed the Ace a place in motoring annals. Chaste, uncluttered, and simple, it makes a Ferrari look top-heavy and clumsy. Purists argue that the Bristol-powered version is the real thoroughbred Ace, closest to its original inspiration, the Bristol-powered Tojeiro prototype of 1953.

ENGINE

Shared by the BMW 328, the hemi-head 125 bhp 2.0 Bristol engine was offered as a performance conversion for the Ace. With triple Solex carbs, push-rod overhead valve gear, a light alloy head, and cast-iron crankcase, the Ace was a club racer's dream.

STEERING WHEEL SHARED WITH THE AUSTIN HEALEY *(SEE PAGES 36–39)* AND THE DAIMLER SP DART *(SEE PAGES 78–81)*

HANDLING
Production cars used Bishop cam-and-gear steering, which gave a turning circle of 11 m (36 ft), and required just two deft turns of the steering wheel lock-to-lock.

INTERIOR
In pure British tradition, the Ace's cockpit was stark, with gauges and switches haphazardly pebble-dashed across the fascia.

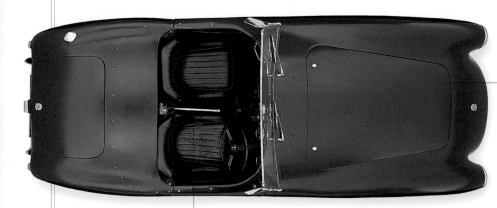

PROPORTION
Simplicity itself – a box for the engine, a box for the people, and a box for the luggage.

— OTHER MODELS —
Founded in 1902, AC was one of the longest established English motor makers, nicknamed "the Savile Row of motordom".

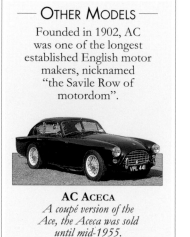

AC ACECA
A coupé version of the Ace, the Aceca was sold until mid-1955.

COOLING
The Ace's wide, toothy grin fed air into the large radiator that was shared by the AC two-litre saloon.

REAR VIEW
Later Aces had a revised rear deck, with square tail lamps and a bigger boot.

FOOT WARMER
For die-hards who always drove with the hood down, the tonneau cover kept your feet warm while your face froze.

AC ACE-BRISTOL

The most handsome British roadster of its day, and as lovely as an Alfa Romeo Giulietta Sprint, the Ace had an Italianate simplicity. Proof of the dictum that less is more, the Ace's gently sweeping profile is a triumph of form over function. Known as *Superleggera* construction, a network of steel tubes was covered by aluminium panels, based on the outline of the 1949 Ferrari 122. Engines were placed well back and gave an 18 per cent rearward bias to the weight distribution.

OWNER DRIVING
An Ace-Bristol recorded an average of 156 km/h (97 mph) over 3,781 km (2,350 miles) at the 1957 Le Mans 24 Hours, the fastest ever for a Bristol-engined car.

SIDESCREENS
Folding perspex sidescreens helped to prevent turbulence in the cockpit at speed.

BONNET CATCHES
Forward-hinged bonnet was locked by two chrome catches, opened by a small T-shaped key.

SPECIFICATIONS

MODEL AC Ace-Bristol (1956–61)
PRODUCTION 463
BODY STYLE Two-door, two-seater sports roadster.
CONSTRUCTION Space-frame chassis, light alloy body.
ENGINE Six-cylinder push-rod 1971cc.
POWER OUTPUT 105 bhp at 5000 rpm (optional high performance tune 125 bhp at 5750 rpm).
TRANSMISSION Four-speed manual Bristol gearbox (optional overdrive).
SUSPENSION Independent front and rear with transverse leaf spring and lower wishbones.
BRAKES Front and rear drums. Front discs from 1957.
MAXIMUM SPEED 188 km/h (117 mph)
0–60 MPH (0–96 KM/H) 9.1 sec
0–100 MPH (0–161 KM/H) 27.2 sec
A.F.C. 7.6 km/l (21.6 mpg)

BRAKES
Front disc brakes were an option in 1957 but later standardized.

AC *Cobra 427*

AN UNLIKELY ALLIANCE BETWEEN AC Cars, a traditional British car maker, and Carroll Shelby, a charismatic Texan racer, produced the legendary AC Cobra. AC's sports car, the Ace *(see pages 20–21)* was turned into the Cobra by shoe-horning in a series of American Ford V8s, starting with 4.2 and 4.7 Mustang engines. In 1965 Shelby, always a man to take things to the limit, squeezed in a thunderous 7-litre Ford engine, in an attempt to realize his dream of winning Le Mans. Although the 427 was not fast enough to win and failed to sell in any quantity, it was soon known as one of the most aggressive and romantic cars ever built.

GTM 777F at one time held the record as the world's fastest accelerating production car and in 1967 was driven by the British journalist John Bolster to record such Olympian figures as an all-out maximum of 265 km/h (165 mph) and a 0–60 (96 km/h) time of an unbelievable 4.2 seconds.

OTHER MODELS

AC Cars Limited began in 1922 and earned themselves a reputation as a maker of good-looking, hand-fettled, luxury sporting cars.

AC COBRA 289
Early Cobras had 260cid engines. Later cars were fitted with Mustang 289 V8s.

INTERIOR
The interior was kept stark and basic, with traditional 1960s British sports car features of black-on-white gauges, small bucket seats, and woodrim steering wheel. 427 owners were not interested in creature comforts, only raw power, great brakes, and wonderful suspension.

SPEEDY APPEAL
Even the "baby" 4.7 Cobras were good for 222 km/h (138 mph) and could squeal up to 60 mph (96 km/h) in under six seconds.

BODYWORK
The body was hand-rolled aluminium wrapped around a tubular steel frame, which proved very light yet extremely strong.

TYRES
Cobra tyres were always Goodyear as Shelby was a long-time dealer.

RADIATOR HEADER TANK KEPT THINGS COOL, HELPED BY TWIN ELECTRIC FANS

UNDER THE AIR CLEANER ARE TWO LARGE FOUR-BARREL CARBURETTORS

ENGINE
The mighty 7-litre 427 block had years of NASCAR (National Association of Stock Car Automobile Racing) racing success and easily punched out power for hours. The street version output ranged from 300 to 425 bhp. Competition and semi-competition versions with tweaked engines could exceed 500 bhp.

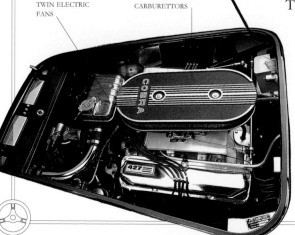

AC COBRA 427

The 427 looked fast standing still. Gone was the lithe beauty of the original Ace, replaced by bulbous front and rear arches, fat 19 cm (7½-in) wheels, and rubber wide enough to roll a cricket pitch. The chassis was virtually all new and three times stronger than the 289's, with computer-designed anti-dive and anti-squat characteristics. Amazingly, the 289's original Salisbury differential proved more than capable of handling the 427's massive wall of torque.

WHEELS
Initially pin-drive Halibrand magnesium alloy but changed for Starburst wheels (designed by Shelby employee Pete Brock) when supplies dried up.

SIDE-SCREENS
Small perspex side screens helped cut down cockpit-wing buffeting at speed.

FRAME
The windscreen frame was hand-made and polished.

COOLING
Wing vents helped reduce brake and engine temperatures.

BUMPERS
Bumpers were token chromed tubes, with the emphasis on saving weight. Racers took them off completely.

EXHAUSTS
Racing Cobras usually had side exhausts which increased power and noise.

GTM 777F

SPECIFICATIONS

MODEL AC Cobra 427 (1965–68)
PRODUCTION 316
BODY STYLE Light alloy, two-door, two-seater, open sports.
CONSTRUCTION Separate tubular steel chassis with aluminium panels.
ENGINE V8, 6989cc.
POWER OUTPUT 425 bhp at 6000 rpm.
TRANSMISSION Four-speed all-synchromesh.
SUSPENSION All-round independent with coil springs.
BRAKES Four-wheel disc.
MAXIMUM SPEED 265 km/h (165 mph)
0–60 MPH (0–96 KM/H) 4.2 sec
0–100 MPH (0–161 KM/H) 10.3 sec
A.F.C. 5.3 km/l (15 mpg)

AC 428

THE AC 428 NEEDS a new word of its very own – "brutiful" perhaps, for while its brute strength derives from its Cobra forebear, the 428 has a sculpted, stately beauty. This refined bruiser was born of a thoroughbred cross-breed of British engineering, American power, and Italian design. The convertible 428 was first seen at the London Motor Show in October 1965; the first fixed-head car – the so-called fastback – was ready in time for the Geneva Motor Show in March, 1966.

But production was beset by problems from the start; first cars were not offered for sale until 1967, and as late as March 1969, only 50 had been built. Part of the problem was that the 428 was priced between the more expensive Italian Ferraris and Maseratis and the cheaper British Astons and Jensens. Small-scale production continued into the 1970s, but its days were numbered and it was finally done for by the fuel crisis of October 1973; the last 428 – the 80th – was built soon afterwards and sold during 1974. But, if you own one of them you have got a rare thing – a refined muscle car, a macho GT with manners and breeding.

BADGING
The letters AC derive from Autocarrier, the company's name until it became known as AC Cars Ltd. in 1922.

SUSPENSION
Front suspension utilizes unequal-length wishbones with combined coil-spring and telescopic-damper units.

ENGINE
Using the same 427 cubic inch (6998cc) V8 engine as the Cobra, the car was known initially as the AC 427. In 1967, it gained the Ford Galaxie engine and an extra cubic inch. Both four-speed manual and three-speed automatic transmissions were available.

UNDER-BONNET HEAT MEANT THAT ON LONG, FAST RUNS THE ENGINE OIL COULD LITERALLY BOIL

HOOD COVER
Early convertibles had a detachable metal tonneau to cover the hood when folded, but this was soon abandoned.

SITTING COMFORTABLY
Interiors are lavishly furnished, with top-quality leather seats and extensive use of chrome-plated fittings.

SUBTLE FILLER
The 82-litre (18-gallon) fuel tank is filled through a flap on the rear deck.

DASHBOARD
Switchgear may be scattered around like confetti, but the instruments are grouped clearly in front of the driver. The speedo *(far left)* reads to an optimistic 180 mph (290 km/h), the tachometer *(far right)* to 8000 rpm.

MAKING AN IMPACT
Slim, wrap-around, chrome-plated bumpers accentuate the 428's length, but provide minimal impact protection.

BODY BEAUTIFUL
Like any Italian or Italian-bodied car of the period, the 428 suffers from corrosion due to poor-quality steel.

SPECIFICATIONS

MODEL AC 428 (1966–73)

PRODUCTION 80 (51 convertibles, 29 fastbacks)

BODY STYLES Two-seat convertible or two-seat fastback coupé.

CONSTRUCTION Tubular-steel backbone chassis/separate all-steel body.

ENGINE Ford V8, 6997cc or 7016cc.

POWER OUTPUT 345 bhp at 4600 rpm

TRANSMISSION Ford four-speed manual or three-speed auto; Salisbury rear axle with limited-slip differential.

SUSPENSION Double wishbones and combined coil spring/telescopic damper units front and rear.

BRAKES Servo-assisted Girling discs front and rear.

MAXIMUM SPEED 224 km/h (139.3 mph) (auto)

0–60 MPH (0–96 KM/H) 5.9 sec (auto)

0–100 MPH (0–161 KM/H) 14.5 sec

A.F.C. 4.2–5.3 km/l (12–15 mpg)

WEATHER BEATER
While the hood has rather large rear quarters which can make the cockpit feel somewhat claustrophobic, the plastic rear "window" is generously proportioned.

SUSPENSION
Salisbury final drive, with limited-slip differential, is bolted to the tubular chassis; short external shafts drive the rear wheels.

AIR VENTS
In an effort to combat engine overheating, later cars have air vents behind the front wheels.

PARTS BIN
The 428 features parts from other manufacturers; rear lights came from Fiat.

AC 428

Styled by Pietro Frua in Turin, the AC 428 was available in both convertible and fixed-head fastback form. It was based on an AC Cobra 427 chassis, virtually standard apart from a 15 cm (6 in) increase in wheelbase. The design contains subtle reminders of a number of contemporary cars, not least the Maserati Mistral – which is hardly surprising really, since the Mistral was also penned by Frua.

THIN SKINNED
Early cars had aluminium doors and bonnet; later cars were all-steel.

LIFTING THE LID
Like the Cobra, the 428's vast bonnet is hinged at the front.

DESIGN CREDIT
Frua are credited with a discreet "Creazione Frua" badge behind each front-wing vent.

ALL LACED UP
Standard wheels were substantial triple-laced, wire-spoked affairs, secured by a three-eared nut.

ALFA ROMEO 1300 Junior Spider

DRIVEN BY DUSTIN HOFFMAN to the strains of Simon and Garfunkel in the film *The Graduate*, the Alfa Spider has become one of the most accessible cult Italian cars. This is hardly surprising when you consider the little Alfa's considerable virtues: a wonderfully responsive all-alloy, twin-cam engine, accurate steering, sensitive brakes, a finely balanced chassis, plus matinee idol looks. Not for nothing has it been called the poor man's Ferrari.

First launched at the Geneva Motor Show in 1966, Alfa held a worldwide competition to find a name for their new baby. After considering 140,000 entries, with suggestions like Lollobrigida, Bardot, Nuvolari, and even Stalin, they settled on Duetto, which neatly summed up the car's two's-company-three's-a-crowd image. Despite the same price tag as the much faster and more glamorous Jaguar E-Type *(see pages 140–143)*, the Spider sold over 100,000 units during its remarkable 26-year production run. Alfa purists favour the pre-1970 "boat-tailed" cars, with the 1600 Duetto and 1750 models among the most collectable. Because of their large production numbers and relatively expensive maintenance costs, not to mention a serious propensity for body decay, prices of Spiders are invitingly low, running at similar levels to MGBs, Triumph TR6s, and Frogeye Sprites.

OTHER MODELS

The Spider has to be one of Alfa's great post-war cars. Next to the Alfasud, GTV, and Giulia, it is perhaps one of their most romantic confections.

ALFA ROMEO GIULIETTA
The Spider's forebear was the comely little Giulietta, available in convertible, two-door coupé, or four-door Berlina versions.

ALFA ROMEO MONTREAL
For six years the Montreal was the jewel in Alfa's crown. A race-bred 2.5 V8 gave a top speed of 225 km/h (140 mph).

REAR VIEW
The "boat-tail" rear was shared by all Spiders up to 1970, replaced by a squared-off Kamm tail. "Duetto" correctly refers to 1600 Spiders only.

LOGO
The Spider was designed by Battista Pininfarina, founder of the Turin-based design house.

HOOD
The Spider's hood is beautifully effective. It can be raised with only one arm without leaving the driver's seat.

BOOT
Spiders have huge boots by sports car standards, with the spare wheel tucked neatly away under the boot floor.

BODYWORK
The Spider's bodywork corrodes alarmingly quickly. Poor-quality steel, scant rustproofing, and inadequate drainage make rust a serious enemy.

ENGINE
*Some of the mid-
'70s Spiders
imported to
the US were
overly restricted
– the catalysed
1750 could
only manage
159 km/h
(99 mph).*

DASHBOARD
The dashboard was painted metal up to
1970. All Spiders had the Italian ape-like
(long arms, short legs) driving
position. Minor controls were
on fingertip stalks, while the
wipers had an ingenious foot
button on the floor.

FLOOR MATS
*Spiders came from the factory with
austere rubber mats, now much
prized by enthusiasts as they do
not absorb water.*

ALFA ROMEO 1300 JUNIOR SPIDER

One of Pininfarina's last designs,
the Spider's rounded front and rear
and deep-channelled scallop
running along the sides attracted
plenty of criticism. One
British motoring
magazine dubbed
it "compact and
rather ugly". The
1300 Junior was
the baby of the
Spider family,
introduced in
1968 to take
advantage
of Italian
tax laws.

STYLISH GRILLE
This hides a twin-cam
energy-efficient engine
with hemispherical
combustion chambers.

SPECIFICATIONS

MODEL Alfa Romeo 1300 Junior
 Spider (1968–78)
PRODUCTION 7,237
BODY STYLE Two-door, two-seater.
CONSTRUCTION All steel
 monocoque body.
ENGINE All-alloy twin-cam 1290cc.
POWER OUTPUT 89 bhp at 6000 rpm.
TRANSMISSION Five-speed.
SUSPENSION *Front:* independent;
 Rear: live axle with coil springs.
BRAKES All disc.
MAXIMUM SPEED 170 km/h (106 mph)
0–60 MPH (0–96 KM/H) 11.2 sec
0–100 MPH (0–161 KM/H) 21.3 sec
A.F.C. 10.3 km/l (29 mpg)

HEADLAMPS
*Perspex headlamp covers look good
and raise the top speed slightly.
They were banned in the United
States and never fitted to
1300 Juniors.*

NOSE SECTION
*Disappearing nose is very
vulnerable to parking
dents. Many a Spider's
snout contains more filler
than it should.*

ASTON MARTIN *DB4*

THE DEBUT OF THE DB4 in 1958 heralded the beginning of the Aston Martin glory years, ushering in the breed of classic six-cylinder DB Astons that propelled Aston Martin on to the world stage. Earlier post-war Astons were fine sporting enthusiasts' road cars, but with the DB4 Astons acquired a new grace, sophistication, and refinement that was, for many, the ultimate flowering of the grand tourer theme. Clothed in an Italian body by Carrozzeria Touring of Milan, it possessed a graceful yet powerful elegance. Under the aluminium shell was Tadek Marek's twin-cam straight-six engine, which evolved from Aston's racing programme.

In short, the DB4 looked superb and went like stink. The DB5, which followed, will forever be remembered as the James Bond Aston, and the final expression of the theme came with the bigger DB6. The cars were glorious, but the company was in trouble. David Brown, the millionaire industrialist owner of Aston Martin and the DB of the model name, had a dream. But, in the early Seventies, with losses of £1 million a year, he bailed out of the company, leaving a legacy of machines that are still talked about with reverence as the David Brown Astons.

UNHINGED
First-generation DB4s have a rear-hinged bonnet.

FUEL FLAP
The single fuel-filler is out of sight behind a discreet flap on the left-hand rear pillar.

SUSPENSION
Front suspension is double wishbones with coil springs and telescopic dampers.

1037 TE

LUXURIOUS LEATHER
While rear seats in the fixed-head offer limited space, just look at the richness and quality of the leather.

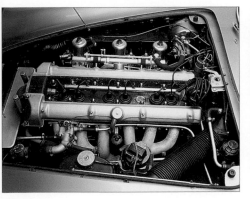

ENGINE
While looking very much like the contemporary Jaguar XK twin-cam straight-six, Tadek Marek's design is more powerful and more complicated. Triple SU carburettors show this to be a Vantage engine with an extra 20 bhp.

IT'S IN THE MIRROR
The dipping rear-view mirror is also found in many Jaguars of the period.

DASHBOARD
The fascia is an unergonomic triumph of form over function; gauges are scattered all over an instrument panel deliberately similar to the car's grinning radiator grille.

SPECIFICATIONS
MODEL Aston Martin DB4 (1958–63)
PRODUCTION 1,040 (fixed head); 70 (convertible); 95 fixed-head DB4 GTs.
BODY STYLES Fixed-head coupé or convertible.
CONSTRUCTION Pressed-steel and tubular inner chassis frame, with aluminium-alloy outer panels.
ENGINE In-line six 3670cc/3749cc.
POWER OUTPUT 240 bhp at 5500 rpm
TRANSMISSION Four-speed manual (with optional overdrive).
SUSPENSION *Front:* independent by wishbones, coil springs and telescopic dampers. *Rear:* live axle located by trailing arms and Watt linkage with coil springs and lever-arm dampers.
BRAKES Discs front and rear.
MAXIMUM SPEED 225+ km/h (140+ mph)
0–60 MPH (0–96 KM/H) 8 sec
0–100 MPH (0–161 KM/H) 20.1 sec
A.F.C. 3.6–7.8 km/l (14–22 mpg)

BRITISH LIGHTWEIGHT
Superleggera, Italian for "super-lightweight", refers to the technique of body construction: aluminium panels rolled over a framework of steel tubes.

ASTON MARTIN DB4
There is no doubt that the DB4 has got serious attitude. Its lines may be Italian, but it has none of the dainty delicacy of some contemporary Ferraris and Maseratis; for the Aston's spirit is somehow true-Brit. Its stance is solid and butch, but not brutish – more British Boxer than lumbering Bulldog, aggressive yet refined – and is an ideal blueprint for a James Bond car.

ASTON SMILE
The vertical bars in this car's radiator grille show it to be a so-called Series 4 DB4, built between September, 1961 and October, 1962.

1037 TE

ASTON MARTIN *V8*

A NEAR TWO-TONNE GOLIATH powered by an outrageous hand-made 5.3-litre engine, the DBS V8 was meant to be Aston's money-earner for the 1970s. Based on the six-cylinder DBS of 1967, the V8 did not appear until April 1970. With a thundering 257 km/h (160 mph) top speed, Aston's new bulldog instantly earned a place on every millionaire's shopping list. The trouble was that it drove into a worldwide recession – in 1975 the Newport Pagnell factory produced just 19 cars.

Aston's bank managers were worried men, but the company pulled through. The DBS became the Aston Martin V8 in 1972 and continued until 1989, giving birth to the legendary 400 bhp Vantage and gorgeous Volante Convertible. Excessive, expensive, impractical, and impossibly thirsty, the DBS V8 and AM V8 are wonderful relics from a time when environmentalism was just another word in the dictionary.

OTHER MODELS

The DBS was sold alongside the DB6, here in convertible Volante form. David Brown Astons were the staple transport of well-heeled British aristocrats.

ASTON MARTIN DB6 VOLANTE
Cars with incredible presence, Astons were good enough for James Bond, King Hussein of Jordan, Peter Sellers, and even the Prince of Wales – who has owned a DB6 Volante from new.

CLASSY INTERIOR
Over the years the DBS was skilfully updated, without losing its traditional ambience. Features included hide and timber surroundings, air conditioning, electric windows, and radio cassette. Nearly all V8s were ordered with Chrysler Torqueflite automatic transmission.

RACING ENGINE
The alloy V8 was first seen in Lola sports-racing cars. The massive air-cleaner box covers a quartet of twin-choke Weber carbs, which guzzle one litre of fuel for every 4.6 km (13 mpg), less if you enjoy yourself.

ASTON LINES
Smooth tapering cockpit line is an Aston hallmark echoed in the current DB7.

SPOILER
Discreet rear spoiler is part of the gently sweeping wing line.

SUSPENSION
Rear suspension was semi-independent De Dion tube with double trailing links, Watts linkage, coil springs, and lever arm dampers.

TYRES
Tyres were massive 18-cm (7-in) Avon Turbospeeds.

REAR VIEW
Prodigious rear overhang makes the rear aspect look cluttered.

TWIN PIPES
Hand-made bumpers cover huge twin exhausts — a gentle reminder of this Aston's epic V8 grunt.

ASTON MARTIN V8

DBS was one of the first Astons with chassis and departed from the traditional Superleggera tubular superstructure of the DB4, 5, and 6. Like Ferraris and Maseratis, Aston prices were ballyhooed up to stratospheric levels in the Eighties. The best examples changed hands for £50,000 plus. But now sobriety has returned to the market, you can buy a decent V8 for the price of a new Nissan.

WHEELS
To handle 300-plus bhp, V8s wore cast alloy wheels instead of wires.

BODYWORK
V8 aluminium body was hand-smoothed and lovingly finished.

SPECIFICATIONS

MODEL Aston Martin V8 (1972–89)
PRODUCTION 2,842 (including Volante and Vantage)
BODY STYLE Four-seater coupé.
CONSTRUCTION Aluminium body, steel platform chassis.
ENGINE Twin OHC alloy 5340cc V8
POWER OUTPUT Never released but approx 345 bhp (Vantage 400 bhp).
TRANSMISSION Three-speed auto or five-speed manual.
SUSPENSION Independent front, De Dion rear.
BRAKES Four-wheel disc.
MAXIMUM SPEED 259 km/h (161 mph); Vantage, 278 km/h (173 mph)
0–60 MPH (0–96 KM/H) 6.2 sec (Vantage 5.4 sec)
0–100 MPH (0–161 KM/H) 14.2 sec (Vantage 13 sec)
A.F.C. 4.6 km/l (13 mpg)

BOND CAR
The 1984 AM V8 Volante from the film *The Living Daylights*, with James Bond actor Timothy Dalton. In 1964 a DB5 was the first Aston to star alongside James Bond in the film *Goldfinger*.

BONNET BULGE
Massive bonnet power bulge is to clear four carburettors.

SPOILER
Chin spoiler and undertray help reduce front-end lift at speed.

FRONT-END
Shapely "cliff-hanger" nose was always a DBS trademark.

AUDI *Quattro Sport*

THE MOST EXPENSIVE AND EXCLUSIVE Audi ever sold was the £60,000, 250 km/h (155 mph) Quattro Sport. With a short wheelbase, all-alloy 300 bhp engine, and a body made of aluminium-reinforced glass-fibre and Kevlar, it has all the charisma, and nearly all the performance, of a Ferrari GTO.

The Quattro changed the way we think about four-wheel drive. Before 1980, four-wheel drive systems had foundered through high cost, weight, and lousy road behaviour. Everybody thought that if you bolted a four-wheel drive system onto a performance coupé it would have ugly handling, transmission whine, and an insatiable appetite for fuel. Audi's engineers proved that the accepted wisdom was wrong and, by 1982, the Quattro was a World Rally Champion. Four-wheel drive cars are now part of most large car makers' model ranges and, along with airbags and anti-lock brakes, have played their bit towards safer driving. We must thank the car that started it all, the Audi Quattro – a technical trail-blazer.

INTERIOR
The interior looks like it may accommodate four people, but in practice it is a two-seater only; unless a rear passenger is willing to travel in the lotus position! Ride is harder than normal Quattros, but steering is quicker.

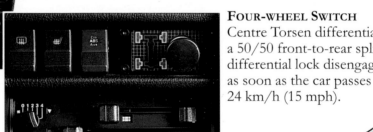

FOUR-WHEEL SWITCH
Centre Torsen differential gives a 50/50 front-to-rear split. Rear differential lock disengages as soon as the car passes 24 km/h (15 mph).

DASHBOARD
While the dashboard layout is nothing special, everything is typically Germanic – clear, tidy, and easy to use. The only touch of luxury in the Quattro is half-leather trim.

BOX WHEELARCHES ARE A QUATTRO HALLMARK, ESSENTIAL TO COVER FAT 9Jx15 WHEELS

INTER-AXLE DIFF ON THE QUATTRO WAS BORROWED FROM THE VW POLO

Turbo lag was a big problem on early Quattros; from 32–96 km/h (20–60 mph) in top it was slower than a 900cc VW Polo

Power output is a monster 304 bhp at 6500 rpm – 0 to 60 in four-and-a-bit seconds is very quick.

ENGINE

The five-cylinder 2133cc alloy engine is 22.7 kg (50 lb) lighter than the stock item, with twin overhead cams, four valves per cylinder, a giant KKK-K27 turbocharger and Bosch LH-Jetronic injection.

BAUER BADGING

Some body parts were made by German coachbuilder Bauer, who were also responsible for the early BMW 3-Series Convertible.

Longer nose and bonnet bulge cover intercooler for the turbo unit

Rear view was limited

SPECIFICATIONS

MODEL Audi Quattro Sport (1983–87)
PRODUCTION 220 (all LHD)
BODY STYLE Two-seater, two-door coupé.
CONSTRUCTION Monocoque body from Kevlar, aluminium, glass-fibre, and steel.
ENGINE 2133cc five-cylinder turbocharged.
POWER OUTPUT 304 bhp at 6500 rpm.
TRANSMISSION Five-speed manual, four-wheel drive.
SUSPENSION All-round independent.
BRAKES Four-wheel vented discs with switchable ABS.
MAXIMUM SPEED 250 km/h (155 mph)
0–60 MPH (0–96 KM/H) 4.8 sec
0–100 MPH (0–161 KM/H) 13.9 sec
A.F.C. 6 km/l (17 mpg)

LIMITED EDITION

Of the 1,700 Audis produced each day in the mid-1980s, only 3 were Quattros, and of a year's output only a tiny amount were Sport Quattros.

Due to breeze-block styling, Quattro aerodynamics were poor at 0.43cd

All-round ventilated discs have selectable anti-lock braking system (ABS). Since ABS is not desirable in all driving conditions, Sport drivers can switch it on and off at will

—QUATTRO RALLY SUCCESS—

In its day the Audi Quattro Sport had the latest four-wheel drive technology, married to the reliability and durability of Prussian engineering perfection.

THE SPORT's capabilities make it not just a fast car, but a superfast supercar, more than able to rub noses with the best from Maranello and Stuttgart. Despite its passing resemblance to the more prosaic Audi GT Coupé, the Quattro Sport is one of the quickest, most sure-footed cars in the world.

In 1984 Stig Blomqvist took Audi to the rank of World Rally Champions, with wins in Greece, New Zealand and Argentina. But it was at the Ivory Coast event, the Sport's first proper outing, that he showed just how competitive this incredible machine could be, trouncing all opposition in his wake. In competition trim, Audi's remarkable turbo-charged engine was pushing out 400 bhp and, by 1987, Audi were admitting to a massive 509 bhp at 8,000 rpm for the fearsome S1 Sport that took Walter Rohrl to victory at Pike's Peak. To meet Group B homologation requirements, only 220 examples of the Sport were built, all in left-hand drive guise, and only a few

AUDI SPORT IN RALLY ACTION

destined for sale to some very lucky private owners.

In its first full competition season in 1985, the Sport took the laurels on the San Remo rally, as well as second place on the Monte Carlo, Swedish, and Acropolis rallies. The San Remo was to be the last Group B Quattro win in the World Rallying Championship because the competition had got to

AUDI
Quattro
Sport

DARKENED REAR LIGHTS WERE INCLUDED ACROSS THE QUATTRO RANGE IN 1984

HOT PROPERTY
From any angle the Sport is testosterone on wheels, with a butch and aggressive four-square stance.

AUDI SPORT, 1983 EAST AFRICA SAFARI RALLY

STIG BLOMQVIST IN ICY CONDITIONS, 1985

grips with the Quattro phenomenon and were producing a growing number of all-driven supercars, purpose built for rallying events. Ultra-quick projectiles like the Metro 6R4, Ford RS 2000, Peugeot 205 T16, and Lancia Delta S4 began to chew away at the Quattro's tail feathers. The reason for the Sport's short life was that all Group B supercars were outlawed after a number of horrendous accidents. Audi withdrew from competition following the ill-fated 1986 Portugal Rally that rewrote the rule book. From 1987, the World Rally Championship would be contested by Group A cars in stock showroom specification, rendering the foreshortened Sport obsolete at a stroke. Gone but not forgotten, the Quattro Sport is now a much admired collector's item, valued at considerably more than its original price.

ROOF SECTIONS ARE ALUMINIUM-BONDED GLASS-FIBRE

HAND-CRAFTED
Body shells were welded together at Ingolstadt, Germany in small batches by a team of just 22 craftsmen.

AUSTIN-HEALEY *Sprite* MK1

Sprite

SOME AUTOMOTIVE ACADEMICS reckon all the best car designs have a recognizable face. If that is the case, few cars have a cuter one than this cheeky little fellow, with that ear-to-ear grinning grille and those wide-open, slightly astonished, eyes. Of course, it is those trademark bulging peepers that prompted the nickname "Frogeye", by which everyone now recognizes this engaging little character. It is a compliment of kinds that the recent retro fad has proffered voguish designs, like the Suzuki Capuccino and Honda Beat, in an attempt to recapture some of the charm of the original. But these modern charm-bracelet trinkets lack one thing – real character. So much of the Frogeye's character was borne of necessity. The Donald Healey Motor Company and Austin had already teamed up with the Austin-Healey 100. In 1958, its little brother, the Sprite, was born, a spartan sports car designed down to a price and based on the engine and running gear of the Austin A35 saloon, with a bit of Morris Minor too. Yet the Frogeye really was a sports car and had a sweet raspberry exhaust note to prove it.

INTERIOR
The Frogeye fits like a glove. Everything is within reach – speedo on the right, rev counter on the left, and a well-placed stubby gear lever.

THE FROG'S EYES
Donald Healey's original design incorporated retracting headlamps like the later Lotus Elan, but extra cost ruled these out and the protruding headlamp pods created a car with a character all its own.

ENGINE ACCESS
Rear-hinged alligator bonnet gives great engine access and makes the Frogeye a delight for DIY tinkerers.

GVS 668

ENGINE
The Austin-Morris A-series engine was a little gem. It first appeared in the Austin A35 saloon and went on to power several generations of Mini *(see pages 40–41)*. In the Frogeye it was modified internally with extra strong valve springs and fitted with twin SU carburettors to give a peppy 50 bhp gross (43 bhp net).

DUAL LIGHTS
Sidelights double as flashing indicators.

BUMPERS
The Frogeye was a budget sports car built down to a price. Bumpers with overrider were a sensible and popular extra that would set you back £6 in 1958.

GV

WHEELS
Drilled steel-disc wheels with AH on plain hub.

AUSTIN-HEALEY SPRITE MK1

At just under 3.5 m (11 ft 5 in), the Frogeye is not quite as small as it looks. Its pert looks were only part of the car's cult appeal, for with its firm, even harsh, ride it had a traditional British sports car feel. A nimble performer, you could hustle it along a twisty road, cornering flat and snicking through the gears on the stubby gearstick.

CLEAN LINES
The design has a classic simplicity, free of needless chrome embellishment; there is no external door handle to interrupt the flowing flanks.

ROUND RUMP
It is not so much a boot, because it does not open; more a luggage locker with access behind the rear seats.

SPECIFICATIONS

MODEL Austin-Healey Sprite Mk1 (1958–61)
PRODUCTION 38,999
BODY STYLE Two-seater roadster.
CONSTRUCTION Unitary body/chassis.
ENGINE BMC A-Series 948cc, four-cylinder, overhead valve.
POWER OUTPUT 43 bhp at 5200 rpm.
TRANSMISSION Four-speed manual, synchromesh on top three ratios.
SUSPENSION *Front:* Independent, coil springs and wishbones *Rear:* Quarter-elliptic leaf springs, rigid axle.
BRAKES Hydraulic, drums all round.
MAXIMUM SPEED 135 km/h (84 mph)
0–60 MPH (0–96 KM/H) 20.5 sec
A.F.C. 12.5–16 km/l (35–45 mpg)

BONNET
The complex one-piece hood is made up of four main panels.

LOW DOWN
The Frogeye's low stance aids flat cornering. Ground clearance is better than it looks; just under 12.7 cm (5 in).

COMPETITION
With its tuneable A-series engine, the Frogeye is still a popular club racer. Sprites also put up spirited performances at Le Mans and Sebring in Florida, USA. Special-bodied Sebring Sprites are rare and prized.

AUSTIN-HEALEY *3000*

THE HEALEY HUNDRED was a sensation at the 1952 Earl's Court Motor Show. Austin's Leonard Lord had already contracted to supply the engines, but when he noticed the sports car's impact, he decided he wanted to build it too – it was transformed overnight into the Austin-Healey 100, with a new badge struck in the wee small hours. Donald Healey had spotted a gap in the American sports car market between the Jaguar XK120 *(see pages 134–35)* and the cheap and cheerful MG T series *(see pages 172–73)*. His hunch was right, for about 80 per cent of all production went Stateside. Over the years this rugged bruiser became increasingly civilized. In 1956, it received a six-cylinder engine in place of the four, but in 1959 the 3000 was born. It became increasingly refined, with front disc brakes, then wind-up windows, and ever faster. Our featured car is the last of the line, a 3000 Mk 3. Although perhaps verging on grand-tourer territory, it is also the fastest of all Big Healeys and still a true sports car.

ENGINE
Under the bonnet of the biggest of the so-called Big Healeys is the 2912cc straight-six that was designated as the 3000. This is the butchest of the big bangers, pumping out a hefty 150 bhp.

COUNTRY CLUB STYLE
Period advertisement emphasizes Austin-Healey's fine pedigree as a sure-footed thoroughbred sports car.

WINDSCREEN
In 1962, the 3000 acquired a wrap-around windscreen and wind-up windows, as the once raw sports car adopted trappings of sophistication.

WHEELS
Wire wheels were options on some models, standard on others.

BONNET SCOOP
All six-cylinder Healeys featured a bonnet scoop; the longer engine pushed the radiator forwards, the scoop clearing the underbonnet protrusion to aid airflow.

THE HEALEY GRIN
From the traditional Healey diamond grille, the mouth of the Austin-Healey developed into a wide grin, initially with horizontal bars and finally with plankton feeder slats.

STOP AND GO
As the Healey 3000 became beefier throughout the Sixties, modern radial tyres helped keep it on course.

SPECIFICATIONS

MODEL Austin-Healey 3000 (1959–68)
PRODUCTION 42,926 (all 3000 models)
BODY STYLES Two-seater roadster, 2+2 roadster, 2+2 convertible.
CONSTRUCTION Separate chassis/body.
ENGINE 2912cc overhead-valve, straight-six.
POWER OUTPUT 3000 Mk1: 124 bhp at 4600 rpm. 3000 Mk2: 132 bhp at 4750 rpm. 3000 Mk3: 150 bhp at 5250 rpm.
TRANSMISSION Four-speed manual with overdrive.
SUSPENSION *Front:* Independent coil springs and wishbones, anti-roll bar. *Rear:* Semi-elliptic leaf springs. Lever-arm dampers all round.
BRAKES Front discs; rear drum.
MAXIMUM SPEED 177–193 km/h (110–120 mph)
0–60 MPH (0–96 KM/H) 9.5–10.8 sec
A.F.C. 6–12 km/l (17–34 mpg)

AUSTIN-HEALEY 3000 MK3

The Austin-Healey put on weight over the years, became gradually more refined too, but stayed true to its original sports car spirit. The two major influences on its changing faces were the all-important needs of the American market and the impositions of Austin, both as parts supplier and as frugal keeper of purse-strings. But from the start, the styling was always a major asset and what you see here in the 3000 Mk3 is the eventual culmination of those combined styling forces.

MORE POWER
In 1959, the 2639cc six-cylinder of the Healey 100/6 was bored out to 2912cc and rounded up to give the model name 3000.

COMFORTS
Updated weather equipment is an improvement on earlier efforts, which took two jugglers 10 minutes to erect.

REFINED REAR
The first prototype rear-end treatments featured faddish fins that were replaced by a classic round rump.

INTERIOR
Once spartan, the cockpit of the Austin-Healey became increasingly luxurious, with a polished veneer fascia and even a lockable glove box to complement the fine leather and rich carpet. One thing remained traditional – engine heat meant the cockpit was always a hot place to be.

AUSTIN *Mini Cooper*

THE MINI COOPER was one of Britain's great motor sport legends, an inspired confection that became the definitive rally car of the Sixties. In the 1964 Monte Carlo Rally, with Paddy Hopkirk at the wheel, the Cooper produced giant-killing performance, trouncing 4.7-litre Ford Fairlanes and coming first; followed in fourth place by yet another Cooper driven by Timo Makinen. After that it never looked back, winning the 1962 and 1964 Tulip Rallies, the 1963 Alpine Rally and the 1965 and 1967 Monte Carlo, as well as notching up more than 25 other prestigious competition wins.

Because of its size, manoeuvrability, and front-wheel drive, the Cooper could dance around bigger, more unwieldy cars and scuttle off to victory. Even driven to the absolute limit, it would still cling limpet-like around corners, long after rear-wheel-drive cars were sliding sideways. The hot Mini was a perfect blend of pin-sharp steering, terrific handling balance, and a feeling that you could get away with almost anything. Originally the brainchild of racing car builder John Cooper, who received two pounds royalty on every car, the Mini's designer, Alec Issigonis, thought it should be a "people's car" rather than a performance machine and did not like the idea of a tuned Mini. Fortunately BMC (British Motor Corporation) did, and agreed to a trial run of just 1,000 cars. One of their better decisions.

ENGINE
The 1071cc A-series engine would rev to 7200 rpm, producing 72 bhp. Crankshaft, con-rods, valves and rockers were all toughened, and the Cooper also had a bigger oil pump and beefed-up gearbox.

INTERIOR
The Cooper has typical rally-car features: wood-rim Moto-Lita wheel, fire extinguisher, Halda trip meter, rev counter, stopwatches, and maplight. Only the centre speedo, heater, and switches are standard equipment.

THE RALLY CAR
Sir Peter Moon and John Davenport leave the start ramp in the 1964 Isle of Man Manx Trophy Rally in 24 PK. But, while leading the pack on the penultimate stage of the rally at Druidale, 24 PK was badly rolled and needed a complete reshell. Many works Coopers led a hard life, often rebuilt and reshelled several times.

SPEEDY CORNERING
With a low centre of gravity and a wheel at each extreme corner, the Mini had the perfect credentials for tram-like handling.

GRILLE
Front grille was quick-release to give access for emergency repairs.

COOPER S
The Cooper S, built between 1963–67, had wider wheels, radial tyres, different badging, and a choice of 970 or 1071cc engines. The 970 S is the rarest of all Coopers, with only 964 made.

SPOTLIGHT
Roof-mounted spotlight could be rotated from inside the car.

WINDSCREEN
Windscreen was glass but all other windows were made out of perspex to save weight.

BRAKES
Lockheed disc brakes and servo provided the stopping power.

NUMBER PLATE
Competitions departments often swapped number plates, bodyshells, and chassis numbers, making it hard to identify genuine ex-works Coopers.

AUSTIN MINI COOPER
24 PK wears the classic Mini rally uniform of straight-through exhaust, Minilite wheels, roll bar, twin fuel tanks, and lightweight stick-on number plates. British Motor Corporation had a proactive Competitions Department, preparing racing Minis with enthusiasm and precision. The Cooper's success in the 1960s is testament to the department's work.

SPECIFICATIONS

MODEL Austin Mini Cooper (1963–69)
PRODUCTION 145,000 (all models)
BODY STYLE Saloon.
CONSTRUCTION All steel two-door monocoque mounted on front and rear sub-frames.
ENGINE Four-cylinder 970cc/ 997cc/998cc/1071cc/1275cc.
POWER OUTPUT 65 bhp at 6500 rpm to 76 bhp at 5800 rpm.
TRANSMISSION Four-speed, no synchromesh on first.
SUSPENSION Independent front and rear suspension with rubber cones and wishbones (Hydrolastic from late 1964).
BRAKES Lockheed front discs with rear drums.
MAXIMUM SPEED 161 km/h (100 mph)
0–60 MPH (0–96 KM/H) 12.9 sec
0–100 MPH (0–161 KM/H) 20 sec
A.F.C. 10.6 km/l (30 mpg)

BENTLEY *R-Type Continental*

IN ITS DAY the Bentley Continental, launched in 1952, was the fastest production four-seater in the world and acclaimed as "a modern magic carpet which annihilates distance"; 43 years later, it is rightly considered one of the greatest cars of all time. Designed for the English country gentleman, it was understated, but had a lithe, sinewy beauty rarely seen in other cars of its era.

Rolls-Royce's brief was to create a fast touring car for plutocrat customers, and to do that they had to reduce both size and weight. Aluminium construction helped the weight, while wind tunnel testing created that slippery shape. Those emergent fins at the back were not for decoration – they actually aided the car's directional stability. The result was a magnificent touring machine that could better 185 km/h (115 mph) and manage a 0–60 mph (96 km/h) time of just over 13 seconds. But such avant-garde development did not come cheap. In 1952, the R-Type Continental was the most expensive production car in the world at £7,608 – today's equivalent of almost half a million pounds.

HALFWAY THROUGH THE CONTINENTAL'S PRODUCTION RUN, AUTO GEARBOXES WERE OFFERED AS AN OPTION AND WERE FITTED TO NO LESS THAN 46 OF THE 208 CARS BUILT

DASHBOARD
Beautifully detailed dash mirrored the Continental's exterior elegance. The first R-Types had manual gearboxes with a right-hand floor-mounted lever, thus reflecting the car's sporting character.

PRODUCTION CARS HAD AN EVEN LOWER ROOF LINE THAN THE ORIGINAL PROTOTYPE

PROTOTYPE HAD SPATS COVERING THE REAR WHEELS TO AID AIR FLOW

BENTLEY S-SERIES CONVERTIBLE
The Bentley S-Series Convertible of the late 1950s and early 1960s may bear a passing family resemblance to the Continental, but it does not possess the same tense urgency of line.

THE CONTINENTAL'S AERODYNAMICS WERE DECADES AHEAD OF ITS TIME

BODY WEIGHT WAS KEPT TO A MINIMUM BECAUSE NO FIFTIES' TYRES COULD COPE WITH SPEEDS OVER 193 KM/H (120 MPH)

SPECIFICATIONS

MODEL Bentley R-Type Continental (1952–55)
PRODUCTION 208
BODY STYLE Two-door, four-seater touring saloon.
CONSTRUCTION Steel chassis, alloy body.
ENGINE 4566 or 4887cc straight-sixes.
POWER OUTPUT Never declared, described as "sufficient".
TRANSMISSION Four-speed synchromesh manual or auto option.
SUSPENSION Independent front with wishbones and coil springs, rear live axle with leaf springs.
BRAKES *Front:* Disc; *Rear:* Drums.
MAXIMUM SPEED 185 km/h (115 mph)
0–60 MPH (0–96 KM/H) 13.5 sec
0–100 MPH (0–161 KM/H) 36.2 sec
A.F.C. 6.9 km/l (19.4 mpg)

GENTLY TAPERING REAR WINGS FUNNEL AIR AWAY INTO A SLIPSTREAM

PILLAR BOX REAR WINDOW WAS A THROWBACK TO PRE-WAR CARS

AERODYNAMIC TESTING

The Continental spent much time in the wind tunnel to establish air drag during forward motion. Sweeping rear quarters directed the wind over the rear wheels.

ALUMINIUM CONSTRUCTION

Not only was the body made from lightweight aluminium – courtesy of H.J. Mulliner & Co. Ltd. – but also the side window and screen frames. The prototype had high quality alloy bumpers; production cars had steel ones.

ENGINE

Continentals used a 4-litre straight-six engine of 4566cc– increased to 4887cc in May 1954 and known as the big bore engine. Carburation was by two SU HD8 units. Speeds ranged from 80 km/h (50 mph) in first to almost 193 km/h (120 mph) in top.

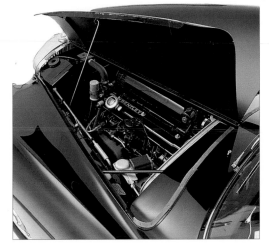

BENTLEY MASCOT

The Continental traded heavily on Bentley's pre-war reputation for quick touring cars. Perhaps more than any other post-war Bentley, it remained loyal to that tradition of aristocratic speed.

DURING PROTOTYPE TESTING NORMAL SIX-PLY TYRES LASTED ONLY 32 KM (20 MILES)

— A POST-WAR CLASSIC —

Designed by Rolls-Royce stylist John Blatchley, the Continental bears an uncanny resemblance to a Pininfarina R-Type prototype shown at the 1948 Paris Salon.

BLATCHLEY INSISTED that he arrived at the Continental's unmistakable shape using only the then new-fangled principles of aerodynamics. He reduced the radiator height to help air distribution and gave the front windscreen a steep rake, joining it to the sides of the body to allow the air to spill away. Such dramatic lines were claimed not to be a product of artistic endeavour, but of scientific research. Such was the lure, and indeed the cost, of the Continental that it was first introduced on an export-only basis – 100 of the total production of 208 went abroad. Only 108 were left in the hands of UK owners. This forced the British motoring magazine *Autocar* to remark: "such a car as the Continental is bound to be costly, and the British, who make it, cannot own it: but it goes abroad as proof that a nation where the creators are constantly subjected to the debasement of their own living standards can still keep alive the idea of perfection for others to enjoy". Nothing, it would seem, has changed.

Another car which possibly pre-empted the Continental's lines is the late Forties Cadillac. And there is the vaguest hint of plagiarism by Bentley. British motoring historian Andrew Whyte declared, "the 1949 Cadillac was certainly an inspiration for the 1952 Bentley Continental". And he

1953 BENTLEY R-TYPE CONTINENTAL

BENTLEY R-Type Continental

BOOT WAS CONSIDERED LARGE ENOUGH TO CARRY LUGGAGE FOR TOURING

REAR FLANKS ARE LIKE THE TENSE HAUNCHES OF A SPRINTER

REPATRIATED CONTINENTALS
During the Classic Car boom of the Eighties, many Continentals were exported to America and Japan. British collectors, anxious to preserve their disappearing heritage, are now actively repatriating as many as possible. A full list of the whereabouts of every Continental made is now being compiled.

GB

UKL 109

might be right. Both had sweeping tails, dorsal fins, and lean, smooth lines. American historian Richard Langworth asserts that, "the Cadillac was one of the industry's all-time design greats. Indeed, the grandly praised Bentley Continental, which appeared in '52, had body styling not unlike that of the '49 Cad".

But that is where the similarity ends. The Bentley handled, the Cadillac did not. America's "Best Car" was happy wallowing along Sunset Boulevard. The Continental was more at home on a hectic run from London to St. Tropez. It was a car that begged you to depress its accelerator pedal to the floorboards and reassured you with its immensely powerful brakes and commendable body control, always exuding the poise and grace of a well-

1947 CADILLAC "62" COUPE

mannered thoroughbred.

And collectors seem to agree that the Continental stands alone as the finest post-war Bentley and one of the world's all-time great cars. Proof that it is a far better car than the Cadillac can be found in the current market values of each. The Cadillac is merely admired, the Bentley is revered. Which is why you can buy ten 1949 Cadillacs for the price of a single R-Type Continental.

DOING THE CONTINENTAL

In 1952, with wartime austerity a fading memory, this was one of the flashiest and most rakish cars money could buy. Today, this exemplar of breeding and privilege stands as a resplendent memorial to the affluence and optimism of Fifties Britain.

DESPITE THE NEED TO KEEP WEIGHT DOWN, IT WAS UNTHINKABLE TO SKIMP ON THAT LAVISH INTERIOR

CLASSIC GOTHIC RADIATOR SHELL WAS CONSIDERED FAR MORE SPORTING THAN ROLLS ROYCE'S DORIC EXAMPLE

FRONT FOG LIGHTS WERE KNOWN AS PASS LIGHTS FOR OVERTAKING

UKL 109

BENTLEY *Flying Spur*

ARGUABLY THE MOST BEAUTIFUL post-war Bentley, the Flying Spur was the first four-door Continental. Initially, Rolls-Royce would not allow coachbuilder H.J. Mulliner to use the name Continental, insisting it should only apply to two-door cars. After months of pressure from Mulliner, R.R. relented and allowed the shapely coach-built car to be known as a proper Continental. More than worthy of the hallowed name, the Flying Spur was launched in 1957, using the standard S1 chassis. In 1959 it inherited R.R.'s 220 bhp, oversquare, light-alloy V8, and by July 1962 the bodyshell was given the double headlamp treatment and upgraded into what some consider to be the best of the breed – the S3 Flying Spur. Subtle, understated, and elegant, Flying Spurs are rare, and in their day were among the most admired and refined machines in the world.

ENGINE
Rolls-Royce's long-serving 6.2-litre V8, still in use today, has aluminium cylinder heads, block, and pistons. The hydraulic tappets were originally supplied by Chrysler, but as this was not good for R.R.'s image, they insisted they were made back home in England.

CAM-AND-ROLLER POWER STEERING PROVIDES 50% ASSISTANCE AT SPEED, 80% WHEN PARKING

INTERIOR
The Interior is pure gentleman's club, with carefully detailed switchgear, the finest hide and walnut, and West of England cloth for the headlining. The large, spindly steering wheel was power-assisted, a standard fitment in 1962. All S3s were automatic, although a few manual S1 Continentals were built.

FRONTAL ASPECT
The four-headlamp nose was shared with the Standard Steel Bentley S3, along with a lowered radiator and bonnet line. The body is hand-rolled aluminium.

FPG 74E

SUSPENSION
Rear suspension was by semi-elliptic leaf springs and radius arm and could be adjusted hydraulically between "firm" and "soft" settings.

BRAKES
Flying Spur has four-shoe drum brakes. Because Rolls-Royce brakes should never squeal, the company waited until 1965 to fit disc brakes to their cars.

OPTIONAL UNIT
Optional air conditioning unit hidden behind the front wheel.

S2 FLYING SPUR
Beautifully proportioned, many believe the Flying Spur to be the most handsome Crewe product of the period.

S3 BENTLEY CONTINENTAL H.J. MULLINER FLYING SPUR

Coachbuilder H.J. Mulliner would receive the chassis from Rolls-Royce and clothe it with a hand-built body. Although customers would often have to wait up to 18 months for their cars to be completed, the finished product was considered the zenith of good taste and refinement.

TYRES
Tyres were 8.20-15 Dunlop tubeless crossplies.

WEIGHTY REAR
Rear view shows sheer bulk of the car, which weighed in at close to two tons. Yet the swooping roof line and tapering tail still manage to lend an air of performance.

SPECIFICATIONS

MODEL S3 Bentley Continental HJ Mulliner Flying Spur (1962–66)
PRODUCTION 291
BODY STYLE Four-door, five-seater.
CONSTRUCTION Aluminium body, separate steel cross-braced box section chassis.
ENGINE V8, 6230cc.
POWER OUTPUT Never officially declared.
TRANSMISSION Four-speed automatic.
SUSPENSION *Front:* independent coil springs and wishbones. *Rear:* semi-elliptic leaf springs.
BRAKES Four-wheel Girling drums.
MAXIMUM SPEED 185 km/h (115 mph)
0–60 MPH (0–96 KM/H) 10.8 sec
0–100 MPH (0–161 KM/H) 34.2 sec
A.F.C. 4.9 km/l (13.8 mpg)

BMW *507*

INSTRUMENT PANEL CONSISTS OF A CLOCK FLANKED BY A BIG SPEEDOMETER AND A 0–6500 RPM TACHOMETER

WHOEVER WOULD have thought that in the mid-Fifties BMW would have unveiled something as voluptuously beautiful as the 507. The company had a fine pre-World War II heritage that culminated in the crisp 328, but it did not resume car manufacturing until 1952, with the curvy, but slightly plump, six-cylinder 501 saloon. Then, at the Frankfurt show of late 1955 they hit us with the 507, designed by Count Albrecht Goertz. The 507 was a fantasy made real; not flashy, but dramatic and with poise and presence. BMW hoped the 507 would straighten out its precarious finances, winning sales in the lucrative American market. But the BMW's exotic looks and performance were more than matched by an orbital price. Production, which had been largely by hand, ended in March 1959 after just 252 – some say 253 – had been built. In fact, the 507 took BMW to the brink of financial oblivion, yet if that had been the last BMW it would have been a beautiful way to die.

INTERIOR
There are gimmicky horn-pulls behind the steering wheel, but other features predicted later innovations; some cars had internally adjusting door mirrors.

RAKISH BODY
The 507's body is an all-aluminium affair atop a simple tubular-steel chassis.

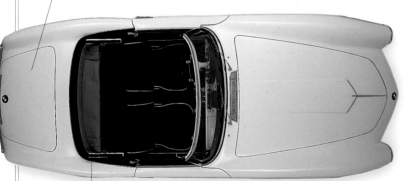

HOOD
You rarely see a 507 with its hood raised, but it is simple to erect and remarkably handsome.

REAR BUMPER
The 507 features minimal brightwork. Rear bumpers have no bulky over-riders.

PIPE MUSIC
The BMW has a brisk, wholesome bark and unmistakable creamy wuffle of a V8.

WHEELS
Bolt-on steel wheels were fitted to many cars, but knock-off Rudge items like these remain the most sought-after option.

LUGGAGE
Inside there is enough room for a reasonable amount of luggage.

DOOR HANDLES
Like the bumpers, the door handles are surprisingly discreet – if not particularly easy to use.

ROUNDELS
Eight BMW stylized propeller roundels, including those on wheel trims and eared spinners, grace the 507, nine if you include the badge in the centre of the steering wheel.

BRAKES
Most 507s were built with all-round Alfin drum brakes. Some later cars have more effective front disc brakes.

HANDLING
The 507 tended towards marked understeer; so instant is throttle response the tail easily snaps out.

RADIATOR GRILLE
BMW's familiar kidney grilles become widely flared "nostrils".

TWIN ZENITH CARBS ARE THE SAME AS THOSE OF CONTEMPORARY PORSCHES

─ **SPECIFICATIONS** ─

MODEL BMW 507 (1956–59)
PRODUCTION 252/3, most LHD
BODY STYLE Two-seater roadster.
CONSTRUCTION Box section and tubular steel chassis; aluminium body.
ENGINE All-aluminium 3168cc V8, two valves per cylinder.
POWER OUTPUT 150 bhp at 5000 rpm; some later cars 160 bhp at 5600 rpm.
TRANSMISSION Four-speed manual.
SUSPENSION *Front:* Unequal-length wishbones, torsion-bar springs and telescopic dampers.
Rear: Live axle, torsion-bar springs.
BRAKES Drums front and rear; front discs and rear drums on later cars
MAXIMUM SPEED 201 km/h (125 mph); 217–225 km/h (135–140 mph) with optional 3.42:1 final drive.
0–60 MPH (0–96 KM/H) 9 sec
A.F.C. 6.4 km/l (18 mpg)

BMW 507

Mounted on a tubular-steel chassis cut down from saloons, Albrecht Goertz's aluminium body is reminiscent of the contemporary – and slightly cheaper – Mercedes-Benz 300SL roadster; from the front it resembles the later AC Aces and Cobra *(see pages 20–23)*. All 252 cars were built as convertibles; a detachable hard-top was available as an option.

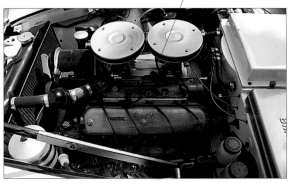

BONNET VENT
The ornate chrome-plated grilles in the front wings cover functional engine-bay air vents.

ENGINE
The 3.2-litre all-aluminium engine was light and powerful and, when mated to an optional 3.42 to 1 final-drive ratio, tuned 160 bhp versions were good for 225 km/h (140 mph).

TOOLKIT
Like all modern BMWs, the 507 has a toolkit – now rarely complete – to carry out minor repairs and adjustments.

BMW *3.0 CSL*

ONE LITTLE LETTER CAN MAKE so much difference. In this case it is the L at the end of the name tag that makes the BMW 3.0CSL so special. The BMW CS pillarless coupés of the late Sixties and early Seventies were elegant and good-looking glasshouse tourers. But add that L and you have a legend. The letter actually stands for "Leightmetall", and when tacked to the rump of the BMW it amounts to warpaint, far more intimidating than today's impotent GTi acronyms. The original CSL of 1974 had a 2985cc engine developing 180 bhp, no front bumper, and a mixture of aluminium and thinner-than-standard steel body-panels. In August 1972, a cylinder-bore increase took the CSL's capacity to 3003cc with 200 bhp and allowed it into Group 2 for competition purposes. But it is the wild-winged, so-called "Batmobile" homologation special that really boils the blood of boy racers. An ultimate road car, great racer, rare, short-lived and high-priced, this charismatic, pared-down Beemer has got copy book classic credentials.

ROAD-GOING RACER
The Batmobile's aerodynamic aids had to be homologated by fitment to at least 500 road cars. They were considered so outrageous that most were supplied as kits for owners to fit – or not – at their discretion.

FLYING MACHINE
The highly effective wings and spoilers of the so-called Batmobile *(left)* were developed to keep the 3.2-litre racing 3.0CSLs firmly on the track at high speed.

DO-IT-YOURSELF
Road-going cars were only slightly lighter than the CS and CSi; they even had BMW's trademark toolkit, neatly hinged from the underside of the aluminium boot lid.

INTERIOR
British-spec CSLs, like this car, retained Scheel lightweight bucket seats, but had carpets, electric windows (front and rear), power steering, and a sliver of wood.

STEERING WHEEL IS STRAIGHT OUT OF THE CS/CSi

RACING TRIM
Optional air guide for rear end of roof.

KS·K 5405

CALLING CARD
The large script leaves no one in any doubt about what has just overtaken them.

SPECIFICATIONS

MODEL BMW 3.0CSL (1971–74)
PRODUCTION 1,208 (all versions)
BODY STYLE Two-door pillarless coupé.
CONSTRUCTION Steel monocoque, steel and aluminium body.
ENGINE 2985cc, 3003cc, or 3153cc in-line six.
POWER OUTPUT 200 bhp at 5500 rpm (3003cc).
TRANSMISSION 4-speed manual.
SUSPENSION *Front:* MacPherson struts and anti-roll bar. *Rear:* semi-trailing swinging arms, coil springs, and anti-roll bar.
BRAKES Servo-assisted ventilated discs front and rear.
MAXIMUM SPEED 217 km/h (135 mph) (3003cc)
0–60 MPH 7.3 sec (3003cc)
0–100 MPH 21 sec (3003cc)
A.F.C. 7.8–8.8 km/l (22–25 mpg)

KS·K 5405

BMW 3.0CSL
Mild rather than wild and winged, the CSL is certainly one of the best-looking cars of its generation. With its pillarless look, the cabin is light and airy, despite the black interior. But all that glass made it hot; air vents behind the BMW rear-pillar badge helped a little.

ENGINE
In genuine racing trim, the Batmobile's 3.2-litre straight-six engine gave nearly 400 bhp and, for 1976, nearly 500 bhp with turbocharging. But road cars like this British-spec 3003cc 3.0CSL gave around 200 bhp on fuel injection.

ORIGINAL 2985CC CAPACITY WAS INCREASED TO THIS 3003CC ENGINE FOR HOMOLOGATION PURPOSES

WHEELS
18 cm (7 in) light-alloy wheels covered by delicate chrome-plated wheelarch extensions.

BUMPER-TO-BUMPER
German-market CSLs had no front bumper and a glass-fibre rear bumper; this car's metal items show it to be a British-spec model.

3.0 CSL

BMW *M1*

THE M1 – A SIMPLE NAME, a simple concept. M stood for Motorsport GmbH, BMW's separate competition division, and the number one? Well, this was going to be a first, for this time BMW were not just going to develop capable racers from competent saloons and coupés. They were going to build a high-profile, beat-all racer, with road-going versions basking in the reflected glory of on-track success.

The first prototype ran in 1977, with the M1 entering production in 1978. By the end of manufacture in 1980, a mere 457 racing and road-going M1s had been built, making it one of the rarest and most desirable of modern BMWs. Though its racing career was only briefly distinguished, it is as one of the all-time ultimate road cars that the M1 stands out, for it is not just a 277 bhp, 257 km/h (160 mph) "autobahnstormer". It is one of the least demanding supercars to drive, a testament to its fine engineering, and is in many ways as remarkable as the gorgeous 328 of the 1930s.

SPECTACLE ON THE TRACK
BMW teamed up with FOCA (Formula One Constructors' Association) to create the spectacular Procar series – M1-only races planned primarily as supporting events for Grand Prix meetings in 1979 and 1980.

INTERIOR
The all-black interior is sombre, but fixtures and fittings are all to a high standard; unlike those of many supercars, the heating and ventilation systems actually work. The driving position is good too, with adjustable steering wheel and well placed pedals in the narrow footwells.

ENGINE
The M1's 3453cc straight-six engine uses essentially the same cast-iron cylinder block as BMW's 635CSi coupé, but with a forged-alloy crankshaft and slightly longer connecting rods. The cylinder head is a light-alloy casting, with two chain-driven overhead cams operating four valves per cylinder.

LEFT HOOKERS
All BMW M1s are left-hand-drive.

AIR DAM
Unlike many of today's high-performance saloon cars, the M1 has only a vestigial lip-type front air-dam.

HEADLAMPS
*Retractable headlamps
are backed up by grille-
mounted driving lamps.*

SLATTED COVER
*Rearward visibility through the slatted,
heavily-buttressed engine cover is restricted.*

BMW M1

The BMW M1 was not a strict in-house
BMW product, but one with widespread
international influences. From a concept
car created in 1972 by Frenchman Paul
Bracq, the final shape of the body was
created in Italy by Giorgio
Giugiaro's ItalDesign in Turin.
Lamborghini also contributed
to the engineering. Yet
somehow it all comes
together in a unified shape
and, with the double kidney
grille, the M1 is still
unmistakably a BMW.

REAR LIGHTS
*Large rear lamp clusters
are the same as those of
the BMW's 6-series coupé
and 7-series saloon models.*

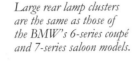

FUEL CAP
*Twin tanks are refilled via an orifice behind
each door. Remarkably, fuel consumption
can be as low as 10.6 km/l (30 mpg).*

MIRROR
*Big door mirrors — essential
for manoeuvring the M1 —
are electrically adjusted.*

AIR VENT
*Strategically positioned
air vents keep the powerful
3.5-litre engine cool.*

> ## SPECIFICATIONS
> **MODEL** BMW M1 (1978–80)
> **PRODUCTION** 457, all LHD
> **BODY STYLE** Two-seater
> mid-engined sports.
> **CONSTRUCTION** Tubular steel space-
> frame with glass-fibre body.
> **ENGINE** In-line six, four valves per
> cylinder, dohc 3453cc.
> **POWER OUTPUT** 277 bhp at 6500 rpm
> **TRANSMISSION** Combined ZF
> five-speed gearbox and limited
> slip differential.
> **SUSPENSION** Coil springs, wishbones
> and Bilstein gas-pressure telescopic
> dampers front and rear.
> **BRAKES** Servo-assisted ventilated discs
> all round.
> **MAXIMUM SPEED** 261 km/h (162 mph)
> **0–60 MPH** (0–96 KM/H) 5.4 sec
> **A.F.C.** 8.5–10.6 km/l (24–30 mpg)

WHEELS
*Slatted Campagnolo
wheels with five-stud
fixing are unique
to the M1.*

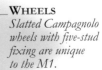

BUICK *Roadmaster*

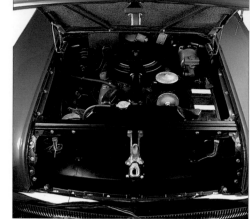

IN 1957, AMERICA WAS GEARING up for the Sixties. Little Richard screamed his way to the top with "Lucille" and Elvis had nine hits in a row. Jack Kerouac penned his immortal novel *On the Road*, inspiring carloads of Americans to seek the adman's "Promised Land" along Ike's new interstates. Fins and chrome were applied with a trowel and General Motors, whose styling had begun to lag behind the rest of Detroit's excesses, spent several hundred million dollars refashioning their Buick model range. Despite celebrating the ninth million Buick built, 1957 sales were down 24 per cent, ranking them fourth in the industry.

The Roadmaster of 1957 was low and mighty, a massive 5.46 m (17 ft 11 in) long and 1.83 m (6 ft) wide. Power was up to 300 bhp, along with trendy dorsal fins, Sweepspear body mouldings, and a trio of chrome chevrons on the rear quarters. Four Ventiports, a Buick trademark harking back to the original 1949 Roadmaster, still graced the sweeping front fenders. But America did not take to Buick's new look, particularly some of the Roadmaster's fashionable jet-age design motifs. The chrome bands separating the three-piece rear windows, for example, encountered huge consumer resistance and were an option that could be deleted on the order form.

V8 HAD 10:1 COMPRESSION RATIO, WHICH MEANT 100 OCTANE FUEL

ENGINE
The hot Buick's 5.9-litre V8 pushed out 300 bhp; it was capable of 180 km/h (112 mph) and 0 to 60 mph (96 km/h) in ten seconds. Dynaflow transmission had variable pitch blades which changed their angle like those of an aeroplane propeller.

FICKLE FASHION
Wrap-around windshields first emerged in 1954 and by 1957 were on virtually every car.

AMERICAN CLASSIC
The 1951 Roadmaster Convertible had become an American icon, the shape of things to come, and one of the first of the great American land yachts with some serious shove.

GRATUITOUS ORNAMENTATION
The Roadmaster's flattened Ventiports were useless vanities, suggesting fire-breathing power.

FILLER CAP
The Roadmaster's rear bumper was home to a new centred fuel filler.

STYLING EXCESS
Vast chrome rear bumper made for a prodigious overhang, with massive Dagmar-like overriders, razor-sharp tail lights and fluted underpanel – a stylistic nightmare.

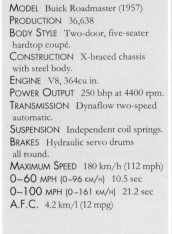

FIN FASHION
The Roadmaster showed that, by 1957, tail-fin fashion was rising to ridiculous heights.

SPECIFICATIONS

MODEL Buick Roadmaster (1957)
PRODUCTION 36,638
BODY STYLE Two-door, five-seater hardtop coupé.
CONSTRUCTION X-braced chassis with steel body.
ENGINE V8, 364cu in.
POWER OUTPUT 250 bhp at 4400 rpm.
TRANSMISSION Dynaflow two-speed automatic.
SUSPENSION Independent coil springs.
BRAKES Hydraulic servo drums all round.
MAXIMUM SPEED 180 km/h (112 mph)
0–60 MPH (0–96 KM/H) 10.5 sec
0–100 MPH (0–161 KM/H) 21.2 sec
A.F.C. 4.2 km/l (12 mpg)

GM BADGE INDICATES THAT BUICKS WERE BUILT AT GM's FACTORY IN FLINT, MICHIGAN

BUICK ROADMASTER
Aircraft design exerted a major influence on automotive styling in the Fifties and the '57 Roadmaster was no exception. With wrap-around windshield, cockpit-like roof area, and turbine-style wheel covers, a nation of Walter Mittys could imagine themselves vapour-trailing through the stratosphere.

DASHBOARD
Roadmaster standard special equipment included a Red Liner speedometer, glovebox lamp, trip mileage indicator, and a colour-coordinated dash panel.

PRESTIGE
The Roadmaster was one of Buick's most luxurious models and wore its bonnet mascot with pride.

JET AGE
Giant chrome protuberances suggested jet-turbine power.

CABIN OR COCKPIT?
Rakish swooping roof line borrows heavily from bubble cockpits of jet fighters.

CADILLAC *Eldorado Convertible*

FOR 1950S AMERICA, cars did not come much more glamorous than the 1953 Eldorado. "A car apart – even from other Cadillacs", assured the advertising copy. The first Caddy to bear the Eldo badge, it was seen as the ultimate and most desirable American luxury car, good enough even for Marilyn Monroe and Dwight Eisenhower. Conceived as a limited edition, the '53 brought avant-garde styling cues from Harley Earl's Motorama Exhibitions. Earl was Cadillac's inspired chief designer, while Motorama were yearly futuristic car shows where his whims of steel took on form. At a hefty $7,750, nearly twice as much as the regular Cadillac Convertible and five times as much as an ordinary Chevrolet, the '53 was special. In 1954, Cadillac cut the price by 50 per cent and soon Eldorados were leaving showrooms like heat-seeking missiles. Today collectors regard the '53 as the one that started it all – the first and most fabulous of the Eldorados.

ENGINE
As Cadillac's finest flagship, the Eldorado had image by the bucketful. The 331 cubic inch V8 engine was the most powerful yet, and the body-line was ultra sleek.

WINDSCREEN
The standard Cadillac wrap-around windscreen was first seen on the '53.

CHROME STYLING
The missile-shaped protuberances on the bumpers were known as Dagmars after a lushly upholstered starlet of the day.

SPARE WHEEL
The boot-mounted spare wheel was an after-market continental touring kit.

INTERIOR
Standard equipment on the Eldo convertible was Hydra-Matic transmission, hydraulic window lifts, leather and cloth upholstery, tinted glass, vanity and side mirrors, plus a self-seeking radio.

FUTURISTIC EXHAUST
The twin exhausts emerge from the rear bumper – the beginnings of "jet-age" styling themes which would culminate in the outrageous 107-cm (42-in) fins on the 1959 Cadillac Convertible (see pages 58–61).

CADILLAC ELDORADO CONVERTIBLE
At the time the '53 was America's most powerful car, with a cast iron V8, four-barrel carburettor, and wedge cylinder head. With the standard convertible weighing 136 kg (300 lb) less, the Eldorado was actually the slowest of the Cadillacs. But despite air conditioning boosting the car's weight to 2,177 kg (4,800 lb), top speed was still a brisk 187 km/h (116 mph).

DOOR HANDLE
Low and sleek, the '53's body-line made a dip near the door handle that imitated the cut-down doors of British sports cars.

SLICK DESIGN
The hood neatly disappeared below a steel tonneau panel, giving the Eldorado a much cleaner uninterrupted line than other convertibles.

HOOD MADE OF ORLON ACRYLIC

WHEELS
Swish whitewall tyres and chrome wire wheels were standard on the Eldorado convertible but a $373 option on all other Cadillacs.

SPECIFICATIONS

MODEL Cadillac Eldorado Convertible (1953)
PRODUCTION 532
BODY STYLE Five-seater convertible.
CONSTRUCTION Steel bodywork.
ENGINE 5424cc V8.
POWER OUTPUT 210 bhp at 4150 rpm.
TRANSMISSION Three-speed Hydra-Matic Dual-Range automatic.
SUSPENSION *Front:* independent MacPherson strut; *Rear:* live axle with leaf springs.
BRAKES Front and rear drums.
MAXIMUM SPEED 187 km/h (116 mph)
0–60 MPH (0–96 KM/H) 12.8 sec
0–100 MPH (0–161 KM/H) 20 sec
A.F.C. 5–7 km/l (14–20 mpg)

TWO-WAY MIRROR
The heavily chromed, hand-operated swivelling spotlight doubled up as a door mirror.

BODY COLOUR
Colours available were Alpine White, Aztec Red, Azure Blue, and Artisan Ochre.

CADILLAC *Convertible*

NO CAR BETTER sums up America at its peak than the 1959 Cadillac – a rocket-styled starship for orbiting the galaxy of new freeways in the richest and most powerful country on earth. With 107-cm (42-inch) fins, the '59 Cad marks the zenith of American car design. Two tonnes in weight, 6.1 m (20 ft) long, and 1.83 m (6 ft) wide, it oozed money, self-confidence, and unchallenged power. Under a bonnet almost the size of Texas nestled an engine almost as big as California, a 390 cubic inch V8 – welcome to the world of 2.8 kilometres a litre (8 mpg). But while it might have looked like it was jet-powered, the '59 handled like the Amoco Cadiz. That enormous girth meant you needed a nine-lane freeway to do a U-turn and two tonnes of metalwork gave it all the get-up-and-go of the Empire State Building.

But the '59 Cad will always be remembered as a glorious monument to the final years of shameless American optimism. And for a brief, hysterical moment the '59 was the pre-eminent American motor car, the ultimate in crazed consumerism. Not a car, but an exemplar of its time that says more about Fifties America than a trunk of history books. The '59 *was* the American dream.

OTHER MODELS

As well as the eight-seater Fleetwood limo, you could have a four-door sedan, convertible, or the cinematic Eldorado Biarritz rag-top, which was the most valuable '59 Cadillac of all.

1959 COUPE DE VILLE
Anybody who was anybody in early Sixties America drove a '59 Cad. It was the best American car money could buy, with the pillarless two-door Coupe de Ville its most popular incarnation.

STYLING
General Motors went crazy in 1959 and the Cadillac pushed car styling to a new peak of absurdity.

LOW PROFILE
The '59's outrageous fins are accentuated by its very low profile, 8 cm (3 in) lower than the '58 model's already modest elevation.

EGG-SHAPED RUBY TAIL-LIGHTS ARE PURE JET AGE

107-CM (42-IN) FINS ARE THE HIGHEST OF ANY CAR IN THE WORLD

EXTRAVAGANT MOUNDS OF CHROME MIGHT LOOK LIKE TURBINES BUT CONCEAL REVERSING LIGHTS

WITH HOOD FURLED, THE CAD HAD AN UNINTERRUPTED, DART-LIKE PROFILE

INTERIOR EXTRAS

As well as power brakes and steering, automatic transmission, central locking, and tinted glass, you could specify automatic headlight dipping, and electrically operated seats, windows, and boot.

ELECTRIC WINDOW PANEL

Four electric window lifts and remote control for the door mirrors live in a neat panel on the driver's door. Detailing can only be described as Baroque, with large helpings of chrome all round.

AUTRONIC EYE WAS A GIMMICK WHICH SOON DISAPPEARED FROM THE BROCHURES

CAR'S THE STAR

The '59 starred in many films. Here, in the aptly named movie *Pink Cadillac*, Clint Eastwood reclines on those dagger-sharp fins.

AUTRONIC EYE

For $55, you could specify the Autronic Eye, which dipped your headlights automatically when it sensed the lights of an oncoming car.

NOSE APPEAL

With a bonnet the size of an aircraft carrier, the '59 Cad was perfect for a society where a car's importance was defined by the length of its nose.

SPECIFICATIONS

MODEL Cadillac Eldorado Convertible (1959)
PRODUCTION 11,130
BODY STYLE Two-door, six-seater convertible.
CONSTRUCTION X-frame chassis, steel body.
ENGINE 6.3-litre (390cid) V8.
POWER OUTPUT 325/345 bhp at 4800 rpm.
TRANSMISSION GM Hydra-Matic three-speed automatic.
SUSPENSION All-round coil springs with optional Freon-12 gas suspension.
BRAKES Four-wheel hydraulic power-assisted drums.
MAXIMUM SPEED 180 km/h (112 mph)
0–60 MPH (0–96 KM/H) 10.3 sec
0–100 MPH (0–161 KM/H) 23.1 sec
A.F.C. 2.8 km/l (8 mpg)

ENGINE

The monster 6.3-litre V8 engine had a cast-iron block, five main bearings, and hydraulic valve lifters, pushing out a not inconsiderable 325 bhp at 4800 rpm.

CHROME DOOR QUARTERLIGHTS COULD BE SWIVELLED FROM INSIDE THE CAR

STEEP, WRAP-AROUND WINDSCREEN COULD HAVE COME STRAIGHT OUT OF A FIGHTER PLANE

CHROME WAISTLINE STRIP GAVE BODY PANELS PROTECTION AGAINST JEALOUS CHEVROLETS

MASSIVE SLAB-SIDED DOORS GAVE EASY ENTRANCE AND EXIT

GLAMOROUS WHITE SIDEWALL TYRES WERE A CONVENIENCE OPTION AT $57

FIN DE SIECLE CADILLAC

Harley Earl, the man responsible for the '59, once said, "You can design a car so that every time you get into it, it's a relief – you have a little vacation for a while". His creations were not just a means of transport but suggested an entire consumer culture and established a new set of national values.

AT THE END of the 1950s, the Russians had put the first Sputnik into orbit, Castro proclaimed a new government in Cuba, Khrushchev got matey with China, and the gathering spectre of nuclear war grew closer and closer. A year later Kennedy would be elected to the White House and America would enter a new decade of stylistic, social, and political change that would alter the fabric of its culture and lifestyle forever.

But the '59 Cadillac really did belong to the Fifties. With tail fins that rose a full 1.07 m (3½ ft) off the ground, it is an artefact, a talisman of its times. Not a car, but a styling icon, wonderfully representative of the end of an

1920s' CIGARETTE CARD SHOWING A "CAR OF THE FUTURE"

era – the last years of American world supremacy and an obsession with space travel and men from Mars.

Harley Earl, directly responsible for the design of 50 million vehicles, completely changed the face of America and the way Americans perceived themselves. No single individual has had such a profound impact on the shape of man-made objects as Earl, and nobody since has been guilty of so many design excesses. On top of the space-age

ONE OF HARLEY EARL'S FUTURISTIC DESIGNS

CADILLAC
Convertible

SEATS SIT 10 CM (4 IN) LOWER THAN THE '57 MODEL

BOOT IS CAVERNOUS AND CAN HOLD FIVE WHEELS AND TYRES

EXTENSIVE INTERIOR
The interior is vast, and a true six-seater, with acres of leg, knee, head, and elbow room. Bucket seats were an optional extra on the Biarritz – only 99 out of 1,320 had them.

AUG PENNSYLVANIA
XSU-385

PONTIAC FIREBIRD PROTOTYPE

theme, Earl grafted on other images to his cars. Grilles had rows of chromium dentures, dashboards looked like flight decks with dozens of gratuitous switches, bonnets sported phallic mascots, and bumpers sprouted enormous breast-shape protrusions known as Dagmars. The grille was a subliminal form of threat display, while the sensuous bumpers were patently erotic. By the late Fifties, the American car was loaded with so many strange and sometimes contradictory symbols that the average American must have felt as though he was in command of a four wheeled, jet-powered bordello.

But the Cad does not have a special place in motoring history because it was an exceptional car. Far from it. '59s had a reputation as rust-raisers, front ends were notorious for

vibration, and the general fit and finish was not up to what the market had come to expect from the premier American car maker. In fact, commentators at the time thought the '59 too garish. So did Cadillac, who took 15.5 cm (6 in) off the fins in the following model year. Yet it is those fins which give the car such a hallowed status in the annals of excess and have guaranteed its collectability as a glorious piece of American Fifties' kitsch.

SKETCH OF JET-POWERED TWO-SEATER DRAWN UP BY FORD'S ADVANCE STYLING SECTION

THE '59 HAD A BIG THIRST, WITH 95.5-LITRE (21-GALLON) FUEL TANK, 13-LITRE (23-PINT) TRANSMISSION, 6.8-LITRE (12-PINT) CRANKCASE, AND 5.7-LITRE (10-PINT) RADIATOR CAPACITY

STEERING ASSISTANCE
The featherlight power steering required only three-and-a-half turns lock-to-lock. The '59 could be hustled around with great panache but you needed a 7.3-m (24-ft) turning circle.

DOUBLE HEADLIGHTS WERE A STYLING ESSENTIAL ON ALL SIXTIES' AMERICAN CARS

XSU-385

CHEVROLET *Corvette Sting Ray*

THE CHEVROLET CORVETTE is America's native sports car. The "plastic fantastic", born in 1953, is still plastic, and still fantastic more than 40 years on. Along the way, in 1992, it notched up a million sales and it is still hanging in there. Admittedly it has mutated over the years, but it has stayed true to its roots in one very important aspect. Other American sports car contenders, like the Ford Thunderbird *(see pages 116–17)*, soon abandoned any sporting pretensions, adding weight and middle-aged girth, but not the Corvette. All Corvette fanciers have their favourite eras: for some it is the purity of the very first generation from 1953; others favour the glamorous 1956–62 models; but for many the Corvette came of age in 1963 with the birth of the Sting Ray.

ENGINE
Sting Rays came in three engine sizes – naturally all V8s – with a wide range of power options from 250 bhp to more than twice that. This featured car is a 1966 Sting Ray with "small block" 5359cc V8 and Holley four-barrel carb.

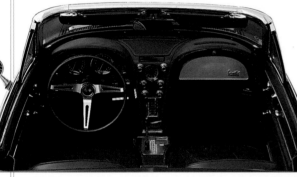

HIDDEN LIGHTS
Twin, pop-up headlights were hidden behind electrically operated covers; more than a gimmick, they aided aerodynamic efficiency.

INTERIOR
The Batmobile-style interior, with twin-hooped dash, is carried over from earlier Corvettes, but updated in the Sting Ray. The deep-dished, wood-effect wheel comes close to the chest and power steering was an option.

─ OTHER MODELS ─

Until 1963, all Corvettes were open roadsters, but with the arrival of the Sting Ray, a fixed-head coupé was now also available.

1963 SPLIT-SCREEN COUPÉ
The distinctive two-piece back window was used for 1963 only; consequently, this "design failing" is now the most sought after of fixed-head Sting Rays.

SPECIFICATIONS

MODEL Chevrolet Corvette Sting Ray
(1963–67)

PRODUCTION 118,964

BODY STYLES Two-door sports
convertible or fastback coupé.

CONSTRUCTION Glass-fibre body; X-
braced pressed-steel box-section chassis.

ENGINE OHV V8, 5359cc (327cid),
6495cc (396cid), 7008cc (427cid).

POWER OUTPUT 250–375 bhp
(5359cc), 390–560 bhp (7008cc).

TRANSMISSION Four-speed, all-
synchromesh manual, optional three-
speed manual, or Powerglide auto.

SUSPENSION Independent all round.
Front: unequal-length wishbones with
coil springs; *Rear:* transverse leaf.

BRAKES Drums to 1965, then four-
wheel discs.

MAXIMUM SPEED 245 km/h
(152 mph, 7008cc).

0–60 MPH (0–96 KM/H) 5.4 sec, 7008cc

0–100 MPH (0–161 KM/H) 13.1 sec

A.F.C. 3–5.7 km/l (9–16 mpg)

CHEVROLET CORVETTE STING RAY

The Sting Ray was a bold design breakthrough, giving concrete
expression to many of the ideas of new GM styling chief,
Bill Mitchell. More than half of all
production was in convertible
roadsters, for which a hardtop
was an option. From the rear,
charismatic fixed-head fastbacks
could be a totally different car.

SIDE EXHAUST
*Aluminium strip conceals side-mounted
exhaust option; standard exhausts
exited through bodywork below
the rear bumper.*

BRAKES
*In 1965 the Sting
Ray got four-wheeled
disc brakes in place
of all-round drums.*

SEATING
*Seats are low and
flat, rather than
figure-hugging, but
the view over the
bonnet is great.*

FLAG WAVING
The chequered flag denotes
sporting lineage, the other flag
bears the GM corporate "Bow
Tie" and a Fleur-de-lis –
lest we forget that Louis
Chevrolet was French.

NAME TRIVIA
*Corvettes from 1963
to 1967 were Sting
Rays; the restyled
1968 model became
Stingray, one word.*

BONNET
*You can tell this is a "small block"
engine – the bonnet power bulge
was widened to accommodate the
"big block" unit.*

BOOT SPACE
*Fuel tank and spare
tyre took up most of the
available boot space, but
at least the boot opened;
it did not on the fastback.*

CHEVROLET *Impala*

THE CHEVY IMPALA was an evergreen best seller and America's favourite family sedan. Chevrolet's product planners reckoned that America's WASP middle classes would be a boom market in the early Sixties – and they were right. The Impala notched up nearly half a million sales in 1960. The fins, chrome, and mock vents meant it was bumper-to-bumper glitz, all at a bumper sticker price of under $3,000.

With a wide range of engine sizes, transmission types, and body styles to choose from, the Impala had it all. And those crossed racing flags were not just empty chromium rhetoric. Enlightened buyers could specify the special Turbothrust V8, making the Impala a "Hot One" with a respectable 0–60 mph (96 km/h) canter of just over nine seconds. Even though the styling was toned down for the 1960 model, the finny Impala remains a perfect embodiment of Sixties' American exuberance.

ENGINE
From a 235cid six cylinder all the way up to a cooking 348cid V8, the Impala could be specified with some serious iron under its hood.

CHEVROLET BADGE
1959 marked a watershed for Chevrolet, moving out of the budget market to seduce aspirational suburbia with new styling themes.

GLASS AREA
With the windows rolled down, the Impala is pillarless, with 90% all-round visibility.

DASHBOARD
Aeronautical styling motifs abound, with gauges enclosed in flight-deck-type binnacles. Lower dash and glove compartment were covered in anodized aluminium for that hi-tech look. Radio and electric clock were optional extras.

LIGHT CLUSTER
Triple tail-lights and an aluminium rear beauty panel were purely glorious pieces of gratuitous kitsch.

ORIGINAL '58 IMPALA
1958 was the first year of the Impala, the flagship of the Chevy fleet and a calculated attempt to catch Ford and Plymouth, who had restyled their products the previous year. Styling was close to Cadillac's, and the Impala's new look rendered Buick and Oldsmobile dated at a stroke. 181,500 Impalas were sold in 1958 – 15% of Chevrolet's model year.

TURN INDICATORS
Clear white lights nestling under the front bumper were not foglamps but direction indicators.

WHEEL COVERS
De Luxe wheel covers and whitewalls helped cut a mild suburban dash.

BADGING
Only crazy stylists would stoop to fixing badges on the rear doors.

TAIL PIPE
Single rear chrome-exhaust exits impudently from behind the rear wheel.

CHEVROLET IMPALA FOUR-DOOR HARDTOP

Low, swish, and beguiling, the Impala looked fast just standing still. Styling was a riot of streaking chrome. Quarter-panel missile ornaments thrust rearwards, while a chromium-finned projectile darted across the rear door, a quaint reminder of Sixties America's obsession with all things space age. And those gullwing rear fins pursue a perfect horizontal line all the way along the waist of the car, ending in a rounded flare on the extreme tip of both front wings. Front and back windscreens could have been taken straight out of the cockpit of a Lockheed Lightning. Even the radio antenna was raked at a provocative angle.

GRILLE
The Impala's slatted frontal aspect is its least pleasing facet. Built to a budget, the Venetian blind grille is an eyesore.

FINS
Compared to the '59, the fins on the '60 Impala were tame. Conventional Chevrolet customers did not like the previous model's weird extravagance.

STYLING
Despite the '60 Impala's supposedly quieter styling, no self-respecting American could bear to be without those voguish double headlamps.

HANDLING
With upper and lower "A" arms and coil springs, the Impala cornered with cinematic tyre squeal and plenty of body roll.

SPECIFICATIONS

MODEL Chevrolet Impala (1960)
PRODUCTION Approx 500,000
BODY STYLE Six-seater, four-door hardtop.
CONSTRUCTION Separate chassis, steel body.
ENGINE Various – 235cid straight-six to 348cid V8.
POWER OUTPUT 230 bhp at 4800 rpm to 335 bhp at 5800 rpm.
TRANSMISSION Three-speed manual, two-speed Powerglide, and three speed Turboglide autos.
SUSPENSION *Front:* Coil springs and wishbones. *Rear:* Coil springs and live axle.
BRAKES Four-wheel drums.
MAXIMUM SPEED 145–217 km/h (90–135 mph)
0–60 MPH (0–96 KM/H) 9]–13 sec
0–100 MPH (0–161 KM/H) 20–27 sec
A.F.C. 5–6.1 km/l (14–17 mpg)

CHEVROLET *Camaro RS Convertible*

RUMOURS THAT General Motors had at last come up with something to steal sales from Ford's massively successful Mustang *(see pages 120–23)* swept through the American motor industry in the spring of 1966. Codenamed Panther, the Camaro was announced to newspaper reporters on 29 June 1966, touching down in showrooms on 21 September. The Pony Car building-block philosophy was simple: sell a basic machine and allow the customer to add their own extras.

The trouble was that the Camaro had an options list as arcane and complicated as a lawyer's library. From Strato-Ease headrests to Comfort-Tilt steering wheel, the Camaro buyer was faced with an *embarras de richesse*. But it worked. Buyers ordered the Rally Sport equipment package for their stock Camaros and suddenly they were kings of the street. Go-faster, twin-lined body striping, hidden headlamps, and matt black tail-light bezels were all calculated to enhance the illusion of performance pedigree. Especially if he or she could not afford the real thing – the hot Camaro SS.

Z28 CAMARO
Trans Am Racing spawned the Z28 Camaro, a thinly veiled street racer designed to take on the Shelby Mustang. Top speed was 200 km/h (124 mph) and 0–60 mph (96 km/h) came up in just 6.7 seconds.

ENGINE
The basic V8 power plant for Camaros was the trusty small block cast-iron 327cid lump, which, with a bit of tweaking, evolved into the 350cid unit of the desirable SS models. Compression ratio was 8.8:1 and it produced 210 bhp at 4600 rpm.

327 POWER RATING
American horsepower was all about cubic inches (cid), not cubic centimetres (cc) as in Europe.

INTERIOR
Standard Camaro interiors included colour-keyed, all-vinyl trim, Strato-bucket front seats, and colour-keyed carpeting. Strato-back bench seat was optional.

NOSE JOB
Lengthening the Camaro's wheelbase created a frontal overhang of 93 cm (36⅔ in).

BRAKES
Disc brakes were a popular option and included special vented steel rally wheels.

REAR LIGHTS
All-red tail-lamp lenses with black bezels were an RS feature.

HOOD
When the Camaro raised its roof, the purity of line was not disturbed.

BACK-UP LIGHTS
On the RS package, reversing lights were moved to the rear valance panel.

FUEL CAP
Centre-mounted fuel filler had RS emblem inscribed.

CHEVROLET CAMARO RS CONVERTIBLE

The market accepted the Camaro as a solid response to the Mustang. Its styling was cleaner, more European, and less boxy, and it drove better than the Ford. Even so, Camaro sales were considerably less than the Mustang.

INTERIOR
Dash was the usual period fare, with acres of plastic and mock wood-grain veneer. This model is fitted with the optional four-speed manual gearbox.

RS PINSTRIPING
Stick-on pinstriping helped flatter the Camaro's curves.

SPECIFICATIONS

MODEL Chevrolet Camaro RS Convertible (first generation, 1967–70)
PRODUCTION 1967 model year: 10,675 RS convertibles, 195,765 coupés, and 25,141 convertibles.
BODY STYLE Two-door, four-seater convertible.
CONSTRUCTION Steel monocoque.
ENGINE 327cid small block V8.
POWER OUTPUT 275 bhp at 4800 rpm.
TRANSMISSION Three- or four-speed manual, two- or three-speed auto.
SUSPENSION Independent front, rear leaf springs.
BRAKES Drums with optional power-assisted front discs.
MAXIMUM SPEED 177 km/h (110 mph)
0–60 MPH (0–96 KM/H) 8.3 sec
0–100 MPH (0–161 KM/H) 25.1 sec
A.F.C. 6.4 km/l (18 mpg)

POWER
The 327cid V8 was puny. Real grunt came from the 375 bhp 396cid cooking SS version.

CITROËN 2CV

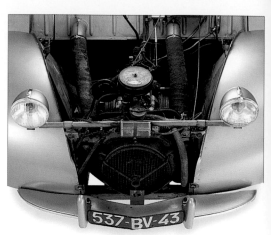

RARELY HAS A CAR been so ridiculed as the Citroën 2CV. At its launch at the 1948 Paris Salon, journalists lashed into this defenceless runabout with vicious zeal and everyone who was near Paris at the time claimed to be the originator of the quip, "Do you get a tin opener with it?" They all missed the point, for this minimal motor car was not meant to be measured against other motor cars; its true rival was the farmer's horse and cart, which Citroën boss Pierre Boulanger hoped to replace with his *toute petite voiture* – or very small car. As the Deux Chevaux it became much more than that and putt-putted into the history books, selling more than five million by the time of its eventual demise in 1990. As devotees of the 2CV say, "You either love them or you don't understand them".

BACK IN FASHION
The two-tone Dolly was a 1985 special edition that, due to strong demand from the fashion conscious who wanted to be seen in a 2CV, became a standard production model.

DRIVER FEEDBACK
Who needs banks of aircraft-style instruments anyway? These days they call it driver feedback, but in a classic 2CV you can tell that you are moving because the scenery changes – albeit slowly. In fact there is a speedo to help reinforce the notion, and in the 2CV's less-is-more idiom the original fuel gauge was a calibrated stick.

INSTRUCTIONS ON HOW TO START AND STOP THE 2CV

SOLE INSTRUMENT ON CONSOLE IS AN AMMETER; THERE IS NO IGNITION KEY

SEATS
Minimal, but handy; lightweight, hammock-style seats lift out to accommodate more goods or provide picnic seating.

TOUGH TWO-POT
The original 375cc air-cooled twin, as seen here, eventually grew to all of 602cc, but all versions are genuinely happy to rev flat out all day. They love it.

DOORS
You were lucky to get them; prototypes featured waxed-cloth door coverings.

CITROËN 2CV
In 1935, Pierre Boulanger conceived a car to woo farmers away from the horse and cart. It would weigh no more than 300 kg (661 lb), and carry four people at 60 km/h (37 mph), while consuming no more than 56 mpg. The suspension should be supple enough to transport a basket of eggs across a ploughed field without breaking a single shell. The car that appears "undesigned" was in fact carefully conceived.

BOOT
Roll-up canvas boot lid of the original saved both weight and cost; a metal boot lid took over in 1957 on French cars.

BODY COLOURS
Grey until late 1959, then the choice doubled to include Glacier Blue, and became kaleidoscopic in 1960 with green and yellow.

SURPRISING HANDLING
The tenacious grip of the skinny tyres is astonishing, providing an exceptional ride.

HEADLIGHTS
Pre-war production prototypes had only one headlight.

SIMPLE CHASSIS
Although designers flirted with notions of a chassis-less car, cost dictated a more conventional sheet-steel platform chassis.

ROLL-TOP REASON
The sober design purpose of the roll-top roof was to allow the transportation of tall, bulky objects.

AIR VENT
Fresh air was obtained by opening the vent on the scuttle; a mesh strained out the insects and leaves.

SPECIFICATIONS

MODEL Citroën 2CV (1949–90)
PRODUCTION 5,114,966 (includes vans)
BODY STYLES Four-door convertible saloon, two-door van.
CONSTRUCTION Separate steel platform chassis, steel body.
ENGINE Air-cooled, horizontally opposed twin of 375cc, 425cc, 435cc, 602cc.
POWER OUTPUT 9, 12, 18, and 29 bhp, respectively.
TRANSMISSION Four-speed manual, front-wheel-drive.
SUSPENSION Independent interconnected coil-sprung.
MAXIMUM SPEED 69 km/h (43 mph), 375cc; 79 km/h (49 mph), 425cc; 85 km/h (53 mph) 435cc; 116 km/h (72 mph), 602cc.
0–60 MPH (0–96 KM/H) 30 sec (602cc)
A.F.C. 16–19.5 km/l (45–55 mpg)

DUAL INDICATORS
A good example of the functional design ethos. Why put indicators on the front and back, when you could give your car "ears" that could be seen front and rear?

BOLT ON
All the body panels simply unbolt, and even the body shell is held in place by only 16 bolts.

SUSPENSION
The sophisticated independent suspension system gave a soft ride, together with that 2CV trademark body roll.

537-BV-43

CITROËN *Traction Avant*

LOVED BY POLITICIANS, poets, and painters alike, the Traction Avant marked a watershed for both Citroën and the world's motor industry. A design prodigy, it was the first mass-produced car to incorporate a monocoque bodyshell with front-wheel drive and torsion-bar springing, and began Citroën's love affair with the unconventional.

Conceived in just 18 months, the Traction Avant cost the French company dear. By 1934, they had emptied the company coffers, laid off 8,000 workers and, on the insistence of the French government, were taken over by Michelin, who gave the Traction Avant the backing it deserved. It ran for over 23 years, with over three quarters of a million saloons, fixed-head coupés, and cabriolets sold. The world lavished unstinting praise on the Traction Avant, extolling its road-holding, hydraulic brakes, ride comfort, and cornering abilities. Citroën's audacious saloon was the most significant and successful production car of its time, eclipsed only by the passage of 20 years and another *voiture revolutionnaire*, the Citroën DS.

LA SIX-H
CITROËN
TRACTION - AVANT
A SUSPENSION
HYDRO-PNEUMATIQUE

SUR LA ROUTE...
LE CONFORT DU HOME

SUSPENSION ATTRACTION
In 1954, the six-cylinder Traction Avant was known as "Queen of the Road" because of its hydro-pneumatic suspension – a mixture of liquid and gas.

STYLISH DESIGN
The Art Deco door handle is typical of Citroën's obsession with form and function.

SIDE-OPENING
BONNET WAS A
PRE-WAR FEATURE

ENGINE REPAIRS
MEANT REMOVING
THE BONNET
COMPLETELY

NEW COLOURS
In 1953, buyers had the option of grey or blue. Until then all Traction Avants had been black.

FRONT SUSPENSION
All-independent suspension with torsion-bar springing, upper wishbones, radius arms, friction dampers, and worm-and-roller steering (later rack-and-pinion) gave crisp handling.

ENGINE
The Traction's Maurice Sainturat-designed engine was new. "Floating Power" came from a short-stroke four-cylinder unit, with a three-bearing crankshaft and push-rod overhead valves – equating to seven French horsepower.

ENGINE, GEARBOX,
RADIATOR, AND
FRONT SUSPENSION
WERE MOUNTED
ON A DETACHABLE
CRADLE FOR EASY
MAINTENANCE

FRONT WHEEL
Front-wheel drive made for tenacious roadholding.

REAR SUSPENSION
Rear suspension was through a trailing axle with twin transverse torsion bars, longitudinal radius arms, and hydraulic dampers.

WINDOW
Minimal rearward visibility.

CITROËN TRACTION AVANT

With aerodynamic styling, unitary steel body, and sweeping wings without running boards, the Traction Avant was a technical and aesthetic *tour de force*. Yet, despite lavish praise, it was this great grand routier that devoured André Citroën's wealth and pushed him to his death bed.

REVISED BOOT
In 1952, Citroën dispensed with the earlier "bob-tail" rear end and gave the Traction a "big boot".

DASHBOARD
Three-speed gearbox was mounted ahead of the engine, with synchromesh on second and third. Drive reached the road by Cardin drive-shafts and constant velocity joints at the axles. The dash-mounted gearshift *(right)* lived on in the DS of 1955 *(see pages 72–75)*.

WHEEL
Michelin produced these Pilote wheels and tyres for the Traction.

SPECIFICATIONS

MODEL Citroen Traction Avant (1934–55)
PRODUCTION 758,858 (including six-cylinder)
BODY STYLE Five-seater, four-door saloon.
CONSTRUCTION Steel front-wheel drive monocoque.
ENGINE 1911cc in-line four-cylinder.
POWER OUTPUT 46 bhp at 3200 rpm.
TRANSMISSION Three-speed manual.
SUSPENSION Independent front and rear.
BRAKES Hydraulic drums front and rear.
MAXIMUM SPEED 113 km/h (70 mph)
0–60 MPH (0–96 KM/H) 25 sec
A.F.C. 8.1 km/l (23 mpg)

CITROËN *DS DECAPOTABLE*

IN 1955, WHEN CITROËN FIRST DROVE prototypes of their mould-breaking DS through Paris, they were pursued by crowds shouting "La DS, la DS, voila la DS!" Few other cars before or since were so technically and stylistically daring and, at its launch, the DS created as many column inches as the death of Stalin. Cushioned on a bed of hydraulic fluid, with a semi-automatic gearbox, self-levelling suspension, and detachable body panels, it rendered half the world's cars out of date at a stroke.

Parisian coachbuilder Henri Chapron produced 1365 convertible DSs using the chassis from the Safari Estate model. Initially Citroën refused to cooperate with Chapron but eventually sold the Decapotable models through their dealer network. At the time the swish four-seater convertible was considered by many to be one of the most charismatic open-top cars on the market, and today genuine Chapron cars command three to four times the price of their saloon counterparts.

ENGINE
The DS 21's rather sluggish 2145cc engine developed 109 bhp and was never highly praised, having its origins in the pre-war Traction Avant *(see pages 70–71).*

SUSPENSION INACTIVE

AERODYNAMICS
The slippery, streamlined body cleaved the air with extreme aerodynamic efficiency. Body panels were detachable for easy repair and maintenance. Rear wings could be removed for wheel changing in minutes, using just the car's wheelbrace. The novel suspension could be raised to clear rough terrain or navigate flooded roads.

THE DS WAS ACKNOWLEDGED TO HAVE THE FINEST RIDE QUALITY OF ANY CAR IN THE WORLD

SUSPENSION RISING

THE DS WAS NICKNAMED THE "SHARK" BECAUSE OF ITS PRODIGIOUS NOSE

SUSPENSION RAISED

MICHELIN-DESIGNED UNIQUE X-TYPE RADIAL PLY TYRES SPECIALLY MADE FOR THE DS

PAST OWNERS OF THE DS INCLUDE
GENERAL DE GAULLE,
BRIGITTE BARDOT, AND
THE POET C. DAY-
LEWIS

DESIGN CLASSIC

Smooth Bertone-designed lines
have made the Citroën DS a cult
design icon and the cerebral
choice for doctors, architects,
artists, and musicians.

GEAR LEVER

The four-speed semi-automatic
gearbox had no clutch and
changes were made by hydraulic
servos. The driver simply lifted
off the accelerator and moved the
lever gently
along the
gate.

DASHBOARD

Bertone's asymmetrical dashboard
makes the interior look as futuristic
as the rest of the car. The
single-spoke steering wheel
was a Citroën hallmark.

CUSTOMER CHOICE

Because the Decapotable was
virtually hand-built, customers could
specify almost any stylistic or
mechanical extra.

ADVERTISEMENT

Citroën's advertising made
much of the car's futuristic
looks; it was once displayed
without wheels to enhance its
rocket-ship styling. The
London Design Museum once
held a special DS exhibition.

THE INSIDE WAS AS INNOVATIVE AS THE
OUTSIDE, WITH CLEVER USE OF CURVED
GLASS AND COPIOUS LAYERS OF FOAM
RUBBER, EVEN ON THE FLOORS

CITROEN KNEW THAT HEAVY FRONT-WHEEL
DRIVE CARS NEEDED POWER-ASSISTED
BRAKES AND STEERING, AND PATENTED
THEIR HYDRAULIC SYSTEM AS EARLY AS 1940

THE DISAPPEARING NOSE
WAS VERY VULNERABLE TO
PARKING MANOEUVRES;
THIN RUBBER OVERRIDER-
TYPE BUMPERS OFFERED
SOME PROTECTION

—CITROËN'S VISION OF THE FUTURE—

Never before in the history of the motor car had a mass market machine achieved such an incredible quantum leap in performance, comfort, and styling.

THE DS's LIST of innovations was nothing short of remarkable. Fully independent gas suspension gave a magic-carpet ride, front-wheel drive gave unerring high-speed control and manoeuvrability, Michelin X-Radial tyres contributed high levels of grip and stopping power was provided by inboard disc brakes with split circuits. Even gear-shifting and clutch action were aided by hydraulic servos, and its pin-sharp rack-and-pinion steering was assisted by high pressure hydraulic

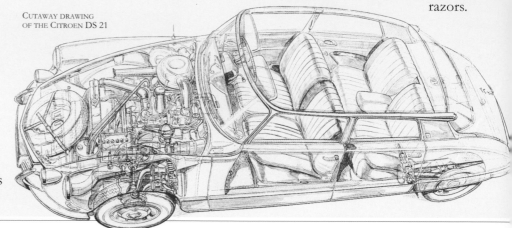

CUTAWAY DRAWING
OF THE CITROEN DS 21

power. Add a body style that looked like something out of a Dan Dare comic and you begin to marvel that all this was achieved in 1955, when the world had just got over the novelty of electric razors.

CITROËN *DS Decapotable*

HIGH PRAISE
The French philosopher Roland Barthes was captivated by the DS's design and compared its technical pre-eminence to the Gothic flourish of medieval cathedrals.

INDICATORS
The Decapotable's trademark was angled chrome-plated indicators perched on the rear wings.

CITROEN'S
DOUBLE
CHEVRONS ARE
MODELLED ON
HELICAL GEARS

ON ALL DSs THE
REAR TRACK WAS
NARROWER THAN
THE FRONT

DS 21

2724 Y 33

Success came soon for the DS. On the first day of the 1955 Paris Motor Show, 749 orders were taken within 45 minutes, 12,000 within the first day and, by the end of the week, Citroën's prodigy had amassed 80,000 confirmed orders. But the French company had launched the DS too early, prompted by scoop pictures in the French magazine *L'Auto Journal* in 1953. Reliability was patchy – the suspension literally let itself down, Citroën dealers had no technical manuals to work from, and owners, whose expectations were understandably high, limped home crestfallen. In 1962, the image of the DS got a shot in the arm when terrorists attacked President General De Gaulle. Despite being sprayed with bullets and two flat tyres, the presidential DS was able to swerve and speed away to safety.

By the time the DS was deleted from the brochures in 1975, no less than 1½ million had been sold worldwide. For a brief period, the DS fell from grace. In the 1970s, it was eclipsed by the CX, and seen as overly complicated and difficult to mend. But by the early 1980s, that shape began to recapture the imagination of car enthusiasts, who rightly hailed it as a style icon and a work of art. Robustly championed as the Car of the Century, the DS was unique, a mechanical invention so

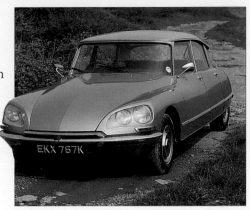

CITROEN DS 21 PALLAS

brilliant that it stood alone as an inspired vision of the future that owed nothing to conventional wisdom and everything to creative genius.

FRONT SHOT

Low, rakish, and space-age in appearance, the DS was so perfectly styled that it hardly altered shape in 20 years. A major change came in 1967 when the headlamps and optional pod spot lamps were faired in behind glass covers.

UNLIKE MANY CHAPRON CONVERTIBLES, THIS CAR IS NOT FITTED WITH A CHROME BONNET HANDLE

EARLY EXPOSED HEADLAMPS MAY HAVE LOOKED GOOD BUT WERE VIRTUALLY USELESS ON DIPPED BEAM

2724 Y 33

CITROËN *SM*

THE CITROËN SM makes about as much sense as Concorde, but since when have great cars had anything to do with common sense? It is certainly a flight of fancy, an extravagant, technical tour de force that, as a 4.9-m (16-ft) long streamliner, offered little more than 2+2 seating.

The SM bristled with innovations – many of them established Citroën hallmarks – like swivelling headlights and self-levelling hydro-pneumatic suspension. It was a complex car – too complex in fact. And of course there was that capricious Maserati V6 motor. Yet once again Citröen had created an enduringly futuristic car where other "tomorrow cars of today" were soon exposed as voguish fads.

THIS IS THE 2.7-
LITRE V6; A 3-
LITRE AUTO WAS
LATER OFFERED,
MAINLY FOR THE
US MARKET

ENGINE
SM stands for Serié Maserati, and here it is – the exquisite Maserati all-aluminium V6 engine, weighing just 140 kg (309 lb) and only 31 cm (12 in) long, but producing at least 170 bhp. Capacity was initially kept below 2.8 litres to escape France's punitive vehicle taxation system.

PURELY FUNCTIONAL
This bulge in the tailgate above the rear number plate is for purely functional, aerodynamic reasons. It also suited the deeper licence plates used in the USA.

REAR CRAMP
Citroën's publicity material tried to hide the fact, but rear-seat legroom and headroom are barely sufficient for two large children.

SUPPORTING ROLE
Like that of most front-wheel-drive cars, the SM's rear suspension does little more than hold the body off the ground.

COMPOUND CURVES
The tinted rear window, with compound curves and heating elements, must have cost a fortune to produce.

ROLLING ALONG
Despite its size and weight the SM can be thrown around like a sports car. It rolls, as here, like a trawler in a heavy sea and, like all front-wheel-drivers, it understeers strongly, but resolutely refuses to let go.

US INFLUENCE
Only the SM's over-elaborate chromed rear "fins" betray the General Motors styling influence.

SPATS
Rear spats were a rare throwback to an earlier age, but necessary to allow the removal of the rear wheel.

WHEELS
Lightweight wheels reinforced with carbon-fibre were optionally available.

IT TOOK PRACTICE
TO DECIDE IN A
HURRY WHAT EACH
OF THE TINY
WARNING LAMPS
ACTUALLY MEANT

DASHBOARD
The SM's controls owe more to style than
ergonomics. The oval speedo and tachometer
are visible through the single-spoke steering
wheel, and the perennially confusing cluster
of warning lights *(above)* are to the right.

SPECIFICATIONS
MODEL Citroën SM, SM EFI, and
SM Auto (1970–75)
PRODUCTION 12,920 (all types, all LHD)
BODY STYLE Two-door, 2+2 coupé.
CONSTRUCTION All-steel unitary, with
steel body and aluminium bonnet.
ENGINE All-aluminium 90-degree V6
of 2670cc (2974cc for SM Auto).
POWER OUTPUT SM: 170 bhp at 5500
rpm; 2974cc: 180 bhp at 5750 rpm.
TRANSMISSION Citroën five-speed
manual or Borg-Warner three-speed
automatic; front-wheel-drive.
SUSPENSION Hydro-pneumatic
springing; independent transverse arms
front, independent trailing arms rear.
MAXIMUM SPEED 220 km/h
(137 mph) (SM EFI).
0–60 MPH (0–96 KM/H) 8.3 sec (SM EFI)
0–100 MPH (0–161 KM/H) 26–30 sec
A.F.C. 5.3–6.1 km/l (15–17 mpg)

HARD TO PLACE
Slim windscreen pillars should
have meant excellent visibility
but, in practice, the left-hand-
drive SM was sometimes difficult
to place on the road.

SPOT LIGHTS
The SM had
an array of six
headlights, with
the inner light
on each side
swivelling with
the steering.

WIND CHEATER
The tapering body is
apparent in this
overhead view.

BACK-TO-FRONT
The SM's engine is mounted
behind the transmission, and
thus well behind the front axle.

CITROËN SM
The SM's striking low-drag body was
designed by ex-General Motors stylist
Henri de Segur Lauve. The sleek nose
and deep undertray, together with
the noticeably tapered rear
end, endow it with a drag
coefficient of 0.27, still
creditable today.

BRAKES
Inboard front disc-brakes
incorporate the handbrake
mechanism.

DAIMLER *SP250 Dart*

AN ECCENTRIC HYBRID, the SP250 was the car that sunk Daimler. By the late Fifties, the traditionalist Coventry-based company was in dire financial straits. Hoping to woo the car-crazy Americans, Daimler launched the Dart, with its odd pastiche of British and American styling themes, at the 1959 New York Show.

Daimler had been making buses out of glass-fibre and the Dart emerged with a quirky, rust-free glass-reinforced-plastic body. The girder chassis was an unashamed copy of the Triumph TR2 *(see pages 208–09)* and, to keep the basic price down, necessities like heater, windscreen washers, and bumpers were made optional extras. Hardly a great car, the SP250 was a commercial failure and projected sales of 7,500 units in the first three years dissolved into just 2,644, with only 1,200 going Stateside. Jaguar took over Daimler in 1960 and, by 1964, Sir William Lyons had axed the sportiest car Daimler had ever made.

TRADITIONAL INTERIOR
The cockpit was pure British trad, with centre gauges mounted on an aluminium plate, leather seats and dash, an occasional rear seat, fly-off handbrake, wind-up windows, and thick-pile carpets.

BOOT WAS HUGE DESPITE ACCOMMODATING PETROL TANK AND SPARE WHEEL

VESTIGIAL REAR SEAT COULD JUST ACCOMMODATE ONE CHILD OR A VERY TOLERANT ADULT

ENGINE
The turbine-smooth, Edward Turner-designed V8 was the Dart's *tour de force*. If you were brave enough, it could reach 201 km/h (125 mph).

SPEED STRAIN
At speed, the Dart was hard work; the chassis flexed, doors opened on bends, and the steering was very heavy.

EARLY CARS HAD TO HAVE A STEEL HOOP AROUND THE BULKHEAD TO STOP SCUTTLE SHAKE

FLUTED WINGS LOOK GOOD AND GIVE THE BODY EXTRA RIGIDITY

GLASS-FIBRE BODY IS 25 MM (1 IN) THICK IN PLACES

EMPTY RHETORIC
The Dart's sales brochure was total misrepresentation. The superlatives "featherlight handling", "impeccable cornering" – betrayed the truth. By 1961, the chassis had to be stiffened to improve the poor roadholding.

SPECIFICATIONS

MODEL Daimler SP250 Dart (1959–64)

PRODUCTION 2,644 (1,415 lhd, 1229 rhd)

BODY STYLE Two-door, two-seater sports convertible.

CONSTRUCTION Glass-fibre body, steel girder chassis.

ENGINE Iron-block 2548cc V8.

POWER OUTPUT 140 bhp at 5800 rpm.

TRANSMISSION Four-speed manual or three-speed Borg-Warner Model 8.

SUSPENSION Independent front with wishbones and coil springs. Rear live axle with leaf springs.

BRAKES Four-wheel Girling discs.

MAXIMUM SPEED 201 km/h (125 mph)

0–60 MPH (0–96 KM/H) 8.5 sec

0–100 MPH (0–161 KM/H) 19.1 sec

A.F.C 8.8 km/l (25 mpg)

STEERING WHEEL
Heavy worm-and-peg steering made manoeuvring in tight spaces a real chore, and in the Seventies many Darts were converted to the rack-and-pinion type.

RACING DAIMLER
Quick enough in a straight line, corners were the Dart's Achilles' heel and it never achieved any significant competitive success. This period shot shows a Dart pirouetting around Brands Hatch in 1962, complete with optional hardtop, pass lights, bumpers, and badge bar.

CENTRE GAUGES WERE FOR OIL PRESSURE, FUEL, AMMETER, AND ENGINE TEMP

PADDED LEATHER GLOVEBOX HAD A QUALITY CHROME LOCK

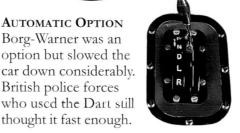

AUTOMATIC OPTION
Borg-Warner was an option but slowed the car down considerably. British police forces who used the Dart still thought it fast enough.

B-SPEC BUMPERS
Dart development had three phases: 1959–61 A-spec cars came with no creature comforts; April 1961-on B-specs had standard bumpers, windscreen washers, and chassis modifications; while the last and most refined C-specs, produced from April 1963 to September 1964, boasted a heater and cigar lighter as standard.

DUNLOP RS5 TYRES WERE STANDARD; WIRE WHEELS WERE EXTRA-COST OPTIONS

PROVOCATIVE TWIN EXHAUSTS EMITTED A DEEP BURBLE, RISING TO A THUNDEROUS ACK-ACK AT SPEED

—THE DAIMLER MISFIT—

The Dart belongs here not because it is dynamically brilliant, but because it perfectly chronicles the influence of American styling on British cars of the period.

SO PENETRATING was the genius of Harley Earl, Cadillac's chief stylist and the man who gave shape to fifty million American cars, that almost every other contemporary car maker jumped on the bandwagon. The fashion for fins even percolated down to a tiny company like Daimler and there is a sad irony in their fundamental incompatibility. Daimler had been churning out stuffy establishment saloons with all the charisma of an old shoe. Cars like the Majestic and Conquest Century bore no family resemblance to the rakish Dart and, in attempting to

seduce the Americans, Daimler simply alienated their deeply conservative home market as a result.

When it was launched, Dodge, who had registered the trademark Dart, forbade them to use it. And, if that

CHRYSLER IMPERIAL CROWN SEDAN, WITH REAR FINS RESEMBLING THOSE OF THE LATER DAIMLER DART

1950 DAIMLER MAJESTIC

wasn't enough, enthusiasts sniggered at the Dart's unhappy styling, which, compared to the smooth MGA, Triumph TR3, and Sunbeam Alpine, looked downright clumsy. With a hefty initial price tag of £1,395, the Dart was not competitive either.

But the Dart's prime attraction was that light, compact, and powerful engine, Britain's only V8 other than Rolls-Royce's Silver Cloud II unit. The British car magazine *Motor* said of

DAIMLER
SP250 Dart

CHROME-ON-BRASS REAR LIGHT FINISHERS WERE MONOGRAMMED WITH A DAINTY "D"

HOOD FURLED AWAY NEATLY BEHIND REAR SEAT AND WAS COVERED WITH A FABRIC HOOD BAG

QUALITY TOUCHES
In the Fifties, few sports cars had wind-up windows. The Dart had beautifully finished chrome-surrounded glass which, when raised, kept cockpit buffeting to a minimum.

4068 WK

Daimler's engine: "quite exceptional in its torque output and turbine-like smoothness over an incredibly wide range of speeds. Other aspects of the car are quite overshadowed by the performance, and its chassis and coachwork are made to seem undistinguished by the engine which propels them". With alloy heads and hemispherical combustion

DAIMLER CONQUEST CENTURY ROADSTER

chambers, it was a gem of a unit which survived until 1969, providing sterling service as power for the Jaguar Mk II-bodied Daimler 250 Saloon.

Underdeveloped and rushed into production, Dart sales were slow. In 1959, Jaguar produced and sold 22,000 cars, while Daimler managed only a few hundred Darts. Never enjoying any reflected glory from racing or celebrity

1961 DAIMLER SP250 DART POLICE CAR

ownership, the only unusual Dart buyers were the British Metropolitan Police, who ran a fleet of around 30 black automatics with brass bells on the front.

The Dart was a Fifties concept born too late to compete with the New Wave of monocoque sports cars headed by the stunning E-Type. It stands as a memorial to both the haphazard Sixties British motor industry and its self-destructive love affair with all things American.

FRONT VIEW
The guppy-style front could never be called handsome but, when Sixties drivers caught it in their rear-view mirrors, they knew to move over. The drastic plastic Dart was seriously quick.

GLASS-FIBRE BONNET HAD A NASTY HABIT OF SPRINGING OPEN AT SPEED

DART HAS MANY DELICATE PERIOD DETAILS, LIKE TINY CHEVRON-SHAPED SIDELIGHTS PERCHED NEATLY ON BOTH FRONT WINGS

4068 WK

DATSUN *Fairlady 1600*

Fairlady

THE SIMILARITY BETWEEN the Datsun Fairlady and the MGB *(see page 175)* is quite astonishing. The Datsun actually appeared first, at the 1961 Tokyo Motor Show, followed a year later by the MGB. Hardly a great car in its early 1500cc guise, the Fairlady improved dramatically over the years, a foretaste of the Japanese car industry's culture of constant improvement. The later two-litre, twin-carb, five-speed variants of 1967 could reach 200 km/h (125 mph) and even raised eyebrows at American sports car club races.

Aimed at the American market, where it was known as the Datsun 1500, the Fairlady sold only 40,000 in nine years. But it showed Datsun how to make the legendary 240Z *(see pages 84–87),* which became one of the world's best-selling sports cars.

EUROPEAN LINES
Higher and narrower than the MGB, the Fairlady had an unmistakable and deliberate European look. However, of the 7,000 1500cc models sold, half went to the United States.

DATSUN FAIRLADY 1600
Low and rakish with classically perfect proportions, the Fairlady has a certain period charm and is one of the best-looking Datsuns produced before 1965. Side-on views show the car at its best, while the messy rear and cluttered nose do not work quite so well. But compared to some of the awkward Oriental offerings of the time, the Fairlady was catwalk material.

OTHER MODELS

Over nine years, Datsun refined the Fairlady until, by the late 1960s, it had evolved into quite a reasonable machine.

DATSUN 1500
Early cars had a less-than-willing 1500cc engine which lacked both mid-range heave and top-end power.

DATSUN 2000 ROADSTER
2000s pushed out 145 bhp and boasted a five-speed overdrive gearbox.

STYLING
Rear three-quarter view has echoes of both the MGB and Midget.

THIRD SEAT
Early Fairladies had a third seat set across the car behind the front bucket seats.

MUF 625F

SNUG INTERIOR IS
DOMINATED BY FULL-
LENGTH CENTRE CONSOLE

INTERIOR
The cockpit was typical of the period, with acres of black plastic. Interestingly, no attempt was made to make the interior harmonize with the Fairlady's traditional exterior lines. Note how the square clock clashes with the circular instruments, plus a steering wheel that would not look out of place in a pick-up truck.

POINTS OF SALE
Although the Fairlady was aimed at a worldwide market – America in particular – it was never actually listed in Britain.

BODY PANELS
In common with the MGB, the Fairlady also had bolt-on removable front wings for easy repair.

SPECIFICATIONS
MODEL Datsun Fairlady 1600 (1965–70)
PRODUCTION Approx 40,000
BODY STYLE Two-seater sports convertible.
CONSTRUCTION Steel body mounted on box-section chassis.
ENGINE 1595cc four-cylinder.
POWER OUTPUT 90 bhp at 6000 rpm.
TRANSMISSION Four-speed all-synchro.
SUSPENSION *Front:* independent; *Rear:* leaf springs.
BRAKES Front wheel discs, rear drums.
MAXIMUM SPEED 169 km/h (105 mph)
0–60 MPH (0–96 KM/H) 13.3 sec
0–100 MPH (0–161 KM/H) 25 sec
A.F.C. 8.8 km/l (25 mpg)

ENGINE
The 1595cc 90 bhp unit was the mainstay of the Fairlady range until 1970. The simple four-cylinder engine had a cast-iron cylinder block and alloy head, breathing through twin Hitachi carbs made under licence from SU in England. Later 1600s were uprated to 96 bhp with a five-bearing engine.

HANDLING
Handling was poised and sure-footed, endearing the car to amateur racers.

FRONT SUSPENSION
Front damping was independent, courtesy of telescopic shock absorbers, wishbones, and coil springs.

MUF 625F

DATSUN *240Z*

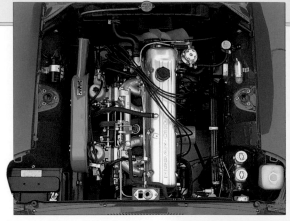

THROUGHOUT THE 1960s, Japanese car makers were teetering on the brink of a sports car breakthrough. Toyota's 2000 GT *(see page 207)* was a beauty, but with only 337 made, it was an exclusive curio. Honda was having a go too, with the dainty S600 and S800. As for Datsun, the MGB-lookalike Fairladies were relatively popular in Japan and the United States, but virtually unknown elsewhere. The revolution came with the Datsun 240Z, which at a stroke established Japan on the world sports car stage.

The breakthrough had been on the cards for a while. The E-Type Jaguar *(see pages 140–43)* was not in its first flush of youth and at the lower level the Austin-Healey *(see pages 36–37)* was on its last legs; neither was the MGB exactly factory fresh. There was a gaping hole, particularly in the US, and the Datsun 240Z filled it handsomely. It was even launched in the States in October 1969, a month before its official Japanese release, and on a rising tide of Japanese exports to the US it scored a massive hit. It had the looks, performance, handling, and equipment levels. A great value sporting package that outsold all rivals.

ENGINE
The six-cylinder twin-carb 2.4-litre engine, developed from the four-cylinder unit of the Bluebird saloon range, provided smooth, reliable power. Japanese buyers had the option of a tax-break 2-litre version, and there were also 420 cars built for the home market with a more powerful 24-valve twin-cam 2-litre unit.

Z IDENTITY
The model was launched in Japan as the Fairlady Z, replacing the earlier Fairlady range; export versions were universally known as 240Z and badged accordingly.

RACK-AND-PINION STEERING WAS LIGHT AND PRECISE AND ADDED TO DRIVING ENJOYMENT

BOOT-LID AEROFOIL WAS NOT A STANDARD 240Z FITMENT IN ALL MARKETS

REAR QUARTER-LIGHT WAS TINY, BUT WITH NO REAR PASSENGERS NOTHING BIGGER WAS NEEDED

INTERIOR
Cockpit layout was tailored to American tastes of the time, with hooded instruments and beefy controls. The vinyl-covered bucket seats offered generous rear luggage space, but the low seating position marred otherwise excellent visibility.

HANDLING
With independent suspension all round, the 240Z handled well, with a true sporting character to match its beefy good looks. One of the few criticisms was the harsh ride.

TACKY PLASTIC WHEEL-TRIM IS AN ORIGINAL FITMENT

STYLING CUES

As with the recessed lights at the front, there is an echo of the E-Type Jaguar fixed-head coupé at the rear, with a little Porsche 911, Mustang fastback, and Aston Martin DBS of 1969.

240Z OFFERED EXCELLENT FUEL ECONOMY; YOU COULD GET 10.6 KM/L (30 MPG) FROM A 60-LITRE (13-GALLON) TANK

DESIGN

The lines of the 240Z were based on earlier styling exercises by Albrecht Goertz, master stylist of the BMW 507 *(see pages 48–49)*.

BALANCE

This view shows that the engine was placed far forwards of the centre-line, with the occupants well behind it; yet the Z was noted for its fine balance.

DATSUN BADGE

Cars were sold in some markets as Nissans, but were badged as Datsuns in the US and the UK.

LARGE REAR WINDOW GAVE GOOD REARWARD VISION

BIG REAR HATCH GAVE MUCH BETTER LUGGAGE ACCESS THAN THE E-TYPE FIXED-HEAD COUPÉ

STEEPLY RAKED WINDSCREEN AIDED AERODYNAMIC EFFICIENCY

THIN, ROT-PRONE BODY PANELS WERE ONE OF THE FEW THINGS THAT LET THE 240Z DOWN

BONNET WAS UNCLUTTERED BY UNNECESSARY LOUVRES; IT LATER BECAME FUSSIER

JAPANESE SPORTING SUCCESS

When the Datsun 240Z's sleek and aggressive lines broke on the world stage late in 1969, it was a sporting breakthrough that once and for all transformed the image of Japanese motor cars.

AGAINST A RISING tide of post-war recovery and growing Japanese exports, the Datsun 240Z was somehow inevitable. The British sports car invasion of America was, if not quite in retreat, at least losing momentum, and Japanese cars were notching up ever increasing sales in the land of Uncle Sam. In fact, the impetus for the 240Z came from North American Nissan executives who spotted the gap and demanded a true sporting contender to fill it. The first Datsun Fairlady, the SP211 of 1959 (a 1960

model is illustrated), was a pretty car but really little more than a sporting pretender; its successor, the re-modelled,

1952 DATSUN SPORTS ROADSTER

bigger-engined Fairlady SP213 of 1962, was closer to the mark. But, in fact, as early as 1952 Datsun had given expression to its sporting ambitions with a quirky little Sports Roadster. About the only sporting aspect was its fold-flat screen. The 240Z, when it appeared, had an instant pedigree, for it was designed by none other than Albrecht Goertz, master stylist of the beautiful BMW 507 and the shortlived

DATSUN 240Z

DESIGNER ALBRECHT GOERTZ INSISTED THE 240Z SHOULD SEAT TWO 1.9 M (6 FT 3 IN) ADULTS

FIRST-OF-BREED
As with so many long-lived sports cars, the first-of-breed 240Z is seen as the best sporting package – lighter and nimbler than its successors.

SOPHISTICATED SUSPENSION SPEC WAS INDEPENDENT WITH MACPHERSON STRUTS ON ALL FOUR WHEELS

Toyota 2000GT. As if to underline its true sports car status, its evolution is an uncanny mirror of the E-Type's, for sporting Datsun devotees generally opt for the sporting purity of the original. The process of fattening up began with the 260Z of 1973–78. With a bigger 2565cc engine to cope with American anti-smog laws, it was not quite as quick and weighed more. In 1974, a stretched 260Z 2+2 was offered, and in 1978 the Z series added more weight and girth with the 280ZX, which was nevertheless immensely popular.

As for the figures, they speak volumes. Add them all together and you have over a million. In fact, the 240Z alone sold twice as many as the E-Type total of 70,000 in less than half the time. To underline its sports car status, the 240Z also accumulated a creditable cabinet of trophies. Its ruggedness earned it a 1–2 in the 1971 East African Safari Rally, and a repeat win in 1973. And in 1983, the 240 name was briefly revived with the Group B competition 240RS, again on the East African Safari.

1960 DATSUN FAIRLADY SP2111

TIMO SALONEN'S 240RS, 1983 EAST AFRICA SAFARI RALLY

ULTIMATE 240Z

If you wanted to cut a real dash in a 240Z, the ultimate Samurai performance option had what it takes. Modifications gave six-second 0–60 (96 km/h) figures.

THE LATER 280ZX OFFERED A POPULAR TARGA-TOP OPTION

THE NAME DATSUN – LITERALLY SON OF DAT – FIRST APPEARED ON A SMALL DAT IN 1932

RECESSED FRONT LIGHT TREATMENT IS VERY REMINISCENT OF E-TYPE JAGUAR

RHX 156L

DeLorean *DMC 12*

MANUFACTURED BY
DELOREAN MOTOR CARS LTD.
MONTH AND YEAR
OF MANUFACTURE OCT.81
GROSS VEHICLE WEIGHT RATING 3180 LBS
GROSS AXLE WEIGHT RATING FRONT 1244 LBS
REAR 1936 LBS
THIS VEHICLE CONFORMS TO ALL
APPLICABLE FEDERAL MOTOR VEHICLE
SAFETY AND BUMPER STANDARDS IN
EFFECT ON THE DATE OF MANUFACTURE
SHOWN ABOVE.
V.I.N. SCEDT26T1BD004579
PASSENGER CAR. 105196

"THE LONG-AWAITED transport revolution has begun" bellowed the glossy brochures for John Zachary DeLorean's mould-breaking DMC 12. With a unique brushed stainless steel body, gullwing doors, and an all-electric interior, the DMC was intended as a glimpse of the future. Today its claim to fame is as one of the car industry's greatest failures, on a par with Ford's disastrous Edsel *(see pages 114–15).* Despite £65m worth of government aid to establish a purpose-built factory in West Belfast, DeLorean shut its doors in 1982 with debts of £25m.

As for the hapless souls who bought the cars, they were faced with a litany of quality control problems, from doors that would not open, to windows that fell out. Even exposure in the film *Back to the Future* did not help the DeLorean's fortunes. Success depended on American sales and the company's forecasts were wildly optimistic. After the initial novelty died down, word spread that DeLoreans were dogs and sales completely evaporated.

STARRING ROLE
The 1985 film *Back to the Future* used a DeLorean as a time machine to travel back to 1955; in reality the car was very orthodox.

GULLWINGS
The DeLorean's most celebrated party trick was gullwing doors that leaked and did not open or close properly.

ENGINE
The overhead cam, Volvo-sourced 2.8 V6 engine used *Bosch K-Jetronic* fuel injection, developing a modest 145 bhp. Standard spec was five-speed manual with optional three-speed automatic.

COMPLEX ELECTRICS WERE THE RESULT OF LAST-MINUTE COST-CUTTING MEASURES

INTERIOR
The leather-clad interior looked imposing, with electric windows, tilting telescopic steering column, double weather seals, air conditioning, and a seven-position climate control function.

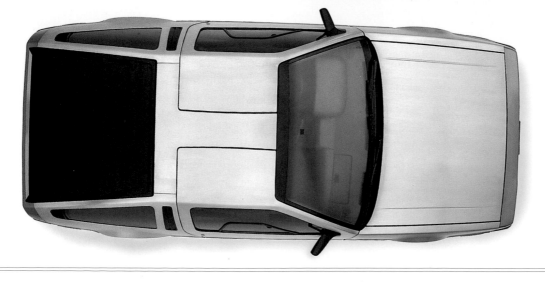

LIGHT FRONT
With rear-engined layout, the weight distribution was split 35 per cent front to 65 per cent rear.

WHEELS
Custom-made spoked alloys were larger at the back than the front.

DeLorean DMC 12

The DeLorean was targeted at "the bachelor who's made it!" and part of the design brief was that there had to be room behind the front seats for a full set of golf clubs. Designed by Giugiaro and overseen by Colin Chapman of Lotus fame, the gullwing doors and stainless-steel body were cynical marketing ploys which, as everybody involved in the prototype agreed, were more trouble than they were worth.

DISASTER DOORS
Overloaded doors were crammed with locks, glass, electric motors, mirrors, stereo speakers, and ventilation pipery. Held by a puny single gas strut, it was an act of the purest optimism to expect them to work properly.

AIR CONDITIONING
With tiny windows and climate control that regularly failed, temperatures got very hot indeed.

SEVENTIES' STYLING
By the time of its launch in 1979, the DeLorean was old before its time. '70s styling motifs abound, like the slatted rear window and cubed rear lights.

STAINLESS STEEL BODY
Brushed stainless steel was disliked by Colin Chapman but insisted upon by DeLorean himself. Soon owners found that it was impossible to clean.

SPECIFICATIONS

MODEL DeLorean DMC 12 (1979–82)
PRODUCTION 6,500
BODY STYLE Two-seater rear-engined sports coupé.
CONSTRUCTION Y-shaped chassis with stainless-steel body.
ENGINE 2850cc ohc V6.
POWER OUTPUT 145 bhp at 5500 rpm.
TRANSMISSION Five-speed manual (optional three-speed auto).
SUSPENSION Independent with unequal length parallel arms and rear trailing arms.
BRAKES Four-wheel discs.
MAXIMUM SPEED 201 km/h (125 mph)
0–60 MPH (0–96 KM/H) 9.6 sec
0–100 MPH (0–161 KM/H) 23.2 sec
A.F.C. 7.8 km/l (22 mpg)

DE TOMASO *Pantera GT5*

AN UNCOMPLICATED SUPERCAR, the Pantera was a charming amalgam of Detroit grunt and Italian glam. Launched in 1971 and sold in North America by Ford's Lincoln-Mercury dealers, it was powered by a mid-mounted Ford 5.7-litre V8 that could muster 256 km/h (159 mph) and belt to 60 mph in under six seconds. The formidable 350 bhp GT5 was built after Ford pulled out in 1974 and De Tomaso merged with Maserati.

With a propensity for the front lifting at speed, hopeless rear visibility, no headroom, awkward seats, and impossibly placed pedals, the Pantera is massively flawed, yet remarkably easy to drive. Handling is poised and accurate, plus that wall of power which catapults the car to 48 km/h (30 mph) in less time than it takes to pronounce its name.

ENGINE
The Pantera is really just a big power plant with a body attached. The monster V8 lives in the middle, mated to a beautifully built aluminium-cased ZF transaxle, which was also used in the Ford GT40 *(see pages 124–127)* and cost more to make than the engine.

INTERIOR
The Pantera requires a typical Italian driving position – long arms and short legs. Switches and dials are all over the place, but the glorious engine tone is right next to your ears.

PANTERA TRIVIA
Elvis Presley shot his Pantera when it wouldn't start.

LIMITED HEADROOM
Do not buy a Pantera if you are over 178 cm (5 ft 10 in) tall – there is no headroom.

De Tomaso Pantera GT5

Fat arches, aggressive GT5 graphics down the flanks, 11-in wide wheels and ground clearance you could not slide an envelope under make the Pantera look evil. Americans were not able to buy the proper GT5 due to the car's lack of engine-emission controls and had to settle for just the GT5 badges.

SPECIFICATIONS

MODEL De Tomaso Pantera GT5 (1974–93)
PRODUCTION N/A
BODY STYLE Mid-engined two-seater coupé.
CONSTRUCTION Pressed-steel chassis body unit.
ENGINE 5763cc V8.
POWER OUTPUT 350 bhp at 6000 rpm.
TRANSMISSION Five-speed manual ZF Transaxle.
SUSPENSION All-round independent.
BRAKES All-round ventilated discs.
MAXIMUM SPEED 256 km/h (159 mph)
0–60 MPH (0–96 KM/H) 5.5 sec
0–100 MPH (0–161 KM/H) 13.5 sec
A.F.C. 5.3 km/l (15 mpg)

WIDE NOSE
Top view shows just how wide the nose really is.

THE PANTERA AT SPEED
The huge wing helps rear down-force, but actually slows the Pantera down. At the General Motors Millbrook proving ground in England, a GT5 with the wing in place made 238 km/h (148 mph); without the wing it reached 244 km/h (151.7 mph).

COCKPIT
With the engine so close to the interior, the cabin temperature could get very hot.

WHEELARCH
Wheelarches strain outwards to cover 33-cm (13-in) rear tyres.

COOLING
Early Panteras would overheat, with the temperature creeping past 110°C (230°F).

RAISED BOOT
Lift-up rear panel gives total engine accessibility for maintenance.

CONSTRUCTION
The underside is old-fashioned welded pressed steel monocoque.

TYRES
Giant Pirelli P7 345/45 rear rubber belongs on the track and gives astonishing road traction.

AERODYNAMICS
With little weight upfront, at over 193 km/h (120 mph) the nose would lift and the steering would lighten up alarmingly.

DODGE *Charger* R/T

COLLECTORS RANK THE 1968 Dodge Charger as one of the fastest and best-styled muscle cars of its era. This, the second generation of Charger, marked the pinnacle of the horsepower race between American car manufacturers in the late 1960s. At that time, gasoline was 10 cents a gallon, Americans had more disposable income than ever before, and engine capacity was everything to the aspiring car buyer.

With its hugely powerful 7.2-litre engine, the Charger 440 was, in reality, a thinly veiled street racer. The Rapid Transit (R/T) version was a high-performance factory option, which included heavy-duty suspension and brakes, dual exhausts, and wider tyres. At idle, the engine produced such massive torque that it rocked the car body from side to side. Buyers took the second generation Charger to their hearts in a big way, with sales outstripping the earlier lacklustre model by a factor of six.

STAR OF THE SCREEN
A car with star quality, the Charger featured in the classic nine-minute chase sequence in the film *Bullitt*. It also had major roles in the the 1970s cult movie *Vanishing Point*, and the American television series, *The Dukes of Hazzard*.

DASHBOARD
The standard R/T cockpit is functional to the point of being stark. There are definitely no distractions here – just a matt black dash with six gauges, a 150 mph (241 km/h) speedometer and, of course, *de rigueur* bucket seats. Factory options included cruise control and wood-grained steering wheel.

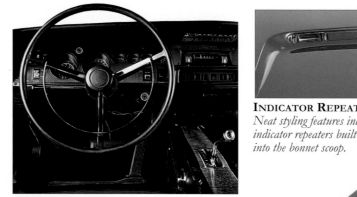

COLOUR
Options originally included Plum Crazy, Go Mango, and Top Banana.

INDICATOR REPEATERS
Neat styling features include indicator repeaters built into the bonnet scoop.

WICKED ENGINE RETURNED JUST 2.8 KM/L (8 MPG)

LIGHTS
Hazard-warning lights and remote mirrors were groovy features for 1967.

ENGINE
The wall-to-wall engine found in the R/T Charger is Dodge's immensely powerful 440 Magnum – a 7.2-litre, V8. This stump-pulling power plant produced maximum torque at a lazy 3200 rpm – making it obscenely quick, yet as docile as a kitten in town traffic.

TYRES
Transferring all the power to the road requires ultra-wide 235 x 14 tyres.

SPECIFICATIONS

MODEL Dodge Charger (1967–70)
PRODUCTION 96,100
BODY STYLE Two-door, four-seater.
CONSTRUCTION Steel monocoque body.
ENGINE V8 7.2 litre.
POWER OUTPUT 375 bhp at 3,200 rpm.
TRANSMISSION Three-speed Torqueflite auto, or Hurst four-speed manual.
SUSPENSION *Front:* heavy duty independent. *Rear:* leaf-spring.
BRAKES Heavy duty, 280 mm (11 in) drums, with optional front discs.
MAXIMUM SPEED 241 km/h (150 mph)
0–60 MPH (0–96 KM/H) 6 sec
0–100 MPH (0–161 KM/H) 13.3 sec
A.F.C. 3.5 km/l (10 mpg)

DODGE CHARGER R/T

The Charger was the creation of Dodge's chief of design, Bill Brownlie, and its clean, voluptuous lines gave this car one of the most handsome shapes of the day. It left you in no doubt as to what it was all about: guts and purpose. The mean-looking nose, blacked-out grille, and low bonnet made drivers of lesser machines move over fast.

SECURITY
The chrome, quick-fill, racing-style gas cap is attached to the car by wire to stop souvenir-hunters.

REAR VIEW
"Buttress-backed" styling was America's version of a European 2+2 sports coupé.

HEADLAMPS
These were hidden under electric flaps to give the Charger a sinister grin.

STEERING WHEEL
Huge steering wheel was essential for keeping all that grunt in a straight line.

ENGINE
The potent engine has enough power to spin the rear wheels in every gear.

ANTI-ROLL BARS
Enormous 25 mm (1 in) diameter anti-roll bars ensure that the Charger handles well, despite its bulk.

FACEL *Vega* II

WHEN SOMEONE LIKE PABLO PICASSO chooses a car, it is going to look good. In its day, the Facel II was a poem in steel and easily as beautiful as anything turned out by the Italian styling houses. Small wonder then that Facels were synonymous with the Sixties' jet set. Driven by Ringo Starr, Ava Gardner, Danny Kaye, Tony Curtis, François Truffaut, and Joan Fontaine, Facels were one of the most charismatic cars of the day. Even death gave them glamour; the novelist Albert Camus died while being passengered in his publisher's FVS in January 1960.

In 1961, the HK 500 was reskinned and given cleaner lines, an extra 15 cm (6 in) in length, and dubbed the Facel II. At 1.5 tonnes, the II was lighter than the 500, could storm to 225 km/h (140 mph), and squeal from 0–161 km/h (100 mph) in a breathless 17 seconds. Costing more than the contemporary Aston Martin DB4 *(see pages 28–29)* and Maserati 3500, the Facel II was as immortal as a Duesenberg, Hispano Suiza, or Delahaye. We will never see its like again.

FABRIC, ROLL-BACK, FULL-LENGTH SUNROOF WAS A PERIOD AFTER-MARKET ACCESSORY

— OTHER MODELS —

Early Facels such as the HK 500 had appalling drum brakes until 1960, when pressure from the press made Facel bolt on Dunlop disc brakes.

FACEL HK 500
The HK 500 was the most popular Facel, with 5.8 and 6.2 Chrysler V8s married to three-speed Torqueflite or four-speed Pont-a-Mousson automatic gearboxes.

TOP VIEW
Facel II used the same wheelbase and engine as the HK 500, but the shape was refined to make it look more modern, losing such cliches as the dated wrap-around windscreen.

SMOOTH LIGHTING
Brake-indicator lights are cut out of the rear wings and help to enhance the Facel's seamless lines.

REAR VIEW
The enlarged rear window gave a much greater glass area than the HK 500 and almost 90% visibility, helped by slimmer screen pillars.

BUMPER IS NOT CHROME BUT RUST-RESISTANT STAINLESS STEEL

BONNET LID IS HUGE, BUT THEN SO IS THE ENGINE

SPECIFICATIONS

MODEL Facel Vega Facel II (1962–64)
PRODUCTION 184
BODY STYLES Two-door, four-seater Grand Tourer.
CONSTRUCTION Steel chassis, steel/light alloy body.
ENGINE 6286cc cast-iron V8.
POWER OUTPUT 390 bhp at 5400 rpm (manual) 355 bhp at 4800 rpm (auto).
TRANSMISSION Three-speed Torqueflite auto or four-speed Pont-a-Mousson manual.
SUSPENSION Independent front coil springs, rear live axle leaf springs.
BRAKES Four-wheel Dunlop discs.
MAXIMUM SPEED 240 km/h (149 mph)
0–60 MPH (0–96 KM/H) 8.3 sec
0–100 MPH (0–161 KM/H) 17.0 sec
A.F.C. 5.4 km/l (15 mpg)

FACEL WHEELS

Light alloy, chromed knock-off disc wheels were the most common fitment on Facel IIs. Optional Borrani-Rudge "record" wire wheels were also listed in the brochures, but rarely specified.

PANELS WERE HAND-FINISHED AND MATED TO EACH OTHER TO CREATE A ONE-PIECE LOOK

KNOCK-OFF WHEEL SPINNERS WERE REMOVED WITH A SOFT-HEADED HAMMER

DASH MIGHT HAVE LOOKED LIKE WOOD BUT WAS ACTUALLY PAINTED METAL

REAR SEATING

The leather back seat might look inviting, but is very occasional and folds down to make a luggage platform.

INTERIOR

Steering wheel points straight to the driver's heart. Note the unmistakable aircraft-type panel layout with centre gauges and heater controls like hand throttles.

MANUAL PONT-A-MOUSSON GEARBOX BEGAN LIFE IN A TRUCK

ENGINE

The Facel II was powered by a 6286cc cast-iron Chrysler V8, which, when coupled to the rare and bulky four-speed manual gearbox, pushed out 390 bhp.

RAKISH BODY WAS ARTISTICALLY SIMILAR TO THE FACELLIA COUPÉ

— The Fascinating Facel —

The first products of the Facel stable were known as Vegas, a name deliberately chosen for its American associations.

MADE BETWEEN 1954 and 1955, an early Vega is a rare thing and only about a dozen survive out of 46 built. In 1956, the Vega was renamed the FVS, this time powered by a 5.5-litre Chrysler V8 that replaced the 4.6-litre DeSoto unit, but hampered by servoless drum brakes. Despite the heart-stopping brake pedal, skittish front-end geometry, and suspension reliability glitches, some 357 FVSs were built, with over three-quarters of the run going to America.

In terms of finish, image, and quality, Facel Vegas were one of the most successful hand-made supercars. Body

joints were perfectly flush, doors closed like heavy vaults, brightwork was stainless steel, and even the roof line was fabricated from five seamlessly joined sections. Meticulous detailing and engineering panache earned Facel an image of wealthy arrogance, somewhere between a Bentley Continental and a Benz SL. But, more importantly, the HK 500 and Facel II were a unique amalgam of '50s American and European styling motifs. Facels oozed self-confidence, with huge wrap-around windscreens, rocket ship rear lights, and aircraft interiors, yet clothed in a softly curved tapering body style – France's

FRENCH ADVERTISEMENT FOR THE FACEL VEGA EXCELLENCE

answer to Detroit's swank tanks.

The third generation FV was the HK 500, launched in 1959, with even more grunt, courtesy of the frenzied American horsepower race between

FACEL
Vega II

DIMENSIONS
At 1.5 tonnes (30 cwt), 4.57 m (15 ft) long, 1.83 m (6 ft) wide, and only 1.3 m (4 ft 3 in) high, the Facel II aped the girth and bulk of contemporary American iron.

HK 500S HAD A MIRROR ON THE ROOF RAIL; IIS HAD IT MOUNTED ON THE DASH

UNLIKE THE DASHBOARD, THE WOOD-RIM WHEEL WAS THE REAL THING

BADGE
The Facel II represents Facel creator Jean Daninos's last and greatest achievement; few other cars of its era possessed the same cachet.

GM and Ford. As soon as the General came up with another handful of cubic inches, Uncle Henry did too, and engine sizes became progressively madder. The first of the HK 500s had a 290 bhp 5.9-litre V8, which, a year later, was swapped for the hairier 6.3 hemi-head design, bringing the already commendable maximum speed to a wild 225 km/h (140 mph). Over 500 HKs were produced, the majority with the standard Torqueflite self-shifter, but some with the awkward Pont-a-Mousson four-speeder. Up to April, 1960, most 500s still had the fade-prone drum brakes of the FVS, later changed to Dunlop discs.

The Excellence, an Olympian 5.18 m (17 ft) stretched Facel introduced in 1958, was a Quixotic tilt at the RR Silver Cloud and Mercedes 300

market. Production ceased in 1964 with just 230 cars built and only 13 sold in Britain. Unloved for its great thirst and dropping pillarless doors, the Excellence is now significantly cheaper than any other big Facel. Facel IIs, on the other hand, are reckoned to be the most desirable of the breed, with sharper lines and even more power – 390 bhp. Introduced in late 1961, they came with wire wheels, disc brakes, auto-shift, and Selectaride shockers. By far the rarest Facel with only 184 made, IIs are still fiercely admired by Facel fanciers.

The Facellia, a scaled down HK 500, available as a convertible or coupé, was the car that bankrupted Facel. Pont-a-Mousson's first venture into engine building was a disaster and the under-developed 1647cc dohc soon had a reputation as a piston-burner. Even

THE FACEL VEGA IN WHICH ALBERT CAMUS DIED, 1960

ownership by such celebrities as Joan Collins could not prevent the Facellia's reputation for unreliability hastening Facel's demise. After creating one of France's most fashionable supercars, the company slipped quietly into receivership at the beginning of 1965.

PRODIGIOUS BONNET BULGE CLEARED VAST OIL DRUM-LIKE AIR CLEANERS OVER DOUBLE CARBURETTORS. DRIVEN FAST, THE FACEL II WOULD DRINK ONE GALLON OF FUEL EVERY TEN MILES

WINDSCREEN IS EVEN MORE STEEPLY RAKED THAN ON THE HK 500

IN THE '50S, FACEL MADE MOTOR SCOOTERS, JET ENGINES, OFFICE FURNITURE, AND KITCHEN CABINETS

FRONT VIEW
The intimidating frontage is all grille, because the hot-running cast-iron V8 engine needed all the cooling air it could get. HK 500 had four round headlamps, but the Facel II's voguish stacked lights were shamelessly culled from contemporary Mercedes saloons.

FERRARI 250 *GT SWB*

IN AN ERA WHEN FERRARI was turning out some lacklustre road cars, the 250 GT SWB became a yardstick, the car against which all other GTs were judged and one of the finest Ferraris ever. Of the 167 made between 1959 and 1962, 74 were competition cars – their simplicity made them one of the most competitive sports racers of the Fifties. Built around a tubular chassis, the V12 3.0 engine lives at the front, along with a simple four-speed gearbox with Porsche internals. But it is that delectable Pininfarina-sculpted shape that is so special. Tense, urgent, but friendly, those smooth lines have none of the intimidating presence of a Testarossa or Daytona. The SWB stands alone as a perfect blend of form and function – one of the world's prettiest cars, and on the track one of the most successful. The SWB won races from Spa to Le Mans, Nassau to the Nürburgring. Which is exactly what Enzo Ferrari wanted. "They are cars", he said, "which the sporting client can use on the road during the week and race on Sundays". Happy days.

FERRARI CALIFORNIA SPYDER
SWB California Spyders owed much to the 250 GT, with the same type-539 chassis, and were first launched in May 1960, running until February 1963.

HORSE RACING
In the middle Sixties, 250 GTs were cheap enough to be bought by privateers who raced them at club events.

OVERHEAD VIEW
The car has perfect balance. Shape is rounded and fluid and the first 11 SWBs were built in alloy. Road cars had a steel body and aluminium bonnet and doors.

COCKPIT IS SNUG AND AIRY BUT FILLS WITH NOISE WHEN YOU TURN THE KEY

GENTLY TAPERING NOSE IS A MASTERPIECE OF THE PANEL BEATER'S ART

RARE LIGHTWEIGHT COMPETITION CARS SUFFERED FROM STRETCHING ALLOY

SWB SAT ON ELEGANT, CHROME-PLATED BORRANI COMPETITION WIRE WHEELS

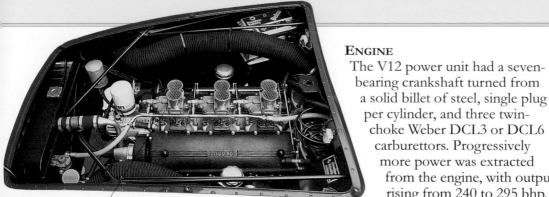

ENGINE

The V12 power unit had a seven-bearing crankshaft turned from a solid billet of steel, single plug per cylinder, and three twin-choke Weber DCL3 or DCL6 carburettors. Progressively more power was extracted from the engine, with output rising from 240 to 295 bhp.

INSTEAD OF AIR CLEANERS, COMPETITION CARS USED FILTERLESS AIR TRUMPETS

⏤ SPECIFICATIONS ⏤

MODEL Ferrari 250 GT SWB (1959–62)
PRODUCTION 167 (10 rhd)
BODY STYLE Two-seater GT coupé.
CONSTRUCTION Tubular chassis with all-alloy or alloy/steel body.
ENGINE 2953cc V12
POWER OUTPUT 280 bhp at 7000 rpm.
TRANSMISSION Four-speed manual.
SUSPENSION Independent front coil and wishbones, rear live axle leaf springs.
BRAKES Four-wheel discs.
MAXIMUM SPEED 237 km/h (147 mph)
0–60 MPH (0–96 KM/H) 6.6 sec
0–100 MPH (0–161 KM/H) 16.2 sec
A.F.C. 4.2 km/l (12 mpg)

250 DOMINATION

Stirling Hamil leads Ed Lowther's Corvette in a mid-1960s American club race duel. For many years the 250 GT dominated hill climbs and track meets at circuits all over the world. The SWB is a small car with wonderfully predictable handling.

INTERIOR

Despite the matinée idol exterior, the interior is a place of work. Functional fascia is basic crackle black with no frills. Sun visors were notably absent.

TWIN EXHAUSTS

Two sets of aggressive drainpipe twin exhausts dominate the SWB's rump and declare its competition bloodline.

COMPETITION VERSIONS HAD LIGHT, BUT EASILY SCRATCHED, PLEXIGLASS WINDOWS. ROAD CARS USED HEAVIER GLASS

EXPANSIVE REAR WINDOW SITS ABOVE ENORMOUS 123-LITRE (27-GALLON) FUEL TANK

INTERIOR SEAT

Roll-cage and modern harnesses were sops to safety. Bucket seats look supportive, but were thinly padded.

AERODYNAMICS

In Pininfarina's wind tunnel with the radiator grille closed, a 250 GT achieved a drag coefficient of only 0.33, a figure that would shame many cars 20 years younger.

—FERRARI'S LEGENDARY RACER—

Although the 250 GT SWB was based on Ferrari's first real mass produced car, the 250 Europa, it was anything but mainstream. More race than road, it was soon feted as one of the finest sports cars of the time.

THERE WERE TWO versions of the SWB, the steel-bodied Lusso for the road or the alloy-bodied Competizione for the track, and it was on those tortuous tarmac chicanes that the SWB really shone. Its most famous win in the UK was at the hands of Stirling Moss in the 1960–61 Tourist Trophy. Moss thought it was a "really comfortable grand touring car with good brakes, a super engine and crisp gearbox ... a very well mannered, well balanced car, especially good for Le Mans or any other circuit where one could give it its head".

Yet, despite its loose pretensions towards being a road machine, one walk around the SWB tells you that this is no aimless boulevardier. A racer stripped of all superfluous fat, there were front air-scoops to cool the disc brakes, wing air extraction vents for under-bonnet cooling, and reinforced points for racing-type quick-action jacks. Even the fuel filler-cap, an alloy quick-fill variety, was essential on all the best Le Mans racers. This was a road rocket in a Savile Row suit, an elegant projectile equally at home crunching up the gravel drive of an English country house or howling round a circuit locked in mortal combat with its deadliest rival, the Aston Martin DB4GT.

ENZO FERRARI ON THE FRONT OF ITALIAN MAGAZINE, *MIRACOLO A MARANELLO*, IN 1955

FERRARI
250 GT SWB

RUDIMENTARY REAR WINDOW VENT WAS FOR COCKPIT COOLING

HUGE ALLOY FILLER CAP WAS FOR FAST PETROL STOPS

DESIGN CREDITS
Soft, compact, and rounded, Pininfarina executed the design, while Scaglietti took care of the sheet metal. The result was one of the most charismatic cars ever produced.

REAR STOP-LIGHT AND INDICATORS WERE USED ON MANY OTHER FERRARIS

MI
1E6000

GUT-WRENCHING THUDS BETRAY THE SWB'S CART-SPRUNG LIVE AXLE

1960s' FERRARI PRODUCTION LINE

third saw the needle touching 249 km/h (155 mph), with a gear to spare. More than enough to give today's V12s a very nasty fright. In the 1961 Tourist Trophy at Goodwood, England, Moss won the four-hour race at an average speed of 141.15 km/h (87.73 mph) and in the same year recorded the seventh fastest lap at Le Mans at the time.

One of the first Ferraris with a well-constructed chassis, the 250 GT not only had a lightness and fluidity found only in a handful of the world's most precocious sports cars, but also possessed a stunning catwalk beauty. The SWB was one of the final

flowerings of that great Grand Touring tradition – cars you could drive to the track, annihilate all comers, and then drive home again. A true gentleman's sports car.

ENZO FERRARI, 1987

Fitted with a 4:1 final drive, it would accelerate from standstill to 161 km/h (100 mph) in a head-jerking 14 seconds. First gear was good for 98 km/h (61 mph), second 137 km/h (85 mph), and

IMPOSING FRONT

The 250 GT is a polished gem, hugging the road limpet-low. Front combines beauty and threat with steely grin and squat wheel-arch-filling attitude. Nothing is exaggerated for effect.

DRAMATIC PILLAR-BOX BONNET VENT SUCKED AIR INTO A TRINITY OF DOUBLE-CHOKE WEBER CARBURETTORS

ROAD CARS HAD PRANCING HORSE BADGE IN GRILLE AND VESTIGIAL FRONT BUMPERS

SWEEPING BODY PANELS ARE NEAR PRICELESS. EACH WAS HAND-MADE, WITH SCANT REGARD FOR REPAIR OR REPLACEMENT

FERRARI *Daytona*

KNOWN TO EVERY SCHOOLBOY as the world's fastest car, the classically sculptured and outrageously quick Daytona was a supercar with a split personality. Under 193 km/h (120 mph), it felt like a truck with heavy inert controls and crashing suspension. But once the needle was heading for 225 km/h (140 mph), things started to sparkle. With a romantic flat-out maximum of 280 km/h (170 mph), it was the last of the great front-engined V12 war horses.

Launched at the 1968 Paris Salon as the 365 GTB/4, the press immediately named it "Daytona" in honour of Ferrari's success at the 1967 American 24-hour race. Faster than the contemporary Lamborghini Miura *(see page 146)*, De Tomaso Pantera *(see pages 90–91)*, and Jaguar E-Type *(see pages 140–43)*, the chisel-nosed Ferrari won laurels on the racetrack as well as the hearts and pockets of wealthy enthusiasts all over the world.

(see page 146), *(see pages 90–91)*, *(see pages 140–43)*

SPECIFICATIONS

MODEL Ferrari 365 GTB/4 Daytona (1968–73)
PRODUCTION 1,426 (165 RHD)
BODY STYLE Two-seater fastback.
CONSTRUCTION Steel/alloy/glass-fibre body, separate multi-tube chassis frame.
ENGINE V12 4390cc.
POWER OUTPUT 352 bhp at 7500 rpm
TRANSMISSION Five-speed all synchromesh.
SUSPENSION Independent front and rear.
BRAKES Four-wheel discs.
MAXIMUM SPEED 280 km/h (174 mph)
0–60 MPH (0–96 KM/H) 5.4 sec
0–100 MPH (0–161 KM/H) 12.8 sec
A.F.C. 5 km/l (14 mpg)

INTERIOR

With hammock-type racing seats, a cornucopia of black-on-white instruments, and a provocatively angled, extra-long gear shift, the cabin promises some serious excitement.

CLASH OF THE TITANS

On the track the Daytona did battle with the best of them and destroyed all comers. With racing modifications, it not only handled but could muster 306 km/h 190 mph) on the straight.

FERRARI 365 GTB/4 DAYTONA

A poem in steel, only a handful of other cars could be considered in the same aesthetic league as the Daytona. Beneath the exterior is a skeleton of chrome-molybdenum tube members, giving enormous rigidity and strength. Body panels were hand-fettled on wooden bucks, with no two exactly the same.

HEADLIGHTS
American safety regulations dictated that the double retractable headlights could be raised in 3 seconds.

SUSPENSION
Double wishbone front suspension was strong enough for hell-raising speeds.

GRAND TOURING BOOT
As a GT car, the Daytona has an accommodating boot.

WIPERS
The windscreen wipers disappear neatly behind the raised edge of the bonnet.

TOUGH TYRES
200-15 G70 Michelin XVRs were the only rubber then available to cope with the top speed.

FERRARI *400 GT*

THE FIRST FERRARI ever offered with automatic transmission, the 400 was aimed at the American market, and was meant to take the prancing horse into the boardrooms of Europe and the US. But the 400's automatic box was a most un-Ferrari-like device, a lazy three-speed GM Turbo-Hydramatic as used in Cadillac, Rolls-Royce, and Jaguar. It may have been the best self-shifter in the world, but it was a radical departure for Maranello, and met with only modest success.

The 400 was possibly the most discreet and refined Ferrari ever made. It looked awful in Racing Red – the colour of 70 per cent of Ferraris – so most were finished in dark metallics. The 400 became the 400i GT in 1973 and the 412 in 1985. It became a fashionable alternative for the Eighties executive bored with Daimler Double-Sixes and BMW 750s.

SPECIFICATIONS

MODEL Ferrari 400 GT (1976–79)
PRODUCTION 501
BODY STYLE Two-door, four-seater sports saloon.
CONSTRUCTION Steel/alloy body, separate tubular chassis frame.
ENGINE 4390cc twin ohc V12.
POWER OUTPUT 340 bhp at 6800 rpm.
TRANSMISSION Five-speed manual or three-speed automatic.
SUSPENSION Independent double wishbones with coil springs, rear as front with hydro-pneumatic self-levelling.
BRAKES Four-wheel ventilated discs.
MAXIMUM SPEED 241 km/h (150 mph)
0–60 MPH (0–96 KM/H) 7.1 sec
0–100 MPH (0–161 KM/H) 18.7 sec
A.F.C. 4.2 km/l (12 mpg)

INTERIOR
The 400 was a genuine 2+2, with ample accommodation for four.

WINDSCREEN
Massive glass area and thin pillars gave the 400 the best visibility of any Ferrari.

MIRROR
Driver's door mirror was remotely controlled from a switch in the interior.

DASHBOARD
The 400's cockpit was a study in luxury, with leather dash and real wood plus the option of a second rear air conditioning unit to keep tired tycoons cool. Rear passengers could also benefit from a four-speaker sound system.

HEADLIGHTS
Four headlights were retracted into the bodywork by electric motors.

PININFARINA BADGE
The Turin-based Pininfarina company is perhaps the most famous name in automotive styling in the world.

BOOT
Boot line was raised to limit drag.

FERRARI 400 GT
Apart from the delicate chin spoiler and bolt-on alloys, the shape was pure 365 GT4 2+2. The rectangular design of the body was lightened by a plunging bonnet line and a waist-length indentation running along the 400's flanks.

AN-48-TA

FERRARI *Dino 246 GT*

PRETTY ENOUGH TO STOP a speeding train, the Dino came not from Enzo Ferrari's head, but from his heart. The Dino was a tribute to the great man's love for his son, Alfredino, who died of a kidney disease. Aimed at the Porsche 911 buyer *(see pages 194–95)*, the 246 Dino engine came with only half the number of cylinders usually found in a Ferrari. Instead of a V12 configuration, it boasted a 2.4-litre V6 engine, yet was nonetheless capable of a very Ferrari-like 241 km/h (150 mph).

With sparkling performance, small girth, and mid-engined layout, it handled like a go-kart, and could be hustled around with enormous aplomb. Beautifully sculpted by Pininfarina, the 246 won worldwide acclaim as the high point of 1970s automotive styling. In its day, it was among the most fashionable cars money could buy. The rarest Dino is the GTS, with Targa detachable roof panel. The Dino's finest hour was when it was driven by Tony Curtis in the Seventies' ITC television series *The Persuaders*. One of the most accessible Ferraris, Dino prices went berserk in the Eighties, but are now half that value.

ENGINE
The transversely mounted 2418cc V6 has four overhead-cams, a four-bearing crankshaft, and breathes through three twin-choke Weber 40 DCF carburettors. The engine's distinctive throaty roar is a Ferrari legend.

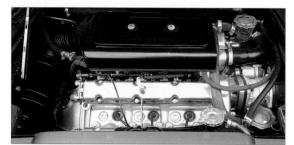

AERODYNAMICS
Sweeping roofline is unmistakable from any angle. The Dino's sleek aerodynamic shape helps to give the car its impressively high top speed.

INTERIOR
The dashboard is suede and strewn with switches, while the cramped-looking interior is actually an ergonomic triumph. Slotting the five-speed gearbox though its chrome gate is much like spooning honey.

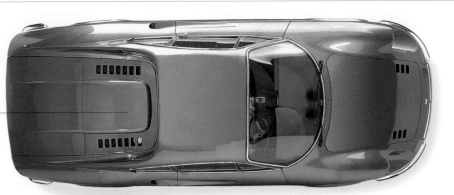

POSITIONING
The engine is positioned in the middle, while the spare wheel and battery are located in the front.

COCKPIT
Interior is cramped, but no-one cared with a car that looked this good.

FERRARI 246 GT

Early Dinos were constructed from alloy, later ones from steel, with the bodies built by Italian designer Scaglietti. Unfortunately, little attention was paid to to rust protection. Vulnerable interior body joints and cavities were covered with only a very thin coat of paint and most surviving Dinos will have had at least one body rebuild by now.

SPECIFICATIONS

MODEL Ferrari Dino 246 GT (1969–74)
PRODUCTION 2,487
BODY STYLE Two-door, two seater.
CONSTRUCTION Steel body, tubular frame.
ENGINE Transverse V6/2.4 litre.
POWER OUTPUT 195 bhp at 5000 rpm.
TRANSMISSION Five-speed, all synchromesh.
SUSPENSION Independent front and rear.
BRAKES Ventilated discs all round.
MAXIMUM SPEED 238 km/h (148 mph)
0–60 MPH (0–96 KM/H) 7.1 sec
0–100 MPH (0–161 KM/H) 17.6 sec
A.F.C. 7.8 km/l (22 mpg)

COLOUR
Metallic brown is a rare colour – 75 per cent of Dinos were red.

STYLING
The sensuous curves are supplied by Ferrari. The Ferrari badge and prancing horse were fitted by a later owner.

SCREEN
Windscreens do not come much more steeply raked than this one.

EXHAUSTS
Four exhausts mean the V6 sounds almost as musical as a V12.

FERRARI *Testarossa*

THE TESTAROSSA WAS NEVER one of Modena's best efforts. With its enormous girth and overstuffed appearance, it perfectly sums up the Eighties credo of excess. As soon as it appeared on the world's television screens in *Miami Vice*, the Testarossa, or Redhead, became a symbol of everything that was wrong with a decade of rampant materialism and greed. The Testarossa fell from grace rather suddenly. Dilettante speculators bought them new at £100,000-odd and ballyhooed their values up to a quarter of a million. By 1988, secondhand values were slipping badly and many an investor saw their car shed three-quarters of its value overnight. Today, a decent used Testarossa struggles to command much more than £50,000. *Sic transit gloria mundi.*

1958 FERRARI TESTA ROSSA
Ferrari bestowed on its new creation one of the grandest names from its racing past – the 250 Testa Rossa, of which only 19 were built for retail customers. The distinctive bodywork, with its sloping nose separated from the cutaway front wheel arches, was known as "pontoon-fendered".

INTERIOR
The cockpit was restrained and spartan, with a hand-stitched hide dashboard and little distracting ornamentation. For once a Ferrari's cockpit was accommodating, with electrically adjustable leather seats and air conditioning as standard.

ENGINE
The flat-12 mid-mounted engine was 4942cc, producing 390 bhp at 6500 rpm. With four valves per cylinder, coil ignition, and fuel injection, it was one of the very last flat-12 GTs.

STYLING
Striking radiator cooling ducts obviated the need to pass water from the front radiator to the mid-mounted engine, freeing the front luggage compartment.

WHEELS
Wheel rims were 20 cm (8 in) at the front and 25 cm (10 in) at the rear.

REAR END TREATMENT
Pininfarina's grille treatment was picked up on the rear end, giving stylistic continuity.

DOOR MIRRORS
Prominent door mirrors on both sides gave the Testarossa an extra 20 cm (8 in) in width.

REAR WING VENTS
Borrowed from Grand Prix racing experience, these cheese-slicer cooling ducts are for the twin radiators, located forward of the rear wheels to keep heat away from the cockpit.

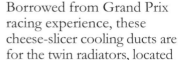

SPECIFICATIONS

MODEL Ferrari Testarossa (1988)
PRODUCTION 1,074
BODY STYLE Mid-engined, two-seater sports coupé.
CONSTRUCTION Steel frame with aluminium and glass-fibre panels.
ENGINE Flat-12, 4942cc with dry sump lubrication.
POWER OUTPUT 390 bhp at 6300 rpm.
TRANSMISSION Five-speed manual.
SUSPENSION Independent front and rear.
BRAKES *Front:* disc; *Rear:* drums.
MAXIMUM SPEED 291 km/h (181 mph)
0–60 MPH (0–96 KM/H) 5.3 sec
0–100 MPH (0–161 KM/H) 12.2 sec
A.F.C. 4.2 km/l (12 mpg)

ORIGINAL GRILLES
The Testarossa's distinctive side grilles are now among the most widely imitated styling features.

REAR-VIEW MIRROR
The curious, periscope-like rear-view mirror was developed by Pininfarina and manufactured by Gilardina.

FERRARI TESTAROSSA

Design was determined with the help of Pininfarina's full-sized wind tunnel, but enthusiasts were initially cool about the Testarossa's size and shape. Wider than the Ferrari 512 BB, the Corvette *(see pages 62–63),* and the Countach *(see pages 148–49),* it measured a portly 1.83 m (6 ft) across. While this meant a bigger cockpit, the ultra-wide door sills collected mud in wet weather and the headlights were inadequate for a 290 km/h (180 mph) road rocket.

AERODYNAMICS
Front spoiler keeps the nose firmly attached to the tarmac and channels cooling air to the front brakes.

FIAT *500D*

WHEN THE FIAT 500 NUOVA appeared in 1957, long-time Fiat designer Dante Giacosa defended his frugal flyweight by saying, "However small it might be, an automobile will always be more comfortable than a motor scooter". Today though, the diminutive scoot-about needs no defence, for time has justified Giacosa's faith – over four million 500s and derivatives were produced up to the demise of the Giardiniera estate in 1977. In some senses the Fiat was a mini before the British Mini *(see pages 40–41)*, for the baby Fiat not only appeared two years ahead of its British counterpart, but was also 7.6 cm (3 in) shorter. With its 479cc tiddler of a two-pot motor, the original 500 Nuova was rather frantic. 1960 saw it grow to maturity with the launch of the 500D, shown here, which was pushed along by its enlarged 499.5cc engine. Now at last the baby Fiat could almost touch 96 km/h (60 mph) without being pushed over the edge of a cliff.

FIAT'S FIRST BABY
The lineage of the post-war baby Fiat descends from this little mite, the original 500, launched in 1936. To be precise, Fiat called it the 500A, the suffix referring to the aero-engine offices where it was drawn up. But the public instantly dubbed it the *Topolino*, or little mouse.

INTERIOR
The Fiat 500's interior is minimal but functional. There is no fuel gauge, just a light that illuminates when three-quarters of a gallon remains – enough for another 64 km (40 miles).

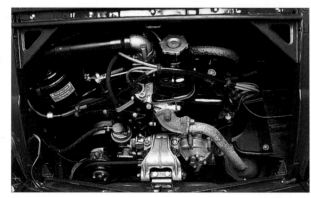

ENGINE
Rear-engined layout, already employed in the Fiat 600 of 1955, saved space by removing the need for a transmission tunnel. The use of an air-cooled engine and only two cylinders in the 500 was a completely new direction for Fiat, and gave an added space-saving bonus by doing away with a radiator. The 500 started with a 479cc engine; the 500D adopted the larger 499cc engine of the 500 Sport, which it replaced. All engines, though, were feisty little devils capable of indefinite flat-out motoring.

EARLY "SUICIDE" DOORS
You can tell this Fiat is pre-1965 because of the rear-hinged, so-called "suicide" doors. After that the hinges moved to the front in line with more modern practice. The Giardiniera estate kept "suicide" doors until its demise in 1977.

BACK-TO-FRONT
Some rear-engined cars aped front-engined cousins with fake grilles and air intakes. Not the unpretentious Fiat.

SUNROOF
Some 500s had small fold-back sunroofs. On cabriolets, the fabric roof with plastic rear screen rolled right back.

FIAT 500D

This pert little package is big on charm. From any angle the baby Fiat seems to present a happy, smiling disposition. When it comes to parking it is a winner, although accommodation is a bit tight. Two average-sized adults can fit up front; realistic backseat permutations are two nippers, one adult sitting sideways, or a large shopping basket.

DRIVING THE 500
The baby Fiat was a fine little driver's car that earned press plaudits for its assured and nimble handling. Although top speed was limited and the gearbox was a touch primitive, the car's poise meant you rarely needed to slow down on clear roads.

"BONNET"
This houses the petrol tank, battery, and spare wheel, with a little space left for a modest amount of luggage.

— SPECIFICATIONS —

MODEL Fiat 500 (1957–77)
PRODUCTION 4 million plus (all models)
BODY STYLES Saloon, cabriolet. Giardiniera estate.
CONSTRUCTION Unitary body/chassis.
ENGINE Two-cylinder air-cooled 479cc or 499.5cc.
POWER OUTPUT 17.5 bhp at 4400 rpm (499.5cc)
TRANSMISSION Four-speed non-synchromesh
SUSPENSION *Front:* Independent, transverse leaf, wishbones. *Rear:* Independent semi-trailing arms, coil springs.
BRAKES Hydraulic drums.
MAXIMUM SPEED 95 km/h (59 mph)
0–40 MPH (0–64 KM/H) 32 sec
A.F.C. 19 km/l (53 mpg)

FORD *Edsel*

THE POOR OLD EDSEL, consigned to the dustbin of history as the ultimate clunker. Everyone blames that unfortunate "horse-collar" frontal treatment, but that is only part of the story. Kinder critics say that its aim was true, but the target moved. Conceived when sales of lower-medium priced cars were booming, the Edsel would be a mass-market winner. The trouble was that by the time it was officially launched on 4 September 1957, the American automobile industry was in a slump, with sales particularly affected in the Edsel's market segment.

The Edsel was also a victim of its own hype. The marketing men had gone into hyperdrive throughout its conception. They forecast 200,000 sales in the first year and would have to build extra factories to cope with demand for a car they claimed had cost US$250,000,000 to develop. The truth is that in its first year the Edsel set an all-time record for deliveries of a brand-new medium-priced model. Yet it fell so short of the grandiose claims that it was almost instantly dubbed a failure. Today the Edsel is an emblem, comforting reassurance for the little man that mighty corporations can get it wrong. And, of course, its comparative failure marks it out as a prized collectors' piece.

INTERIOR
Well over 80 per cent of Edsel buyers chos[e] automatic transmissions. Some 1958 mode[ls] featured auto transmission, operated by push-buttons in the steering-wheel hub. Th[is] is a 1959 automatic Corsair with padded dash. Less than half of all Edsels had power steering.

TELL TAIL LIGHTS
1958 Edsels had a higher rear light-cluster that one cruel critic likened to an ingrowing toenail. The remodelled lights identify this as a 1959 model.

EDSEL MODELS
The Edsel launch line-up featured 18 models in four series, starting with the Ranger and moving up to the Pacer, Corsair, and top-of-the-range Citation. Station wagons were Ranger, Villager, and Bermuda.

EDSEL EXTREMES
The 1958 frontal treatment was muted compared to the 1959, shown here with more chrome than a roadside diner.

HYPE HOPES
Edsel's launch was preceded by a massive marketing build-up. The official launch was in September 1957, but sales for the 1958 model year of 63,110 slumped to 44,891 for 1959, then 2,846 for 1960.

LAST EDSEL
This is a 1959 Edsel. 1960 model year was completely restyled with no "horse collar".

FORD EDSEL

The Edsel is no beauty, for sure, but neither is it as ugly as its reputation. The most controversial aspect is the vertical centre grille; one comic described the Edsel as an "Oldsmobile sucking a lemon" and it certainly has an unhappy frontal aspect. Its sides, though, are clean, almost elegant. Ford advertising gushed "EDSEL ... already an expression of good taste", but that is surely pushing it a bit.

COLLECTOR PLATE
The collector plate underlines the classic cachet of a car once considered a clunker.

"GUN SIGHTS"
The 1958 Edsel had a single central "gun-sight" mascot, which was doubled up into two side-sights in 1959.

EDSEL EMBLEM
The car was named after Henry Ford's son, Edsel, who had died in 1943.

BUMPERS
Bumpers on 1959 models are far more substantial; another tell-tale of the year is the lowered sidelight.

SPECIFICATIONS

MODEL Ford Edsel (1958–59)
PRODUCTION 108,001 (110,847 including 1960 model year)
BODY STYLES Two- and four-door sedan, two- and four-door hardtop coupé, station wagon, two-door con'ble.
CONSTRUCTION Steel body, separate chassis frame.
ENGINES 223cid straight six. V8s from 292 to 410cid.
POWER OUTPUT 145 bhp at 4500 rpm (223cid); 345 bhp at 4600 rpm (410).
TRANSMISSION Three-speed manual; two- and three-speed automatic.
SUSPENSION *Front:* independent, coil springs. *Rear:* live axle, leaf springs.
BRAKES Drums all round.
MAXIMUM SPEED 145–174 km/h (90–108 mph) depending on engine.
0–60 MPH (0–96 KM/H) 10–17 sec
A.F.C. 3.5–5.3 km/l (10–15 mpg)

OPEN AIR OPTIONS
Convertibles are the rarest of the Edsel family. In 1959, the only rag-top was the Corsair convertible, with only 1,343 built.

EDSEL EVOLUTION
For 1959, the headlights were lowered and the bonnet was much more shelf-like. All the chrome took emphasis away from the "horse collar".

OPTIONS
Dual spotlights were just one option in a wide choice of electric and power options ranging from electric windows to power seats.

FORD *Thunderbird*

LAUNCHED IN 1955 as a stylish, personal sports compact, the Thunderbird broke new ground in American car styling. Against the backdrop of overstyled and overchromed land yachts, Ford came up with an altogether more subtle creation which suggested youth, money, and success. An instant hit, the T-Bird was pitched against the first generation Chevrolet Corvette *(see pages 62–63)*. While the Chevy had an asthmatic straight-six engine, simple glass-fibre body, and few creature comforts, the Thunderbird boasted a Mercury V8, steel body, and wind-up windows. In the showrooms of 1955 the T-Bird annihilated the 'Vette, outselling it twenty-four to one and whetting America's appetite for sports cars. The two-seater Thunderbird of 1955–57 has become a design icon, a romantic piece of Fifties American ephemera that features in the lyrics of half a dozen cult songs and as many films.

ENGINE
The Thunderbird's cast-iron V8 breathed through a Holley carburettor and developed 200 bhp with three-speed manual transmission and 202 bhp with Ford-O-Matic automatic transmission.

HOOD
Glass-fibre hardtop was standard, with a rayon convertible hood an extra-cost option at $290.

CARB SPACE
Bonnet bulge was for the beefy four-barrel carburettor.

FORD THUNDERBIRD
The Thunderbird was a brilliantly successful blend of luxury and prestige. The sporting overtones and snug two-seater shape were exactly right for the lifestyles of a new generation of baby boomers.

FORD STYLING
The Thunderbird's rear lights, rear wing, and hooded headlights were all styling themes present in other Ford saloons.

RETRO SHAPE
To many, the long bonnet and short boot recalled the Lincoln Continental of the early 1940s.

WINDSCREEN
By 1956 curved windscreens were fitted to virtually everything.

LOW FRONT
Ground clearance was only 14 cm (5½ in).

SPORTY BADGING
Although Ford's marketeers tried to sell the T-Bird as a sports car, it had a softer image, with comfort and convenience emphasized over raw speed and power.

JET EXHAUST
On the '55 and some '56 models exhausts were routed through the bumper overriders.

BACK END
Rear wing treatment was more restrained than other contemporary American cars and has a definite European feel.

INTERIOR
Dashboard sports a tachometer and high-mount speedometer. 1956 models had softer springs and slower steering than the '55 models. Buyers preferred it that way.

SPECIFICATIONS

MODEL Ford Thunderbird (1955–56)
PRODUCTION 31,786
BODY STYLE Two-door two-seater.
CONSTRUCTION Steel ladder chassis.
ENGINE V8/4785cc (292cid).
POWER OUTPUT 200 bhp at 4400 rpm.
TRANSMISSION Three-speed manual with optional overdrive or automatic.
SUSPENSION *Front:* coil springs; *Rear:* leaf springs.
BRAKES Drums front and rear.
MAXIMUM SPEED 183 km/h (114 mph)
0–60 MPH (0–96 KM/H) 9.5 sec
0–100 MPH (0–161 KM/H) 21 sec
A.F.C. 6.4 km/l (18 mpg)

SUSPENSION
Rear suspension was courtesy of old-fashioned cart springs under a live rear axle.

FORD *Fairlane 500 Skyliner*

FORD REALLY RAISED the roof with this one, and eyebrows too, for a Ford Fairlane Skyliner pulling up at the kerb was an engaging spectacle. All you had to do was flick a switch and watch the amazed faces of onlookers as your Skyliner performed its remarkable and unique tin-top disappearing act. The "world's only hide-away retractable hardtop", as Ford billed it, was based on an earlier development project. That plan proved hopelessly grandiose and to redeem the $2 million development costs Ford created the remarkable Skyliner. Ford was pleased with its party trick and gushed in ads that the Skyliner was "just about the most revolutionary change in transportation since the Ford replaced the horse on the American road". Well, not quite. It was a technical *tour de force* certainly, but also an expensive gimmick whose novelty wore off in three short years. By the end of 1959 the disappearing tin-top had disappeared.

LIFTING THE LID
This press ad from 1957 shows how the drama unfolds. To run the show it took 186 m (610 ft) of electrical wire, 10 power relays, 10 limit switches, four lock motors, three drive motors, and eight circuit breakers. Despite its complexity, the mechanism was surprisingly reliable.

INTERIOR
As the top-of-the-line Fairlane, the glamorous Skyliner was luxuriously appointed, with colour co-ordinated seats and dash, and power-assisted steering and brakes. This 1959 car has *Cruise-O-Matic* automatic transmission.

ENGINE OPTIONS
All Skyliners were V8-powered. Base models were 272cid for 1957, then 292cid. The most potent option was a 352cid unit pushing out 300 bhp.

SEATING
Hood mechanics do not infringe passenger space; the Skyliner, with benches front and rear, is a spacious six-seater.

JET STYLING
Fifties' rocket ship themes are expressed here by big red rear lights mimicking jet afterburners.

FIN TALE
To you and I they are fins, but Ford called them "high-canted fenders".

FORD FAIRLANE 500 SKYLINER

Each of the three Skyliner model years have their own distinct identity. The original of 1957 had full-length side trim, kinked at the rear of the door to create hips; the full-width grille was a simple slatted affair. In 1958 the trim was revised; the bonnet received a fake air intake and twin headlights appeared (grille resembled the '58 Thunderbird, *see pages 116–17*). Further revisions followed in 1959 to create this, the final expression of the Skyliner theme.

SPECIFICATIONS

MODEL Ford Fairlane Skyliner (1957–59)
PRODUCTION 48,394
BODY STYLE Retractable hardtop.
CONSTRUCTION Steel box-section chassis, steel body.
ENGINE Various overhead-valve V8s, 272cid (1957) & 292cid (1958–59). Options of 312, 332, and 352cid.
POWER OUTPUT 190 bhp at 4,500 rpm (272cid); 205 bhp at 4,500 rpm (292cid); 300 bhp at 4600 rpm (352cid).
TRANSMISSION Three-speed manual with optional overdrive; automatic.
SUSPENSION *Front:* independent, coil-springs; *Rear:* leaf springs with live axle.
BRAKES Drums all round.
MAXIMUM SPEED 154–161+ km/h (96–100+ mph)
0–60 MPH (0–96 KM/H) 10–18 sec
A.F.C. 5 km/l (14 mpg)

LUGGAGE LOCKERS
Retracting hardtop reduced luggage space to a small tub in the centre of the boot.

FAIRLANE ORIGINS
The car took its name from Henry Ford's mansion, Fair Lane. Up to 1958, the car was called Ford Fairlane 500 Skyliner; in 1959 it became the Ford Fairlane 500 Galaxie Skyliner.

EXTRA LENGTH
At nearly 5.3 m (17½ ft) the Skyliner is slightly longer than standard Fairlanes to accommodate the retracting hard top; extra length is in the rear deck.

FORD *Mustang*

THIS ONE HIT THE GROUND RUNNING – galloping in fact, for the Mustang rewrote the sales record books soon after it burst on to the market in April 1964. It really broke the mould, for it was from the Mustang that the term "pony car" was derived to describe a new breed of sporty "compacts". The concept of an inexpensive sports car for the masses is credited to dynamic young Ford vice-president, Lee Iacocca. In realization, the Mustang was more than classless, almost universal in appeal. Its extensive options list meant there was a flavour to suit every taste. There was a Mustang for mums, sons, daughters, husbands, even young-at-heart grandparents. Celebrities who could afford a ranch full of thoroughbred race horses and a garage full of Italian exotics were also proud to tool around in Mustangs. Why, this car's a democrat.

MASSIVE AIR CLEANER, HERE IN BODY COLOUR, DOMINATES ENGINE BAY

302, 390, 427, AND 428CID OPTIONS WERE SOON ADDED TO THE STANDARD FORD 289 V8

ENGINE CHOICES
Mustangs were offered with the option of V8 (289cid pictured) or six-cylinder engines; eights outsold sixes two-to-one in 1964–68. Customers could thus buy the car just for its good looks and make do with 100 bhp – or they could order a highway-burner producing four times that much, and enjoy real sports car performance.

1965 MUSTANG FITTED WITH FORD CRUISE-O-MATIC THREE-SPEED AUTO

THE SPORTS WHEEL IS A STANDARD 1965 FITMENT; MUSTANG BOSS SERVES AS HORN

V-SIGN
V8s advertised engine size and their V configuration. Less powerful sixes kept quiet about their lack of horsepower.

INTERIOR
The first Mustangs shared their instrument layout with more mundane Ford Falcons, but in a padded dash. The plastic interior is a little tacky, but at the price no one was going to complain.

BANDED, TINTED WINDSCREEN WAS YET ANOTHER OPTION

BOTH FRONT AND REAR USE OF CHROME IS RESTRAINED AND TASTEFUL

FRONT DISCS WERE A NEW OPTION FOR 1965

PILLARLESS COUPÉ
Both front and rear side windows wound completely out of sight to enhance the hardtop's looks and keep things cool.

SPECIFICATIONS

MODEL Ford Mustang (1964–68)
PRODUCTION 2,077,826
BODY STYLES Two-door, four-seat hardtop, fastback, convertible.
CONSTRUCTION Unitary chassis/body.
ENGINE Six-cylinder 170cid to 428cid V8. Featured car: 289cid V8.
POWER OUTPUT 195–250 bhp at 4000–4800 rpm or 271 bhp at 6000 rpm (289cid).
TRANSMISSION Three- or four-speed manual or three-speed automatic.
SUSPENSION Independent front by coil springs and wishbones; semi-elliptic leaf springs at rear.
BRAKES Drums; discs optional at front.
MAXIMUM SPEED 177–204 km/h (110–127 mph) (289cid)
0–60 MPH (0–96 KM/H) 6.1 sec (289)
0–100 MPH (0–161 KM/H) 19.7 sec
A.F.C. 4.6 km/l (13 mpg)

RACE WINNER
Mustangs enjoyed success on both sides of the Atlantic. The big engine in a relatively small package meant they were more at home on many European tracks than previous American contenders.

FLANK EXPRESSION
Scalloped, simulated air-scoop serves no function but is an enjoyable styling flourish.

POPULAR VINYL-COVERED ROOF OPTION ON THE HARDTOP SIMULATES THE CONVERTIBLE; IT LOOKS LEANER THAN HARDTOPS WITH BODY-COLOURED ROOFS

STYLING
The Mustang's almost understated styling was a breath of fresh air compared with the extravagant size-is-everything excesses of the Fifties and early Sixties.

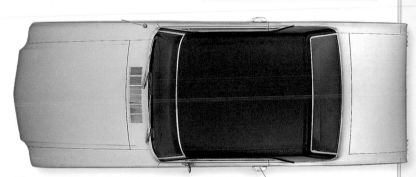

THREE TOPS
In April 1964, first Mustangs were hardtops or convertibles; semi-fastback arrived in October. Three quarters of 1964–68 cars were hardtops; fastbacks and convertibles split the balance.

LONG DOORS HELPED ENTRY AND EXIT FOR REAR PASSENGERS

THE MUSTANG WAS SO SUCCESSFUL THAT A MICHIGAN BAKER ADVERTISED "OUR HOTCAKES ARE SELLING LIKE MUSTANGS"

MYRIAD OPTIONS INCLUDED SMALLER WHEELS, WIDER TYRES, WIRE WHEEL COVERS, AND KNOCK-OFF STYLE HUB EMBELLISHERS

FORD *GT40*

TO APPLY THE term "supercar" to the fabled Ford GT40 is to demean it; in the modern idiom Jaguar XJ220s, Mclaren F1s, and Bugatti EB110s are all the acme of supercar superlatives, but when did any one of them win Le Mans outright? The Ford GT40 though, was not only the ultimate road car but also the ultimate endurance racer of its era, a twin distinction no one else can match. In fact, the GT40 was so good that arguments are still going on over its nationality, as both Britain and America are proud to claim the honour. Let us call it a joint design project between the American manufacturer and independent British talent, with a bit of Italian and German input as well.

What really matters is that it achieved what it was designed for, claiming the classic Le Mans 24-hour race four times in a row. And there is more to the GT40 than its Le Mans legend. You could, if you could afford it, drive around quite legally on public roads in this 320 km/h (200 mph) projectile. The cockpit might be cramped, but the GT40's impracticability is all part of its extreme extravagance.

Ultimate supercar? No, it is better than that. Ultimate car? Maybe.

WIND CHEATER

The graceful and muscular shape was penned in Ford's Dearborn design studios. Essential requirements included a mid-engined layout and aerodynamic efficiency, vital for burning off Ferraris on the straights of Le Mans.

INTERIOR

As befits a purpose-built racer, the cockpit is designed for business rather than pleasure. Height and width of the door sills make entry and exit a chore, but once in place everything falls to hand. Racers had a side gear-change, road versions a central location.

SHORT NOSE

There is just enough room in this road car for the radiator, spare tyre, and a bit of plumbing.

LIP ON TAIL HELPED HIGH-SPEED STABILITY

KNOCK-OFF HUBS FOR QUICK CHANGES; SIMPLE SIX-SPOKED WHEEL FROM 1967

STILL WINNING FOR BRITAIN

GT40s can still be seen in retrospective events such as the 1994 Tour de France rally, which the featured car won. The circuit is the Montlhéry track outside Paris, scene of many minor GT40 successes. The British-owned car proudly displays the British Racing Drivers' Club badge.

SPECIFICATIONS

MODEL Ford GT40 MkI, II, III & IV (1964–68)
PRODUCTION 107
BODY STYLE Two-door, two-seat coupé.
CONSTRUCTION Sheet-steel monocoque (honeycomb MkIV), glass-fibre body.
ENGINE Ford V8, 4195cc (MkI), 4727cc (MksI & III), 6997cc (MksII & IV).
POWER OUTPUT From 350 bhp at 7200 rpm (Mk1 4195cc) to 500 bhp at 5000 rpm (MkIV).
TRANSMISSION Transaxle and four- or five-speed ZF gearbox.
BRAKES Ventilated discs all round.
SUSPENSION Independent by coil springs and wishbones all round.
MAXIMUM SPEED 249–322 km/h (155–200 mph, depending on gearing)
0–60 MPH (0–96 KM/H) 4.5 sec
0–100 MPH (0–161 KM/H) 8.5 sec
A.F.C. 4.2–5.7 km/l (12–16 mpg)

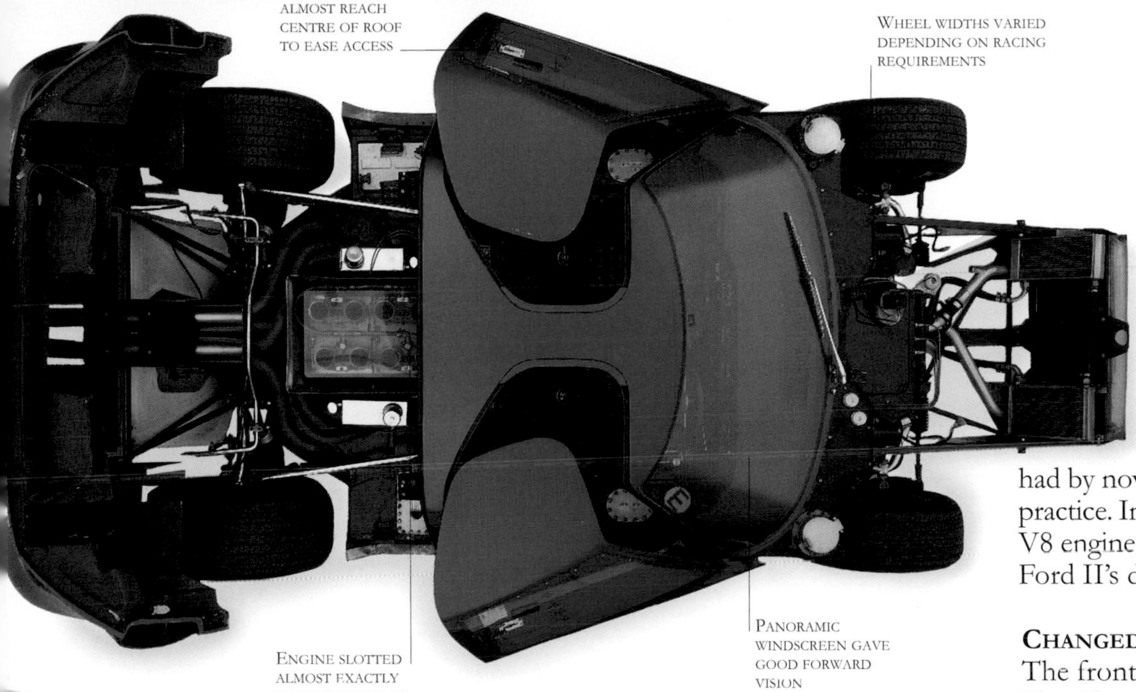

LARGE DOORS ALMOST REACH CENTRE OF ROOF TO EASE ACCESS

WHEEL WIDTHS VARIED DEPENDING ON RACING REQUIREMENTS

ENGINE SLOTTED ALMOST EXACTLY IN MIDDLE OF CAR

PANORAMIC WINDSCREEN GAVE GOOD FORWARD VISION

DESIGN SECRETS

Design of the GT40 was based on an earlier British Lola. Features such as mid-engined layout with gearbox/transaxle at the rear had by now become standard race-car practice. In Ford's favour were the powerful V8 engine, plenty of bucks, and Henry Ford II's determination to win Le Mans.

CHANGED APPEARANCE

The front section is the easiest way to identify various developments of the GT40. First prototypes had sharp snouts; the squared-off nose, as shown here, first appeared in 1965; the road-going MkIII was smoother, and the end-of-line MkIV rounder and flatter.

MANY RACE CARS DISPENSED WITH WING MIRRORS

EARLY VERSIONS AND ROAD CARS HAD DELICATE BORRANI WIRES

THIS IS A RACER, BUT ROAD CARS HAD TINY CHROME BUMPERS

B. BELL

BRDC

—THE ROAD TO LE MANS—

*Le Mans laurels looked a long way off when Ferrari rebuffed Ford's overtures,
but with unwavering determination Henry Ford II
pursued his goal and created a Le Mans legacy that will live forever.*

GT40 AT LE MANS, DRIVEN BY MAGLIOLI AND CASSONI

HENRY FORD'S grandson, Henry Ford II, reckoned the quickest and easiest way of achieving his ultimate Le Mans goal would be to buy the company that was already doing all the winning in the endurance classics of the time – Ferrari. The Commendatore, Enzo Ferrari, would not sell to the Americans, so they had to look elsewhere. Unsuccessful overtures were also made to Colin Chapman's Lotus in England.

The project finally started to gain momentum when Ford took over a race-car project begun by the small British firm of Lola, which by coincidence used a Ford V8 racing engine. Other British racing people were hired to join the team based near London and to produce a Ferrari-beater. American input was in the form of the V8 racing engine, and the distinctive body design. Everything else was created in England, and the first series cars completed there. But it was American determination which insisted that the cars ran at Le Mans in 1964, before they were really ready. They were the fastest cars in the race, but did not have the reliability. On the other hand, the American policy which dictated that the early engines be replaced by a monstrous 7-litre unit for

FORD GT40 MKIV AT LE MANS IN 1967

FORD
GT40

FUZZY SLIT ABOVE ENGINE COVER
GIVES JUST ENOUGH REAR VISION
TO WATCH A FERRARI FADE AWAY

EXHAUST NOTE RISES
FROM GRUFF BELLOW
TO EAR-SPLITTING YOWL

VITAL STATISTICS
GT, of course, stands for Grand Touring; 40 for the car's height in inches. Overall length was 4.2 m (13 ft 9 in), width 1.78 m (5 ft 10 in), and unladen weight 832 kg (1,835 lb).

FELIC

1965, brought the first breakthrough – victory in the world championship round at Daytona in Florida.

Still the Le Mans jewel remained elusive, and the cars again broke down after setting the early pace. But Henry Ford remained single-minded in the dogged pursuit of his ambition, and it was a matter of third time lucky for the Anglo-American enterprise, which finally enjoyed the fruits of its

GULF FORD GT40 LE MANS WINNER, 1968

1966 FORD GT40 AT SPA, BELGIUM

effort with a stunning Le Mans 1-2 in 1966. Now they had cracked the formula, they could not be beaten – again in 1967, 1968, and 1969 as well, the 24-hour enduro fell to Ford.

The last two victories were achieved after the Ford company, honour satisfied, had withdrawn from the fray and left the operation in the hands of the independent Gulf team. Headed by John Wyer, who had been the first manager of the GT40 racing team, Gulf achieved the incredible distinction of winning at Le Mans two years in a row – with the same car.

GT40's LE MANS VICTORIES
1966: CHRIS AMON (NZ)/BRUCE McLAREN (NZ); *1967*: AJ FOYT (US)/DAN GURNEY (US); *1968*: PEDRO RODRIGUEZ (MEX)/LUCIEN BIANCHI (B); *1969*: JACKY ICKX (B)/JACKIE OLIVER (GB).

THE LUCKY FEW WHO HAVE DRIVEN THE GT40 REPORT PLEASINGLY LIGHT STEERING

DUCTS HELPED HOT AIR ESCAPE FROM RADIATOR

ONE OF THE SEVEN MKIII ROAD CARS WAS ACTUALLY FITTED WITH A TV

FEL IC

GORDON KEEBLE GT

IN 1960, THIS WAS THE MOST electrifying car the British magazine *Autocar & Motor* had ever tested. Designed by Giugiaro in Italy and built in an aircraft hanger in Southampton, it boasted good looks, a glass-fibre body, and a 5.4-litre, 300 bhp V8 Chevrolet Corvette engine *(see pages 62–63)*. But, despite plenty of publicity, good looks, epic performance, and a clientele as glamorous as Jackie Kennedy and Diana Dors, the Gordon Keeble was a commercial disaster, with only 104 built.

"The car built to aircraft standards", read the advertising copy. And time has proved the Keeble's integrity; a space-frame chassis, rust-proof body, and that unburstable V8 has meant that over 90 Gordons have survived, with 60 still regularly used today. Born in an era where beauty mattered more than balance sheets, the Gordon Keeble failed for two reasons. Firstly the workers could not make enough of them, and secondly the management forgot to put a profit margin in the price. How the motor industry has changed...

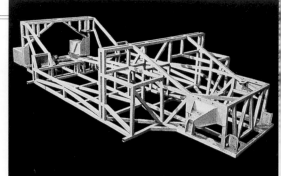

COMPOSITE SKELETON OF SQUARE TUBES

SPACE FRAME
The prototype space-frame chassis was finished in February 1960, flown to France, then overland to Turin, where Giugiaro fitted a handsome grp body.

HIGH-QUALITY BODY
In its day the Keeble's hand-finished, glass-reinforced plastic body was among the best made.

CARTER FOUR-BARREL CARB LIVES UNDER RESPLENDENT CHROMED AIR CLEANER

WINDOWS
Electric windows used the same motors as the Rolls-Royce Silver Shadow.

ENGINE
The small block Sting Ray engine, supplied by General Motors, is an aristocrat among American V8s, delivering a massive 300 bhp of high compression power. The engine's brutal performance means 113 km/h (70 mph) in first gear and a mighty wall of torque which, even when flooring the throttle in top gear, meant you could destroy most other cars.

LIGHTS
Twin slanted headlamps were distinctly sporting in the 1960s.

BUMPERS
The Keeble's delicate three-piece chrome bumpers were specially hand-made.

FEW 555

FUEL TANKS
Twin fuel tanks say much about an era when petrol was cheap and 5.3 km/l (15 mpg) was considered reasonable.

POWER
Despite restrained elegance and concealed twin exhausts, the Keeble could top 225 km/h (140 mph).

GORDON KEEBLE GT
Only 21 when he designed the car, Giugiaro gave the bonnet a dummy intake scoop and fashionably raked twin headlights. The roof was lengthened and the slant of the C pillar decreased to give wider glass areas and maximum visibility.

LAVISHLY EQUIPPED, THE KEEBLE CAME WITH A PUSH-BUTTON RADIO, SEAT BELTS, AND A FIRE EXTINGUISHER

FOUR-SPEED CHEVROLET GEARBOX WAS UNBREAKABLE

AERO VENTILATION
Built at Eastleigh airport, Southampton, England, many aircraft parts found their way into the Keeble, like this period swivelling ventilation nozzle.

INTERIOR
The inside is like the flight deck of an old Clipper flying boat – quilted aircraft PVC, black-on-white gauges, toggle switches, and that *de rigueur* accessory of all Sixties GT cars, a wood-rimmed steering wheel.

THIS IRONIC BADGE WAS CHOSEN AFTER A TORTOISE WALKED INTO SHOT DURING THE PHOTO SHOOT FOR THE SALES BROCHURE

STYLE
For a '60s' design, the Gordon Keeble is crisp, clean, and timeless.

HOLDEN *FX*

AT THE END OF WORLD WAR II, Australia was up against a problem – an acute shortage of cars and a newly civilianized army with money to burn. Loaded with Government handouts, General Motors-Holden came up with a four-door, six-cylinder, six-seater that would eventually become an Australian legend on wheels.

Launched in 1948, the 48-215, more generally known as the FX, was Australia's Morris Minor *(see pages 178–81)*. Tubby, conventional, and as big as a Buick, it had a sweet, torquey engine, steel monocoque body, hydraulic brakes, and a three-speed column shift. Light and functional, the FX so impressed Lord Nuffield (of Morris fame) with its uncomplicated efficiency that he had one shipped to England for his engineers to pull apart. The Australians did not care about the FX's humble underpinnings and bought 120,000 with grateful enthusiasm.

DOOR HANDLE
The extravagant door handle looked strangely out of place on such an austere shape and was one of the FX's few styling excesses.

SPEEDO CALIBRATED TO 100 MPH (161 KM/H) WAS A TAD OPTIMISTIC

BIJOU WHITE STEERING WHEEL WAS AN AMERICAN INHERITANCE

DASHBOARD
The dash echoes the Australian culture for utilitarianism, with centre speedo, two occasional gauges, precise three-speed column change, and only five ancillary switches. The umbrella handbrake and chrome horn-ring were hangovers from Detroit design influences.

FRONT SUSPENSION
Front springing was by tough coil and wishbone with lever arm damper.

ENGINE
Power came from a sturdy 2170cc cast-iron straight-six, with an integral block and crankcase, push-rod overhead valves, and a single-barrel downdraught Stromberg carburettor, which developed a modest 60 bhp.

HORN
Strident horn mounted behind the front grille was to warn roaming wildlife in the Australian outback.

TK · 377 NSW

HANDLING
The Holden was too powerful for its suspension and many ended up on their roofs.

LIGHTING
Simple and unadorned, the FX had no indicators or sidelights, just a six volt electrical system with a single rear lamp.

SPACE
Endlessly practical, the FX had a cavernous luggage compartment.

BROCHURES
General Motors-Holden started life as an Adelaide saddlery and leather goods manufacturer, later diversifying into Holden Motor Body Builders, who were sole supplier to General Motors Australia.

ECONOMY
Post-war fuel shortages meant that the Holden was parsimonious.

BODY FLEX
Taxi drivers complained of body flexing – doors could spring open on corners.

MASCOT
Recumbent lion bonnet mascot lent the FX an illusion of pedigree. In reality, Holden had no bloodline at all.

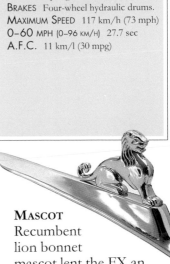

HOLDEN 48-215 FX

The "Humpy Holden" was a warmed-over pre-war design for a small Chevrolet sedan that General Motors US had created in 1938. A Detroit-Adelaide collaboration, the FX emerged as a plain shape that would not date, with high ground clearance for bad roads and dust-proof body. It became the standard transport of the Australian middle classes.

REAR WING STYLING
Rear wing line was cut into the rear doors but was much milder than Detroit's styling men would have liked. Rear wing spats were fitted to make the car look lower and sleeker.

REAR WING STONE-GUARDS WERE MADE NOT FROM CHROME BUT RUBBER

CHROME
Lavish Baroque grille looks like a stylistic afterthought.

HUDSON *Super Six*

IN 1948, HUDSON'S FUTURE could not have looked brighter. The feisty independent was one of the first with an all-new post-war design. Under the guidance of Frank Spring, the new Hudson Super Six not only looked stunning, it bristled with innovation. The key was its revolutionary "step-down" design, based on a unitary construction, with the floor pan suspended from the bottom of the chassis frame. The Hudson was lower than its rivals, handled with ground-hugging confidence, and with its gutsy six-cylinder engine, outpaced virtually all competitors. In 1951, it evolved into the Hudson Hornet, dominating American stock car racing from 1951 to 1954. But the complex design could not adapt to the rampant demand for yearly revision; the 1953 car looked much like the 1948, and in 1954 Hudson merged with Nash, disappearing for good in 1957.

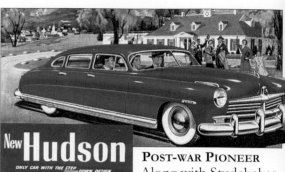

POST-WAR PIONEER
Along with Studebaker, the 1948 Hudson was one of the very first all-new post-war designs. It created a sensation, but its complex structure made it difficult to update.

ENGINE
The gutsy new 262cid six arrived the same year as the new-style Hudsons in 1948. It made the Hudson one of the swiftest cars on America's roads and, bored out to 308cid for the 1951 Hornet, it became a racing legend.

THIS IS A RARE RIGHT-HAND DRIVE CAR, ORIGINALLY EXPORTED TO SOUTH AFRICA, NOW IN THE UK

DASHBOARD
This is not wood at all, but painted metal. Main instruments are a speedo and 30-hour wind-up clock, both of which were later moved ahead of the driver. "Idiot lights" for oil pressure and amperes – rather than gauges – were a traditional Hudson feature.

LOW RIDER
Chassis frame runs outside the rear wheels, serving as "invisible side bumpers" and contributing to low height.

HEIGHT
The Super Six stood only 1.53 m (60.4 in) high when contemporary Buicks and Chryslers were more than 38 cm (15 in) taller. Yet Hudson's interior space was exceptional.

LOGO
Hudson triangle dated back to 1909 when department store owner Joseph L. Hudson gave his name and financial backing to the venture. White triangle is illuminated.

INTERIOR
All passengers were cradled between axles for comfort. Reviewers raved that rear passengers were treated to a front-seat ride.

SPECIFICATIONS

MODEL Hudson Super Six (1948–51)
PRODUCTION 180,499
BODY STYLES Four-door sedan, Brougham two-door sedan, Club coupé, hardtop coupé, two-door Brougham convertible.
CONSTRUCTION Unitary chassis/body.
ENGINE 262cid L-head straight-six.
POWER OUTPUT 121 bhp at 4000 rpm.
TRANSMISSION Three-speed manual, optional overdrive; semi-automatic.
SUSPENSION *Front:* independent, wishbones, coil springs, telescopic dampers, anti-roll bar. *Rear:* live-axle, semi-elliptic leaf springs, telescopic dampers, anti-roll bar.
BRAKES Hydraulic drums all round.
MAXIMUM SPEED 145 km/h (90 mph)
0–60 MPH (0–96 KM/H) 14–18 sec (depending on transmission)
A.F.C. 4.2–6.4 km/l (12–18 mpg)

HUDSON SUPER SIX

It is the smooth beauty of the profile that really marks the Hudson out. The design team was led by Frank Spring, a long-time Hudson fixture, whose unusual blend of talents combined styling and engineering. He had also designed aeroplanes, and the new Hudson shape that evolved from a series of wartime doodles was one of the most aerodynamic of its time. The famed "step-down" chassis kept the centre of gravity and overall height low without compromising levels of comfort.

MONOBILT
All Hudsons from 1932 had unitary chassis and body, Monobilt in company speak. Many reckoned the Super Six's step-down design made it the safest automobile of its time.

REAR ASPECT
The rear of the Hudson is least pleasing, a slightly settled blancmange; but it is the view most other motorists and stock-car racers saw.

SPLIT SCREEN
Each segment of the split screen was well curved for semi-wrap-around effect and good visibility.

JAGUAR *XK120*

A CAR-STARVED BRITAIN, still trundling around in perpendicular, pre-war hangover motors, glimpsed the future in October of 1948 at the Earl's Court Motor Show in London. The star of the show was the Jaguar Super Sports. It was sensational to look at from any angle, with a purity of line that did not need chrome embellishment. It was also sensationally fast; in production as the Jaguar XK120 it would soon be proven that 120 really did stand for 120 mph (193 km/h), making it the fastest standard production car in the world.

Once again Jaguar boss William Lyons had pulled off his favourite trick: offering sensational value for money compared with anything else in its class. In fact this time there was nothing else in its class. The only trouble was that you could not actually buy one. Lyons had planned the XK120 as a short production-run, prestige show-stopper, but overwhelming interest at the 1948 show changed all that. Hand-built alloy-bodied cars dribbled out of the Jaguar factory in 1949 and you needed a name like Clark Gable to get your hands on one. In 1950, tooling for steel-bodied cars was ready and the XK120 took off as an export earner, with over 85 per cent of all XK120s going to foreign climes. Today the XK120 remains one of the most captivating Cats ever.

HANDSOME
SMITH dials

WALNUT TRIM WAS
A FEATURE OF FIXED-
HEAD COUPÉS AND
DROPHEADS ONLY

CAT MOTIF
ON IMPOSING
STEERING WHEEL

ENGINE
The famed XK six-cylinder engine was designed by Bill Heynes and Wally Hassan, and went on to power the E-Type *(see pages 140–43)* and other Jaguars up until 1986. Even this was "styled"; William Lyons insisted it had twin camshafts to make it resemble GP cars of the Thirties.

INTERIOR
Surrounded by leather and thick-pile carpet, you feel good just sitting in an XK120. With its lush interior, purposeful instruments, and the bark of the exhaust from behind, you will hardly notice that it is a little cosy — if not downright cramped.

REAR VIEW
Fixed-head coupés had limited rear vision.

SELLING THE DREAM
The original sales brochure for the XK120 used airbrushed photographs of the very first car built.

SPECIFICATIONS

MODEL Jaguar XK120 (1949–54)
PRODUCTION 12,055
BODY STYLES Two-seater roadster, fixed-head coupé, and drophead coupé.
CONSTRUCTION Separate chassis, aluminium/steel bodywork.
ENGINE 3442cc twin overhead cam six-cylinder, twin SU carburettors.
POWER OUTPUT 160 bhp at 5100 rpm.
TRANSMISSION Four-speed manual, Moss gearbox with syncromesh on upper three ratios.
SUSPENSION *Front:* independent, wishbones and torsion bars; *Rear:* live rear axle, semi-elliptic.
BRAKES Hydraulically operated 30-cm (12-in) drums.
MAXIMUM SPEED 203 km/h (126 mph)
0–60 MPH (0–96 KM/H) 10 sec
0–100 MPH (0–161 KM/H) 35.3 sec
A.F.C. 6.1–7.8 km/l (17–22 mpg)

JAGUAR XK120 FIXED-HEAD COUPÉ

Many rate the fixed-head coupé as the most gorgeous of all XK120s, with a roof-line and teardrop window reminiscent of the beautiful Bugatti Type 57SC Atlantic. The fixed-head model did not appear until March 1951 and is much rarer than the roadster. Even though numbers were trimmed further in the late Eighties' scrabble to restore roadsters, their flowing curves and perfect proportions are now more widely appreciated.

SIDELIGHTS
XK spotters can tell this is a 1953 XK120 because of the body-coloured sidelights fared into the wing. Early XKs had chrome sidelight pods.

THE CAT'S PAWS
Skinny cross-ply tyres gave more thrills than needed on hard cornering.

WHEELS
Standard wheels were the same steel discs as on the Jaguar saloons. Wire wheels were a popular option and helped to reduce the build-up of heat in the brake drums, which could lead to alarming fade.

XK120 HALLMARKS
Slim split bumpers and thin grille slats distinguish the XK120 from the thicker bumpered XK140 which superseded it.

JAGUAR *XK150*

THE XK150 APPEARED IN THE SPRING of 1957 and was the most refined of the XK trio. One of the last Jaguars to have a separate chassis, it carried all-round Dunlop disc brakes, a 210 bhp version of the legendary XK straight-six power plant, plus a Borg Warner automatic gearbox option. The 150 marked the beginning of the civilization of the Jaguar sports car. With its wider girth and more creature comforts, it was to hold the market's interest admirably until the then secret E-Type project *(see pages 140–43)* was ready for unveiling in 1961.

In the late 1950s, the XK150 was a seriously glamorous machine, almost as swish as an Aston Martin, but £1,500 cheaper. March 1958 saw more power in the form of the "S" performance package, which brought the 3.4 up to 250 bhp, and in 1959 the 3.8's output soared to a heady 265 bhp. Available as a roadster, drophead, or fixed-head coupé, the 150 sold a creditable 9,400 examples in its four-year run, the rarest model being the XK150S drophead coupé, with a mere 193 cars built. Despite being eclipsed by the sinewy E-Type, the 150 was charismatic enough to be the personal transport of Fifties racing ace Mike Hawthorn and starlet Anita Ekberg. Currently undervalued, a well-restored 150 costs half the price of the equivalent E-Type and is much more individual.

INTERIOR
The interior was much more refined than previous XKs, with a wrap-around windscreen and adjustable steering column. On the last 1960 cars, the indicator switch was on the steering column instead of the dashboard.

LIGHT INDICATOR
A tiny red peak on the sidelight was to remind the driver that lights were on.

The XK150 Roadster

SLEEK PROMOTION
Introduced in 1958, the two-seater XK150 Roadster was the last model in the series and also the sportiest. Ever since the 120, all XKs had been a hit in America and the 150 was no exception.

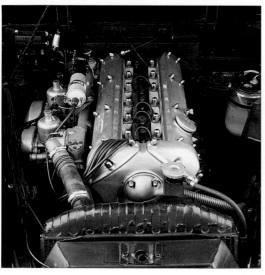

ENGINE
This classic, twin overhead-cam design first saw the light of day in 1949, and was phased out as recently as 1986. Some say it is one of the finest production engines of all time. Sturdy, powerful, and handsome, the 3.8 powered the legendary D-Type Jaguars which could top 317 km/h (197 mph).

TYRES
Standard tyres were Dunlop Crossply RS5s.

REAR VIEW
From the rear, the fixed-head has definite saloon lines, with a curved rear screen, big wrap-around bumper, wide track, and cavernous boot.

JAGUAR XK150

The gorgeous curved body sits on a conventional chassis. Joints and curves were smoothed off at the factory using lead. The 1950s' motor industry paid little thought to rustproofing, so all Jaguars of the period are shameful rust-raisers.

WHEELS
Wire wheels were the most common, although steel wheels with hubcaps were available.

BODYWORK
The body is mounted on a massive box-section chassis, which hardly differs from the original XK120 design. All the XK150's body panels were new, with a higher scuttle and wing line, wider bonnet, and broader radiator grille than earlier models.

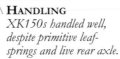

VENTILATION
Vent in front wing was for ventilation of passenger compartment.

HANDLING
XK150s handled well, despite primitive leaf-springs and live rear axle.

RACING SUCCESS
Jaguar XKs won laurels all over the world.

SO MUCH FOR SO LITTLE

At £1,800, the 150 was resounding value. This is a very early car wearing a 1958 Coventry-issued registration number, probably a factory demonstrator.

┌─── **SPECIFICATIONS** ───┐

MODEL Jaguar XK150 FHC (1957–61)
PRODUCTION 9,400
BODY STYLES Two-seater roadster, drophead, or fixed-head coupé.
CONSTRUCTION Separate pressed-steel chassis frame with box section side members.
ENGINE Straight-six, twin overhead-cam 3442cc or 3781cc.
POWER OUTPUT 190 bhp at 5500 rpm (3.4); 210 bhp at 5500 rpm (3.8); 265 bhp at 5500 rpm (3.8S).
TRANSMISSION Four-speed manual, with optional overdrive, or three-speed Borg Warner Model 8 automatic.
SUSPENSION Independent front, rear leaf springs with live rear axle.
BRAKES Dunlop front and rear discs.
MAXIMUM SPEED 217 km/h (135 mph)
0–60 MPH (0–96 KM/H) 7.6 sec (3.8S)
0–100 MPH (0–161 KM/H) 18 sec
A.F.C. 6.4 km/l (18 mpg)

JAGUAR *C-Type*

THE C-TYPE IS THE CAR that launched the Jaguar racing legend and began a Le Mans love affair for the men from Coventry. In the 1950s, Jaguar boss Bill Lyons was intent on winning Le Mans laurels for Britain, just as Bentley had done a quarter of a century before. After testing mildly modified XK120s in 1950, Jaguar came up with a competition version, the XK120C (C-Type) for 1951. A C-Type won that year, failed in 1952, then won again in 1953. By then the C-Type's place in history was assured, for it had laid the cornerstone of the Jaguar sporting legend that blossomed through its successor, the D-Type, which bagged three Le Mans 24-hour wins in four years. C-Types were sold to private customers, most of whom used them for racing rather than road use. They were tractable road cars though, often driven to and from meetings; after their days as competitive racers were over, many were used as high-performance highway tourers.

THE CAT FAMILY
Grille reflects family resemblance to the XK120 production model which company boss Bill Lyons had insisted on.

HOME COMFORTS
Snug-fitting seats supported well during hard cornering.

ENGINE
The engine was taken from the XK120 and placed into the competition version. Horsepower of the silky six was boosted each year until some 220 bhp was available.

AERO HERITAGE
Designer Malcolm Sayer's aircraft industry background shows through in the smooth aerodynamic styling.

FAST FUELLING
Quick-release filler-cap was another racing feature, and could save valuable seconds in a race.

ACCESSIBILITY
It was easier to step over the door than open it; passenger did not even get one.

BONNET HINGES FORWARDS TO EASE MID-RACE ADJUSTMENTS

ENGINE SNUGGLES NEATLY INTO ITS BAY, READY FOR ACTION

WIRE WHEELS HAVE KNOCK-OFF HUB-CAPS FOR QUICK TYRE CHANGES

JAGUAR C-TYPE
Jaguar's Bill Lyons dictated that the C-Type racer should bear a strong family resemblance to production Jaguars and the Malcolm Sayer body, fitted to a special frame, achieved that aim. The clever blend of beauty and function retained the pouncing-cat Jaguar "look", while creating an aerodynamically efficient tool for the high-speed Le Mans circuit. In racing trim, cars ran with single aero-screen; this car has an additional full-width screen.

SPECIFICATIONS

MODEL Jaguar C-Type (1951–53)
PRODUCTION 53
BODY STYLE Two-door, two-seater
  sports racer.
CONSTRUCTION Tubular chassis,
  aluminium body.
ENGINE Jaguar XK120 3442cc, six-
  cylinder, double overhead camshaft
  with twin SU carburettors.
POWER OUTPUT 200–210 bhp at
  5800 rpm.
TRANSMISSION Four-speed XK
  gearbox with close-ratio gears.
SUSPENSION Torsion-bars all round;
  wishbones at front, rigid axle at rear.
BRAKES Lockheed hydraulic drums;
  later cars used Dunlop discs all round.
MAXIMUM SPEED 232 km/h (144 mph)
0–60 MPH (0–96 KM/H) 8.1 sec
0–100 MPH (0–161 KM/H) 20.1 sec
A.F.C. 5.7 km/l (16 mpg)

ON THE TRACK
The C-Type was always most at home on the track, though more at Le Mans – where it won the 24-hour classic twice from three attempts – than on shorter circuits such as Silverstone, where this picture was taken in July 1953.

INTERIOR
The cockpit was designed for business, not comfort, but was roomy enough for two adults; passengers were provided with a grab-handle in case the driver thought he was at Le Mans.

LUGGAGE SPACE
A car built for racing does not need to carry baggage; rear deck covers the massive fuel tank.

STOP SIGNAL
Stop-lights were a racing necessity as well as safety feature for road use, particularly with later disc-braked versions.

PUR 120

SPARE WHEEL
Removable panel in the tail hides the spare wheel.

ATTENTION TO DETAIL
Louvres on the bonnet help hot air escape; engine cover is secured by quick-release handles and leather safety straps.

SUSPENSION
Telescopic dampers smoothed the ride; C-Type introduced disc brakes to road racing as a secret weapon in 1952, though most examples used drums.

JAGUAR *E-Type*

WHEN JAGUAR BOSS WILLIAMS LYONS, by now Sir William, unveiled the E-Type Jaguar at the Geneva Motor Show in March 1961, its ecstatic reception rekindled memories of the 1948 British launch of the XK120 *(see pages 134–35)*. The E-Type, or XKE as it is known in America, created a sensation. British motoring magazines had produced road tests of pre-production models to coincide with the launch – and yes, the fixed-head coupé really could do 242 km/h (150.4 mph). OK, so the road-test cars were perhaps tweaked a little and early owners found 233 km/h (145 mph) a more realistic maximum, but the legend was born. It was not just a stunning, svelte sports car though; it was a trademark Jaguar sporting package, once again marrying sensational performance with superb value for money. Astons and Ferraris, for example, were more than double the money.

FIXED HEAD
A two-seater, fixed-head coupé was available from the outset. In 1966, a longer wheelbase, fixed-head two-plus-two was added to the range and it was this longer wheelbase that the V12 adopted at its launch in 1971.

DETACHABLE HARDTOP WAS AVAILABLE AS A FACTORY OPTION

INTERIM MODEL
This 1965 E-Type is still a Series 1, even though it features the 4.2 engine, better brakes, and an all-synchro gearbox.

SIMPLICITY OF LINE
Designer Malcolm Sayer insisted he was an aerodynamicist and hated to be called a stylist. He claimed the E-Type was the first production car to be "mathematically" designed.

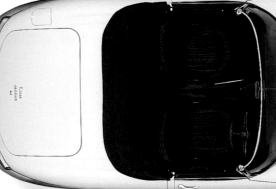

THIN-BACKED BUCKET SEATS OF THE 3.8s WERE CRITICIZED. IN THE 4.2, AS HERE, THEY WERE GREATLY IMPROVED

TELL TAIL
The thin bumpers with lights above are an easy giveaway for E-Type spotters. From 1968, with the introduction of the Series 2, bulkier lamp clusters appeared below the bumpers.

WIRE WHEELS WERE STANDARD ROAD WEAR FOR SIX-CYLINDER E-TYPES; STEEL DISCS WERE FITTED TO V12s

ENGINES

The twin-overhead cam, six-cylinder was a development of the original 3.4-litre XK unit fitted to the XK120 of 1949. First E-Types had a 3.8-litre unit, then 4.2 from 1964. Configuration changed in 1971 to a wholly new V12.

TRIPLE SU CARBS ON UK SIXES; LESS OOMPH FROM TWIN STROMBERGS ON SOME US CARS

ENGINE ACCESS LOOKS GOOD, BUT MIND YOUR HEAD

SPECIFICATIONS

MODEL E-Type Jaguar (1961–74)
PRODUCTION 72,520
BODY STYLES Two-seater roadster and fixed coupé, 2+2 fixed head coupé.
CONSTRUCTION Steel monocoque.
ENGINE 3781cc straight-six; 4235cc straight-six; 5343cc V12.
POWER OUTPUT 265 to 272 bhp.
TRANSMISSION Four-speed manual, optional automatic from 1966.
SUSPENSION *Front:* independent, wishbones and torsion bar; *Rear:* independent, coil and radius arm.
BRAKES Discs all round.
MAXIMUM SPEED 241 km/h (150 mph), 3.8 & 4.2; 230 km/h (143 mph), 5.3.
0–60 MPH (0–96 KM/H) 7–7.2 sec.
0–100 MPH (0–161 KM/H) 16.2 sec, 3.8
A.F.C. 5.7–7 km/l (16–20 mpg)

HANDLING

Jaguar designed an all-new independent set up at the rear. Handling in the wet and on the limit is often criticized, but for its day the E-Type was immensely capable.

RACING

Although intended as a road-going sports car, lightweight and racing E-Types performed creditably on the track in the hands of privateers.

CENTRE PANEL HINGES FOR ACCESS TO ELECTRICS

3.8S HAD ALUMINIUM-FINISHED CENTRE CONSOLE PANEL AND TRANSMISSION TUNNEL

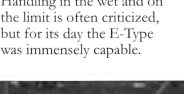

INTERIOR

The interior of this Series 1 4.2 is the epitome of sporting luxury, with leather seats, wood-rim wheel, and an array of instruments and toggle switches – later replaced by less sporting rocker and less injurious rocker switches.

WITH NO SUN VISORS, TINTED SCREEN IS DESIRABLE

LOUVRES ARE NOT FOR LOOKS; E-TYPES, PARTICULARLY EARLY ONES, TENDED TO OVERHEAT IN HOT CLIMES

BONNET

On a sunny day, the view over the long hood from the driving seat is one of the great motoring sensations – but not in congested traffic.

ALL-ROUND DISC BRAKES AS STANDARD WERE PART OF THE SPEC FROM FIRST E-TYPES

JENSEN *Interceptor*

THE JENSEN INTERCEPTOR was one of those great cars that comes along every decade or so. Built in a small Birmingham factory, a triumph of tenacity over resources, the Interceptor's lantern-jawed looks and tyre-smoking power made the tiny Jensen company a household name. A glamorous cocktail of an Italian-styled body, American V8 engine, and genteel British craftsmanship, it became the car for successful swingers of the late 1960s and 1970s.

The Interceptor was handsome, fashionable, and formidably fast, but its tragic flaw was a single figure appetite for fuel – 10 mpg if you enjoyed yourself. After driving straight into two oil crises and a worldwide recession, as well as suffering serious losses from the ill-starred Jensen-Healey project, Jensen filed for bankruptcy in 1975 and finally closed its doors in May 1976.

SPECIFICATIONS

MODEL Jensen Interceptor (1966–76)
PRODUCTION 1,500
BODY STYLE All-steel occasional four-seater coupé.
CONSTRUCTION Separate tubular and platform type pressed steel frame.
ENGINE V8, 6276cc.
POWER OUTPUT 325 bhp at 4600 rpm.
TRANSMISSION Three-speed Chrysler Torqueflite automatic.
SUSPENSION Independent front with live rear axle.
BRAKES Four-wheel Girling discs.
MAXIMUM SPEED 217 km/h (135 mph)
0–60 MPH (0–96 KM/H) 7.3 sec
0–100 MPH (0–161 KM/H) 19 sec
A.F.C 4.9 km/l (13.6 mpg)

ADWEST POWER STEERING WAS ALSO USED IN THE CONTEMPORARY JAGUAR XJ6

INTERIOR
Road testers complained that the Interceptor's dash was like the flight deck of a small aircraft, but the interior was beautifully hand-made with the finest hides and plush Wilton carpets.

BODYWORK
Bodies were all-steel, with little attention paid to corrosion proofing.

SUSPENSION
Front suspension was coil spring, wishbone and lever arm dampers borrowed from the Austin Westminster.

TYRES
Original skinny Dunlop RS5 Crossplies had, by 1968, changed to wider Dunlop SP Radials.

JENSEN INTERCEPTOR
The Interceptor's futuristic shape hardly changed over its 10-year life span and was widely acknowledged to be one of the most innovative designs of its decade. The rear screen lifted up to reveal a large luggage compartment.

STYLING
The classic shape was crafted by Italian styling house Vignale. From bare designs to running prototype took just three months.

ENGINE
The lazy Chrysler V8 of 6.2 litres gives drag strip acceleration along with endless reliability. With one huge carburettor and only a single camshaft, the Interceptor has a simple soul.

GEARING
Most Interceptors were automatic apart from 24 ultra rare cars fitted with four-speed manual gearboxes.

LAMBORGHINI *Espada*

FERRUCCIO LAMBORGHINI'S AIM of out-Ferrari-ing Ferrari took a side-step with the four-seater Espada. It was a first and a last for the tractor manufacturer turned dream-maker; the first and only true four-seater Lamborghini, and the last of the front-engined cars, alongside the Jarama. Perhaps underrated today, it was nevertheless the biggest selling Lamborghini ever until the Countach *(see pages 148–49)* overtook it.

With the design constraint of seating four adults in a VIP supercar, the Espada was never going to have conventional 2+2 beauty, but it is still an exhilarating executive express. Propelled by the Miura's muscular four-litre V12, the fastest boardroom on wheels will eat up the autostrada at 225 km/h (140 mph) all day long. Where other cars are merely badged GT, this Bertone beauty needs no acronyms on its rump to excel as the epitome of the term Grand Tourer.

SPECIFICATIONS

MODEL Lamborghini Espada (1968–78). S1 1968–70; S2 1970–72; S3 1972–78.
PRODUCTION 1,217
BODY STYLE Two-door, four-seater fastback saloon.
CONSTRUCTION Pressed-steel platform frame, integral steel body with alloy bonnet.
ENGINE Four-cam V12 of 3929cc.
POWER OUTPUT 325–365 bhp at 6500 rpm.
TRANSMISSION Five-speed manual or, from 1974, Chrysler TorqueFlite auto.
SUSPENSION All independent by unequal-length wishbones & coil springs.
BRAKES Discs on all four wheels.
MAXIMUM SPEED 241–249 km/h (150–155 mph)
0–60 MPH (0–96 KM/H) 7.8 sec
0–100 MPH (0–161 KM/H) 16 sec
A.F.C. 3.6–5.4 km/l (10–15 mpg)

INTERIOR
Sumptuous interior fittings included leather upholstery and electric windows. The hectic fascia improved on later cars, as seen here.

DEEP BREATHS
Six greedy twin-choke Webers gulp in air through bonnet air ducts.

POISE
Four headlights, blacked-out grille, and low stance make for a formidable road presence.

ENGINE
The engine was borrowed from existing models – the 400GT and the Miura. Power from the 4-litre V12 grew from 325 bhp for the first models, through 350 bhp for the S2, to 365 bhp for the last of the S3s.

FAT FEET
Fat tyres, supple ride, and a fine chassis add up to exceptional handling.

LAMBORGHINI ESPADA
The Espada's styling was penned by Marcello Gandini from Bertone's "Marzal" show car. Lamborghini's first true passenger car could carry four people comfortably, as long as two of them were not too tall.

LAMBORGHINI *Miura*

THE LAUNCH OF THE Lamborghini Miura at the 1966 Geneva Motor Show was the decade's motoring sensation. Staggeringly beautiful, technically pre-eminent, and unbelievably quick, it was created by a triumvirate of engineering wizards all in their twenties. For the greater part of its production life the Miura was reckoned to be the most desirable car money could buy, combining drop-dead looks, awesome performance, and unerring stability, as well as an emotive top speed of 282 km/h (175 mph).

From its dramatic swooping lines – even Lamborghini thought it was too futuristic to sell – to its outrageously exotic colours, the Miura perfectly mirrored the middle Sixties. But, as the oil crises of the Seventies took hold, the Miura slipped into obscurity, replaced in 1973 by the unlovely, and some say inferior, Countach *(see pages 148–49)*.

INTERIOR
The cockpit is basic but finely detailed, with a huge Jaeger speedo and tacho. Six minor gauges on the left of the console tell the mechanical story. Only the gearbox is a disappointment, with a truck-like, sticky action that does not do the Miura's gorgeous engine any justice.

ALLOY GEAR-LEVER GATE IS A HAND-MADE WORK OF ART

ENGINE
The V12 4-litre engine was mid-mounted transversely to prevent the car's wheelbase from being too long. The gearbox, final drive, and crankcase were all cast in one piece to save space. Beneath all that pipery slumber twelve pistons, four chain-driven camshafts, 24 valves, and four carburettors.

BERTONE DESIGN
Long, low, and delicate, the Miura is still considered one of the most handsome automotive sculptures ever.

TAIL-END ACTION
Because the Miura sits so low, it displays virtually zero body roll; therefore there is little warning before the tail breaks away.

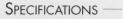

SOUND INSULATION
In an attempt to silence a violently loud engine, Lamborghini put 10 cm (4 in) of polystyrene insulation between engine and cabin.

LIGHT POWERHOUSE
The Miura has a very impressive power-to-weight ratio – output of 385 bhp and yet weighing only 1,200 kg (2,646 lb).

FRONT-END LIFT
Treacherous aerodynamics meant that approaching speeds of 274 km/h (170 mph) both front wheels could actually lift off the ground.

LAMBORGHINI MIURA SV

In looks and layout the mid-engined Lambo owes much to the Ford GT40 *(see pages 124–27)*, but was engineered by Gianpaulo Dallara. At the core of the Miura is a steel platform chassis frame with outriggers front and rear to support the major mechanicals. The last-of-the-line SV was the most refined Miura, with more power, a stiffer chassis, and redesigned suspension. Other changes included wider wheels and a different rear wing profile.

FILLER CAP
The petrol filler hides under one of the bonnet slats.

SPECIFICATIONS
MODEL Lamborghini Miura (1966–72)
PRODUCTION Approx 800.
BODY STYLE Two-seater roadster.
CONSTRUCTION Steel platform chassis, light alloy and steel bodywork.
ENGINE Transverse V12 4.0 litre.
POWER OUTPUT P400, 350 bhp at 7000 rpm; P400S, 370 bhp at 7700 rpm; P400SV, 385 bhp at 7850 rpm.
TRANSMISSION Five-speed with trans axle.
SUSPENSION Independent front and rear.
BRAKES Four-wheel ventilated disc.
MAXIMUM SPEED 282 km/h (175 mph), P400SV.
0–60 MPH (0–96 KM/H) 6.7 sec
0–100 MPH (0–161 KM/H) 15.1 sec
A.F.C. 5.7 km/l (16 mpg)

SV MARQUE
The Miura SV is the most desirable of the species, with only 150 built.

AIR DUCTS
Ducts in front of the rear wheels channel air for cooling the back brakes.

HEADLIGHT POSITION
The car was so low that headlights had to be "pop-up" to raise them high enough for adequate vision.

LIGHTS
Standard Miura headlamps were shared by the Fiat 850.

LAMBORGHINI *Countach 5000S*

THE COUNTACH WAS first unveiled at the 1971 Geneva Motor Show as the Miura's replacement, engineered by Giampaolo Dallara and breathtakingly styled by Marcello Gandini of Bertone fame. For a complicated, hand-built car, the Countach delivered all the reliable high performance that its swooping looks promised. In 1982, a 4.75-litre 375 bhp V12 was shoe-horned in to give the up-coming Ferrari Testarossa *(see pages 110–11)* something to reckon with. There is no mid-engined car like the Countach. The engine sits longitudinally in a multi-tubular space-frame, with fuel and water carried by twin side-mounted tanks and radiators. Weight distribution is close to 50/50, which means that the Countach's poise at the limit is legendary.

On the down side, it takes an epoch to get used to the extra wide body, visibility is appalling, steering is heavy, gear selection recalcitrant and, for all its tremendous cost, the cockpit is cramped, with luggage space restricted to an overnight bag. Yet such faults can only be considered as charming idiosyncrasies when set against the Countach's staggering performance – a howling 301 km/h (187 mph) top speed and a 0–60 (96 km/h) belt of 5 seconds.

NOT ONE BUT FOUR
Everything on the Countach is built on a grand scale. Four exhausts, four cams, 12 cylinders, six 45DCOE Webers, a rev line of 8000 rpm, 118-litre (26-gallon) fuel tank, single-figure thirst, and the widest track of any car on the road.

MANOEUVRABILITY
Reversing the Countach is like launching the Queen Mary. *Preferred technique is to open the door and sit on the sill while looking over your shoulder.*

WHEELS
Steamroller-like 12J five-porthole alloy wheels sit on ultra-low profile Pirelli P7 rubber.

CELEBRATIONS

The 25-year anniversary of Lambo production in 1985 was celebrated with the 5000S and the elite Quattrovalvole 5000S.

SPECIFICATIONS

MODEL Lamborghini Countach (1973–90)
PRODUCTION Approx 1,000
BODY STYLE Mid-engined, two-seater sports coupé.
CONSTRUCTION Alloy body, space-frame chassis.
ENGINE 4754cc four-cam V12.
POWER OUTPUT 375 bhp at 7000 rpm.
TRANSMISSION Five-speed manual.
SUSPENSION Independent front and rear with double wishbones and coil springs.
BRAKES Four-wheel vented discs.
MAXIMUM SPEED 301 km/h (187 mph)
0–60 MPH (0–96 KM/H) 5.1 sec
0–100 MPH (0–161 KM/H) 13.3 sec
A.F.C. 3.2 km/l (9 mpg)

BODY VULNERABILITY
Scant body protection means that most Countachs acquire a tapestry of scars and scratches that require the cost of a small car to repair.

INTERIOR
The cabin is crude, with unsubtle interior architecture. Switches and wands are Fiat- and Lancia-sourced.

HANDLING
The Countach goes exactly where it is pointed with unerring precision thanks to almost perfect weight distribution.

SOUND EFFECTS
Inches away, all occupants are able to hear exactly what this engine has to say.

DOORS
Pivoting doors are works of art that worked perfectly even on the earliest prototypes.

LAMBORGHINI COUNTACH 5000S

The shape is a riot of creative genius that ignores all established rules of car design. Air scoops under the body's side windows break up the wedge-shaped line and form a ready-made indent for a compact door catch and an ideal hand-hold for the huge gullwing doors. Underneath the alloy panels nestles a birdcage space-frame chassis of great complexity.

LANCIA *Aurelia* B24 *Spider*

BEAUTY IS MORE THAN just skin deep on this lovely little Lancia, for underneath those lean Pininfarina loins the Aurelia's innards bristle with innovative engineering. For a start there is the compact alloy V6. Designed under Vittorio Jano, the man responsible for the great racing Alfas of the Twenties and Thirties, this free-revving, torquey little lump was the first mass-produced V6. The revolution was not just at the front though, for at the back were the clutch and gearbox, housed in the transaxle to endow the Aurelia with near-perfect weight distribution. Suspension, although hardly run-of-the mill, was typically Lancia, with the front sliding pillars that Lancia had first employed in the 1920s.

These innovations were first mated with the Pininfarina body in 1951 with the Aurelia B20 GT coupé, often credited as the first of the new breed of modern post-war GTs. And the point of it all becomes clear when you climb behind the wheel, for although the Aurelia was never the most accelerative machine, its handling was so impeccable that 40 years on it still impresses with its masterly cornering poise. With the B24 Spider you got all this and fresh air too, and today this rare and charismatic roadster is the most prized of this illustrious family.

ENGINE
Aurelias featured the world's first mass-production V6, an all-alloy unit which grew from 1754cc to 1991cc, to the 2451cc fitted to the B24 Spider. The flexible 60-degree V6 could pull the Spider from 32 km/h (20 mph) in top gear, yet ran to 5500 rpm.

INTERIOR
The panel has just three major dials and a clutch of switches on a painted metal dash. It was devoid of the walnut-leather trimmings which British car makers of the time considered essential for a luxury sports car.

ELEGANT, ADJUSTABLE NARDI STEERING WHEEL WAS STANDARD EQUIPMENT ON THE SPIDER

LUGGAGE ROOM
The Aurelia Spider scored well in luggage-carrying capabilities compared with other two-seaters of the time.

TWIN TAIL PIPE
As you pile on the revs, the throbbing, gruff sound rises to a rich gurgle that is singularly tuneful from the twin exhausts.

ROADHOLDING
Handling was the Spider's best feature, helped by racing tyres being fitted as part of the original spec.

BALANCE
For perfect balance, the weight of the engine was offset by locating clutch and gearbox in a unit with differential at the rear.

CROSSED FLAGS
These represent the joint input of Lancia, responsible for design and manufacture of the mechanical parts, and Pininfarina, who not only styled the body, but also built the cars.

RIGHT-HAND DRIVE
Until the Aurelia, Lancia had eccentrically persisted with right-hand steering, even for the home market. The adoption of left-hand drive makes this right-hooker a real rarity.

SPECIFICATIONS

MODEL Lancia Aurelia B24 Spider (1954–56)
PRODUCTION 330
BODY STYLE Two-seater sports convertible.
CONSTRUCTION Monocoque with pressed steel and box-section chassis frame.
ENGINE Twin-overhead-valve aluminium alloy V6, 2451cc.
POWER OUTPUT 118 bhp at 5000 rpm.
TRANSMISSION Four-speed manual.
SUSPENSION Sliding pillar with beam axle and coil springs at front, De Dion rear axle on leaf springs.
BRAKES Hydraulic, finned alloy drums, inboard at rear.
MAXIMUM SPEED 180 km/h (112 mph)
0–60 MPH (0–96 KM/H) 14.3 sec
A.F.C. 7.8 km/l (22 mpg)

LANCIA AURELIA B24 SPIDER

The Spider bears a passing family resemblance to the Aurelia saloon, and even more so to the GT models. Neither of the closed versions had the wrap-around windscreen though, or the equally distinctive half-bumpers; the Spider's radiator grille was a slightly different shape, too. The curvaceous Pininfarina profile is characterized by the sweeping front wings and long luggage compartment. High-silled monocoque construction meant small doors; the Spider had a basic hood with plastic sidescreens.

SPIDER SPOTTING
The Spider's bonnet-top air-scoop was a unique feature among Aurelia models.

LANCIA STRATOS

THE LANCIA STRATOS was built as a rally-winner first and a road car second. Fiat-owned Lancia took the bold step of designing an all-new car solely to win the World Rally Championship and, with a V6 Ferrari Dino engine *(see pages 108–09)* on board, the Stratos had success in 1974, '75 and '76. Rallying rules demanded that at least 500 cars be built, but Lancia needed only 40 for its rally programme; the rest lay unsold in showrooms across Europe for years. Never a commercial proposition, the Stratos was an amazing mix of elegance, hard-charging performance, and thrill-a-minute handling.

RALLY SUCCESS
Lancia commissioned Bertone to build a rally weapon, and the Stratos debuted at the 1971 Turin Show. Despite scooping three World Championships, sales of Stratos road cars were so slow that they were still available new up until 1980.

INTERIOR
The Stratos is hopeless as a day-to-day machine, with a claustrophobic cockpit and woeful rear vision. The width of 1.72 m (67 in) and the narrow cabin mean that the steering wheel is virtually in the middle of the car.

DEEP WINDOWS
Perspex side windows are so deeply recessed within the bodywork that they can be fully opened without causing any wind turbulence.

ENGINE
Factory rally versions had a four-valve V6 engine.

REAR COWL
Moulded glass-fibre rear cowl lifts up by undoing two clips, giving access to midships-mounted power plant.

SHARP END
Flimsy nose section conceals spare wheel, radiator, and twin thermostatically-controlled cooling fans.

WHEELS
Campagnallo alloys sit on Pirelli P7F rubber – F stands for a soft compound to give a gentler loss of adhesion.

LANCIA STRATOS

Shorter than a Mk II Escort, and with the wheelbase of a Fiat 850, the stubby Stratos wedge looks almost as wide as it is long. Front and back are glass-fibre with steel centre-section.

COMFORT
Truncated cabin is cramped, cheap, nasty, and hot.

WEIGHT
The Stratos is a two-thirds glass fibre featherweight, tipping the scales at a whisker over 908 kg (2,000 lb).

SPECIFICATIONS

MODEL Lancia Stratos (1973–80)
PRODUCTION 492
BODY STYLE Two-seater, mid-engined sports coupé.
CONSTRUCTION Glass-fibre and steel unit construction body chassis tub.
ENGINE 2418cc mid-mounted transverse V6.
POWER OUTPUT 190 bhp at 7000 rpm.
TRANSMISSION Five-speed manual in unit with engine and transaxle.
SUSPENSION Independent front and rear with coil springs and wishbones.
BRAKES Four wheel discs.
MAXIMUM SPEED 230 km/h (143 mph)
0–60 MPH (0–96 KM/H) 6.0 sec
0–100 MPH (0–161 KM/H) 16.7 sec
A.F.C. 6.4 km/l (18 mpg)

SCREEN
Windscreen is cut from thin cylindrical glass to avoid distortion.

ENGINE

Lifted straight out of the Dino 246, the 190 bhp transverse, mid-mounted V6 has four chain-driven camshafts spinning in alloy heads, which sit just 15 cm (6 in) from your ear. Clutch and throttle are incredibly stiff, which makes smooth driving an art form.

WINDOW SLATS
A 1970s fad, matt black plastic rear window slats do little for rearward visibility.

REAR SPOILER
Raised rear spoiler does its best to keep the rear wheels stuck to the road like lipstick on a collar.

SUSPENSION
Rear springing was by Lancia Beta-style struts, with lower wishbones, and had anti-dive and anti-squat geometry.

LOTUS *Elite*

IF EVER A CAR WAS A MARQUE landmark, this is it. The Elite was the first Lotus designed for road use rather than out-and-out racing, paving the way for a string of stunning sports and GT cars that, at the least, were always innovative. But the first Elite was much more than that. Its all-glass-fibre construction – chassis as well as body – was a bold departure which, coupled with many other innovations, marked the Elite out as truly exceptional, and all the more so considering the small-scale operation that created it. What's more, its built-in Lotus race-breeding gave it phenomenal handling and this, together with an unparalleled power-to-weight ratio, brought an almost unbroken run of racing successes. It also happens to be one of the prettiest cars of its era; in short, a superb GT in miniature.

WINDOW DESIGN
The door shape did not allow for conventional wind-down windows. Quarter lights opened, but on early cars the main side windows were fixed. This later car has a catch to allow outwards opening.

CUBBY-HOLES APLENTY WERE PROVIDED TO SUPPLEMENT BOOT SPACE

SE (SPECIAL EQUIPMENT) MODELS HAD SILVER ROOF AS A "DELETE OPTION"

LOW DRAG
Low frontal area, with air intake below the bumper lip, was a major contribution to Elite speed and economy. Drag coefficient was 0.29, a figure most other manufacturers would not match for 20 years.

QUICK-RELEASE FUEL-CAP WAS AN OPTION MANY CHOSE

LENGTH IS ONLY 3.66 M (12 FT), YET THE BOOT IS VERY USABLE; SPARE WHEEL IS IN THE CABIN

BOTH FRONT AND REAR BUMPERS HID BODY MOULDING SEAMS

GLASS-FIBRE FACTS
Glass-fibre was used both to avoid the tooling costs of traditional construction and to build in lightness. In reality, the Elite was not cheap to produce but, at around 590 kg (1,300 lb), it was certainly light.

INTERIOR

Even tall owners were universal in their praise for driving comfort. The award winning interior is crisp and neat, with light, modern materials. Main instruments are a speedo reading to 140 mph (225 km/h) and a 0–8000 rpm tachometer.

OUTLINE OF INSTRUMENT PANEL MIMICS PROFILE OF THE ELITE BODY

WOOD-RIM WHEEL IS THE ONE TRADITIONAL TOUCH IN THE INTERIOR

COVENTRY CLIMAX ENGINE BADGE SHOWS LADY GODIVA, WHO PARADED NAKED THROUGH THE CITY'S STREETS

VENTILATION

In-built cockpit ventilation system was fed by an intake on the scuttle; outlet vents were above the rear window.

CIRCUIT SUCCESS

Elites were seen on the track even before they were available for sale. They were uncatchable in their class, claiming Le Mans class wins six years in a row from 1959 to 1964. and often embarrassing bigger GT Ferraris and Jaguars.

ENGINE

The lightweight 1216cc four-cylinder engine was developed by Coventry Climax from their successful racing units. Power rose from an initial 75 bhp to 83 bhp in the second series, but over 100 bhp was possible with options.

CONCEALED STEEL HOOP AROUND WINDSCREEN ADDED STIFFNESS AND GAVE SOME ROLL-OVER PROTECTION

CONTEMPORARY ROAD TESTS RECORDED A REMARKABLE 8.8 KM/L (25 MPG) AT A STEADY 161 KM/H (100 MPH)

48-SPOKE CENTRE-LOCK DUNLOP WIRE WHEELS WERE STANDARD

SPECIFICATIONS

MODEL Lotus Elite (1957–63)

PRODUCTION 988

BODY STYLE Two-door, two-seater sports coupé.

CONSTRUCTION Glass-fibre monocoque.

ENGINE Four-cylinder single ohc Coventry Climax, 1216cc.

POWER OUTPUT 75–105 bhp at 6100–6800 rpm.

TRANSMISSION Four-speed MG or ZF gearbox.

SUSPENSION Independent all round by wishbones and coil springs at front and MacPherson-type "Chapman strut" at rear.

BRAKES Discs all round (inboard at rear).

MAXIMUM SPEED 190 km/h (118 mph)

0–60 MPH (0–96 KM/H) 11.1 sec

A.F.C. 12.5 km/l (35 mpg)

THE COVENTRY CLIMAX ENGINE WAS DEVELOPED FROM A WARTIME FIRE-PUMP ENGINE

THE FIRST LOTUS FOR THE ROAD

Against the odds the elegant Elite launched the tiny Lotus company into the world of production car maufacture with a blend of almost amateur enthusiasm, race-bred engineering expertise, dedication, and sure intuition.

THE ELITE WAS THE brainchild of company founder and great racing innovator, Anthony Colin Bruce Chapman. The elegant coupé was a remarkable departure for the small company – and, to most, a complete surprise when it appeared at the London Motor Show in October, 1957. Even more surprising was the nature of the package, for it was not professionally styled, drawn up initially by a friend of Chapman, Peter Kirwan-Taylor – an accountant and design hobbyist.

It bristled with innovation too, for its glass-fibre monocoque – not just body – was an amazing industry first. The engine was the lightweight Coventry Climax that Chapman knew well in competition Lotuses – and yes, it really was developed from a wartime fire-pump engine. Suspension was derived from the Lotus Formula 2 car of 1956, with that elegant weight-saving Chapman strut at the rear. The result was a light fantastic, so nimble and

precise it gave road users an insight into racing-car dynamics; on the race track it was a giant-killer.

That is the glory of the Elite, but in reality customers had to wait to find out. The Elite was already a race winner, but the first customer cars – only two of them – did not go out until

COLIN CHAPMAN AT TRACKSIDE

LOTUS
Elite

AT ITS LAUNCH, THE ELITE COST MORE THAN A JAGUAR XK150

MANY ELITES FROM 1961 WERE SOLD AS NEAR-COMPLETE KITS, WHICH, THE ADVERTISING SAID, COULD BE ASSEMBLED IN 25 MAN HOURS

STRESSED ROOF
The roof was part of the Elite's stressed structure, which meant that popular calls for a convertible – especially from America – could not be answered.

TINY DOOR HANDLE IS LITTLE MORE THAN A HOOK

LJC 322

COLIN CHAPMAN, LOTUS SUPREMO

December 1958, more than a year after the launch. And the Elite's exceptional qualities came at an exotic price, initially a little more than a Jaguar XK150, and twice the price of an MGA. In the end, it was a triumph that 988 were built at all, against a backdrop of early production problems and

Lotus' characteristically convoluted finances and organization – even the production total is far from certain.

But the ultimate testimony to the Elite is the number of survivors – at least 660, possibly 750. It had made its mark and when the end came, the American magazine *Road & Track* published a full-page obituary that serves as a fine epitaph: "A beautiful design was the Elite ... one that seems certain to be looked back upon as a landmark of some sort in automobile design. Without

question it was the best, if not the very best looking Grand Touring car ever built." But it was also a beginning. Current with the Elite was the cult-status Lotus 7, and the Elite laid the foundations for future Lotuses – the Elan, then Europa, Elite again, Eclat, Esprit, and back to a new Elan.

LOTUS 7

SUSPENSION STRUT
Curious conical bulges cover the coil springs and telescopic dampers.

AIR CHEATER
The Elite's aerodynamic make-up is remarkable considering there were no full-scale wind-tunnel tests, only low-speed air-flow experiments. Height of just 1.17 m (46 in) helped, as did the fully enclosed undertray below.

A 2-LITRE ENGINE WAS TOYED WITH FOR A WHILE, BUT IT UPSET THE ELITE'S FINE BALANCE

LJC322

LOTUS *Elan Sprint*

THE LOTUS ELAN RANKS AS one of the best handling cars of its era. But not only was it among the most poised cars money could buy, it was also a thing of beauty. Conceived by engineering genius Colin Chapman to replace the race-bred Lotus 7, the Elan sat on a steel backbone chassis, clothed in a slippery glass-fibre body, and powered by a 1600cc Ford twin-cam engine. Despite a high price tag, critics and public raved and the Elan became one of the most charismatic sports cars of its decade, selling over 12,000 examples.

Over an 11-year production life, with five different model series, it evolved into a very desirable and accelerative machine, culminating in the Elan Sprint, a 193 km/h (120 mph) banshee with a sub-seven second 0–60 (96 km/h) time. As one motoring magazine of the time remarked, "The Elan Sprint is one of the finest sports cars in the world". Praise indeed.

ENGINE
The "Big Valve" engine in the Sprint pushed out 126 bhp and blessed it with truly staggering performance. The Twin 40 DCOE Weber carburettors were hard to keep in tune. The ribbed cam covers were designed to prevent oil leaks. Servo-assisted disc brakes provided tremendous stopping power.

INTERIOR
The Sprint's interior accommodation was refined and upmarket, with all-black trim, wood veneer dashboard, and even electric windows. Safer recessed rocker switches were a legal requirement in most markets.

WHEEL RESPECT
Colin Chapman's signature on the alloy steering wheel.

BOOT SPACE
The Elan was popular as a touring car because, despite housing the battery, its boot was larger than average.

SPORTY PIPE
The rakishly angled exhaust left no-one in any doubt about the car's performance.

HEADLIGHTS
The pop-up headlights worked via a vacuum system, but often failed.

LOTUS ELAN SPRINT

The duo-tone paintwork with dividing strip was a popular factory option for the Sprint. The red and gold combination had racing associations – the same livery as the Gold Leaf racing team cars. Everybody agreed that the diminutive Elan had an elfin charm.

WRAP-AROUND BUMPERS
Front bumper was foam-filled glass-fibre and the Elan was one of the first cars to be fitted with bumpers that followed the car's contours.

STYLING
Perfectly proportioned from any angle, the Elan really looked like it meant business.

WORLD CHAMPION BADGE
Never slow to sing their own praises, Lotus fitted many Elans with this badge as a reminder of the company's string of Grand Prix victories.

WORLD CHAMPION CAR CONSTRUCTORS 1970 1968 1965 1963

SPECIFICATIONS

MODEL Lotus Elan Sprint (1970–73)
PRODUCTION 1,353
BODY STYLE Two-seater drophead.
CONSTRUCTION Steel box section backbone chassis.
ENGINE Four-cylinder twin overhead cam, 1558cc.
POWER OUTPUT 126 bhp at 6500 rpm.
TRANSMISSION Four-speed manual.
SUSPENSION Independent front and rear.
BRAKES Discs all round.
MAXIMUM SPEED 195 km/h (121 mph)
0–60 MPH (0–96 KM/H) 6.7 sec
0–100 MPH (0–161 KM/H) 15 sec
A.F.C. 8.5 km/l (24 mpg)

SPRINT

MASERATI *Ghibli*

MANY RECKON THE GHIBLI is the greatest of all road-going Maseratis. It was the sensation of the 1966 Turin Show, and 30 years on is widely regarded as Maserati's ultimate front-engined road car, a supercar blend of luxury, performance, and stunning good looks that never again quite came together so sublimely on anything with the three-pointed trident. Pitched squarely against the Ferrari Daytona *(see page 104)* and Lamborghini Miura *(see page 146)*, it outsold both. Its engineering may have been dated, but it had the perfect pedigree, with plenty of power from its throaty V8 engine and a flawless Ghia design. It is an uncompromised supercar, yet it is also a consummate continent-eating grand tourer with 24-karat cachet. Muscular and perhaps even menacing, but not overbearingly macho, it is well mannered enough for the tastes of the mature super-rich with hectic social timetables. There will only be one dilemma; do you take the windy back roads or blast along the autoroutes? Why not a bit of both.

GHIBLI NAME
Like the earlier Mistral, the Ghibli takes its name from a regional wind.

ENGINE
The potent race-bred quad-cam V8 is even-tempered and undemanding, delivering loads of low-down torque and accelerating meaningfully from as little as 500 rpm in fifth gear. This is the 4.9-litre engine of the featured 1971 Ghibli SS.

FOUR GREEDY TWIN-CHOKE WEBER CARBS SIT ASTRIDE THE V8

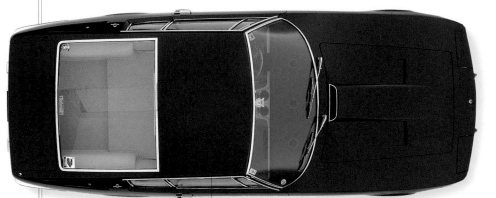

OPEN MASER
Most prized of all Ghiblis are the 125 convertible Spiders.

WIDE VIEW
The front screen is huge but the mighty bonnet can make the Ghibli difficult to manoeuvre.

STEERING
Power steering was a later, desirable option.

HIDE-AWAY HEADLIGHTS
Pop-up headlights improve looks when not needed, but take their time to pop up.

LIFT OFF
Wide front has a tendency to lift above 193 km/h (120 mph) as the steering can become disconcertingly light.

TRIDENT
Masers are instantly recognizable by the three-pointed trident.

DASHBOARD
A cliché certainly, but here you really feel you are on an aircraft flight-deck. The high centre console houses air-conditioning, which was standard Ghibli equipment.

MASERATI GHIBLI SS
The Ghibli's dramatic styling is uncompromised, a sublime and extravagant 4.57 m (15 ft) of attitude that can only accommodate two people. From its blade-like front to its short, bobbed tail, it looks fast even in static pose. It has also aged all the better for its lack of finicky detail; the Ghibli's detail is simple and clean, worn modestly like fine, expensive jewellery.

SPECIFICATIONS

MODEL Maserati Ghibli (1967–73)
PRODUCTION 1274
BODY STYLE Two-door sports coupé or open Spider.
CONSTRUCTION Steel body and separate tubular chassis.
ENGINE Four-cam 90-degree V8, 4719cc or 4930cc (SS).
POWER OUTPUT 330 bhp at 5000 rpm (4719cc); 335 bhp at 5500 rpm (4930cc).
TRANSMISSION ZF five-speed manual or three-speed Borg-Warner auto.
SUSPENSION Wishbones and coil-springs at front; rigid axle with radius arms/semi-elliptic leaf springs at rear.
BRAKES Girling discs on all four wheels.
MAXIMUM SPEED 248 km/h (154 mph), 270 km/h (168 mph, SS)
0–60 MPH (0–96 KM/H) 6.6 sec, 6.2 sec (SS)
0–100 MPH (0–161 KM/H) 15.7 sec
A.F.C. 3.5 km/l (10 mpg)

THIRSTY
The Ghibli was a petrol gobbler, but when was there an economical supercar?

EARLY GIUGIARO
Coachwork by Ghia was one of the finest early designs of their brilliant young Italian employee, Giorgetto Giugiaro.

MASERATI *Kyalami*

THE 1970s PRODUCED some automotive lemons. It was a decade when bare-faced badge engineering and gluttonous V8 engines were all the rage, and nobody cared that these big bruisers cost three arms and a leg to run. The Kyalami is one such monument to excess, a copy of the De Tomaso Longchamp with Maserati's all-alloy V8 on board instead of Ford's 5.8 cast-iron lump.

The Kyalami was meant to take on the Jaguar XJS but failed hopelessly. Plagued with electrical gremlins, this was a noisy, bulky, and unrefined machine that was neither beautiful nor poised. Yet for all that it still sports that emotive trident on its nose and emits a deep and strident V8 bark. The Kyalami might not be a great car, but most of us, at least while looking at it, find it hard to tell the difference.

MASERATI KYALAMI
Maserati designer Pietro Frua retouched the De Tomaso Longchamp design, turning it into the Kyalami. He gave it a new lower nose with twin lights, full width bonnet, new rubber-cap bumpers with integral indicators, and deleted the extractor vents from the C-pillars. By the time he had finished, the only shared body panels were the door pressings.

MASERATI 300S
Maserati's racing bloodline goes back to 1930, when it won five Grand Prix events in a row. After the war, Juan Fangio trounced the opposition in the legendary 250F, and the 300S sports-racing model went on to secure success at Le Mans.

REAR LIGHTS
Dainty rear light clusters were borrowed from the contemporary Fiat 130 Coupé.

THIRSTY
The Kyalami gobbled liquid gold at the rate of 4.2 km/l (14 mpg).

ENGINE

The engine is a four-cam, five-bearing 4.9 V8, with four twin-choke 42DCNF Weber carbs, propelling the Kyalami's considerable bulk to a touch under 241 km/h (150 mph). Physically imposing, the vast air cleaner and cam covers are presented in crackle black as opposed to the usual polished Italian alloy. Transmission was five-speed manual or three-speed automatic.

INTERIOR

The cabin is a study of 1970s tastelessness, with hide seats and Alcantara dash top. Quality control was poor and many components, like the Ford steering column, were sourced from European parts bins.

STYLING

Basic design was originally penned by Tom Tjaarda for De Tomaso and was a unitary construction with a pressed-steel body and a chassis that turned out rather too boxy and angular for its own good.

TYRES

The Kyalami generates lots of commotion and bump thump from fat 205/70 Michelins.

STEERING

Power-assisted steering robs the car of much needed accuracy and feel.

NOT A PRETTY FACE

The frontal aspect is mean but clumsy. The three-part front bumper looks cheap, while the Maserati grille and trident seem to have been bolted on as after-thoughts.

SPECIFICATIONS

MODEL Maserati Kyalami 4.9 (1976–82)

PRODUCTION 250 approx.

BODY STYLE Two-door, 2+2 sports saloon.

CONSTRUCTION Steel monocoque body.

ENGINE 4930cc all-alloy V8.

POWER OUTPUT 265 bhp at 6000 rpm.

TRANSMISSION Five-speed ZF manual or three-speed Borg Warner automatic.

SUSPENSION Independent front with coil springs and wishbones. Independent rear with double coils, lower links, and radius arms.

BRAKES Four-wheel discs.

MAXIMUM SPEED 237 km/h (147 mph)

0–60 MPH (0–96 KM/H) 7.6 sec

0–100 MPH (0–161 KM/H) 19.4 sec

A.F.C. 3.6 km/l (14 mpg)

MAZDA RX7

MAZDA THE RX7 ARRIVED in American showrooms in 1978 and sales promptly went crazy. Even importing 4,000 a month, Mazda could not cope with demand and waiting lists stretched towards the horizon. For a while, RX7s changed hands on the black market for as much as US$3,000 above retail price. By the time production ceased in 1985, nearly 500,000 had found grateful owners, making the RX7 the best-selling rotary car of all time.

Cheaper than the Porsche 924 and Datsun 280Z, the RX7 sold on its clean European looks and Swiss-watch smoothness. Inspired by the woefully unreliable NSU Ro80 *(see page 182)*, Mazda's engineers were not worried about the NSU's ghost haunting the RX7. By 1978 they had completely mastered rotary-engine technology and sold almost a million rotary-engined cars and trucks. As always, the Japanese took a good idea and made it even better. These days the RX7 is becoming an emergent classic – the first car to make Felix Wankel's rotary design actually work and one of the more desirable and better made sports cars of the 1970s.

ENGINE
The twin-rotor Wankel engine gave 135 bhp in later models, although oil consumption was always quite high. Reliable, compact, and easy to tune, there was even a small electric winch on the bulkhead to reel in the choke if owners forgot to push it back in.

INTERIOR
Cockpit and dashboard are tastefully orthodox, with a handsome three-spoke wheel and five-gauge instrument binnacle.

EUROPEAN STYLING
For a Japanese design, the RX7 was atypically European, with none of the garish over-adornment associated with other cars from Japan. Occasional rear seats and liftback rear window helped in the practicality department.

SUSPENSION
Rear suspension was in the best European sports car tradition – wishbones and a Watt's linkage.

HANDLING
Fine handling is due to near equal weight distribution and the low centre of gravity.

HEADLIGHT
Pop-up headlights helped reduce wind resistance and add glamour. But, unlike those on the Lotus Esprit and Triumph TR7, the Mazda's always worked.

Mazda RX7

Originally planned as a two-seater, Mazda had to include a small rear seat in the RX7 as Japanese law stated that all cars had to have more than two seats to encourage car sharing. The RX7's slippery, wind-cheating shape cleaved the air well, with a drag coefficient of only 0.36 and a top speed of 201 km/h (125 mph). Smooth aerodynamics helped the RX7 feel stable and composed with minimal body roll. The body design was perfect from the start and in its seven-year production run few changes were made to the slim and balanced shape.

SPECIFICATIONS

MODEL Maxda RX7 (1978–85)
PRODUCTION 474,565 (377,878 exported to US)
BODY STYLE All-steel two-seater coupé.
CONSTRUCTION One-piece monocoque bodyshell.
ENGINE Twin rotor, 1146cc.
POWER OUTPUT 135 bhp at 6000 rpm.
TRANSMISSION Five-speed all synchromesh/automatic option.
SUSPENSION Independent front. Live rear axle with trailing arms and Watt's linkage.
BRAKES *Front:* ventilated discs; *Rear:* drums.
MAXIMUM SPEED 210 km/h (125 mph)
0–60 MPH (0–96 KM/H) 8.9 sec
0–100 MPH (0–161 KM/H) 24 sec
A.F.C. 7.5 km/l (21.3 mpg)

REAR DESIGN
Original design favoured a one-piece rear tailgate like the Porsche 944, but economics dictated an all-glass hatch instead.

ENGINE FLAWS
The Wankel-designed rotary engine has two weak points – low speed pull and fuel economy.

BONNET
The RX7's low bonnet line could not have been achieved with anything but the compact rotary engine, which weighed only 142 kg (312 lb).

BRAKES
Both front and rear brakes were well cooled with ventilated discs and finned rear drums.

MERCEDES *300SL Gullwing*

WITH ITS GORGEOUS gullwing doors raised, the Mercedes 300SL looked like it could fly. And with them lowered shut it really could, rocketing beyond 225 km/h (140 mph) and making its contemporary supercar pretenders look ordinary. Derived from the 1952 Le Mans-winning racer, these mighty Mercs were early forebears of modern supercars like the Jaguar XJ220 and McLaren F1 in taking race-track technology on to the streets. In fact, the 300SL can lay a plausible claim to being the first true post-war supercar. Awkward to enter, hot once you were inside, noisy, and with twitchy high-speed handling strictly for the "advanced motorist", it was sublimely impractical – it is a virtual supercar blueprint. It was a statement too that Mercedes had recovered from war-time devastation. Mercedes was back, and at the pinnacle of that three-pointed star was the fabulous 300SL, the company's first post-war sports car.

SLANT SIX
The engine was canted at 50 degrees to give a low bonnet-line. It was also the first application of fuel injection in a production car.

GULLWING DOORS ARE MADE OF ALUMINIUM AND ARE SURPRISINGLY LIGHT TO LIFT WITH HELP FROM HYDRAULIC STAYS

GULLWING DOORS
The car's most famous feature was the roof-hinged gullwing doors. With the high and wide sills, they were a functional necessity, rather than a finnicky design flourish.

REAR VISION IS GOOD BUT ALL THAT GLASS CAN TURN THE COCKPIT INTO A HOT HOUSE

AERODYNAMICS
Detailed attention to aerodynamics was streets ahead of anything else at the time and helped make the 300SL the undisputed fastest road car of its era.

SALOON-BASED REAR SUSPENSION COMPROMISED HIGH-SPEED HANDLING AND COULD CATCH YOU OUT IN A BIG WAY

IN BRITAIN YOU COULD BUY TWO AND A BIT JAGUAR XK140S FOR ONE GULLWING. IN THE US ONE GULLWING WAS NEARLY TWO CORVETTES

SOME SAY STEEL DISC WHEELS WERE FITTED TO KEEP COSTS DOWN, BUT THEY ALSO LOOK MORE MUSCULAR THAN FRAGILE WIRES

PRECISION INTERIOR

In the Fifties, the bechromed dash was pure sci-fi. The large two-spoked white wheel gives a good view of the dials. On some cars, mostly for the US, the wheel tilted to ease access and became known as "the fat man's wheel".

PASSENGER AND DRIVER GET EQUAL SHARE OF THE CLOCK.

AERODYNAMIC STYLING

Mercedes insisted that the "eyebrows" over the wheel arches were aerodynamic aids; it is more likely they were US-aimed styling touches.

SPECIFICATIONS

MODEL Mercedes-Benz 300SL (1954–57)
PRODUCTION 1,400
BODY STYLE Two-door, two-seat coupé.
CONSTRUCTION Multitubular space-frame with steel and alloy body.
ENGINE Inline six-cylinder overhead camshaft, 2996cc.
POWER OUTPUT 240 bhp at 6100 rpm.
TRANSMISSION Four-speed all synchromesh gearbox.
SUSPENSION Coil springs all round, with double wishbones at front, swinging half-axles at rear.
BRAKES Finned alloy drums.
MAXIMUM SPEED 217–265 km/h (135–165 mph), depending on gearing.
0–60 MPH (0–96 KM/H) 8.8 sec
0–100 MPH (0–161 KM/H) 21.0 sec
A.F.C. 6.4 km/l (18 mpg)

IF YOU TURN TURTLE IN A GULLWING THERE IS NO GETTING OUT UNTIL SOMEONE TURNS YOU UPRIGHT

ROAD CARS DEVELOPED 240 BHP, MORE EVEN THAN THE RACING VERSIONS OF JUST TWO YEARS EARLIER

PIPE-WORK ON THE SIDE IS FOR FUEL INJECTION

ENGINE

The engine was derived originally from the 300-Series 3-litre saloons, then developed for the 1952 300SL racer, and two years later let loose in the road-going Gullwing, with fuel injection in place of carburettors.

STAR IDENTITY

The massive three-pointed star dominated the frontal aspect and was repeated in enamel on the bonnet edge.

ENGINE BAY COULD GET VERY HOT SO GILL-LIKE SIDE VENTS WERE MORE THAN A MERE STYLING MOTIF

HD·WD 34

SILVER WAS THE OFFICIAL GERMAN RACING COLOUR

THE FLIGHT OF THE GULLWING

The might of Mercedes had been brought low by the ravages of war, but the launch of the staggering 300SL Gullwing prototype at the 1954 New York Motor Show also announced to the world that Mercedes was back – with a bang.

STIRLING MOSS ON THE 1955 MILLE MIGLIA

MERCEDES' RECOVERY had been based on its trademark solid and well-engineered saloons, but with the Gullwing, its proud sporting tradition was once more in full flight. The

STIRLING MOSS AT START OF 1955 MILLE MIGLIA

awesome Silver Arrows were no longer just a misty memory of yesterday's podium glory, but, here in the 300SL, was tomorrow's supercar, today.

The Gullwing is certainly magical and bathed in its own folklore, which centres on the involvement of a New York sports car importer with a coast-to-coast smile – Max Hoffman.

In 1952, Mercedes stormed back into motor sport with a space-frame chassised car that

did not allow for conventional doors. Its engine was a development of the 3-litre engine of the 300-Series saloons. This aluminium-bodied car was called the 300SL – SL stood for Super Leicht – and it was right straight out of the box. In its first race, the 1952 Mille Miglia, it finished second, snatched outright victory at the Berne Grand Prix, took a 1–2 at Le Mans, won at the Nürburgring, and ended the year with 1–2 in the Carrera Panamericana Mexican road race. Mercedes had proved their point, and in 1954 concentrated on Grand Prix goals.

MERCEDES
300SL Gullwing

SMOOTH REAR
The Gullwing's smooth styling extended to the uncluttered rear; the boot lid suggests ample luggage space, but this was not the case.

COSY COCKPIT BECAME PRETTY HOT; AIR VENTS AT REAR HELPED REMOVE STALE AIR

LIMITED SPACE
With the spare tyre mounted atop the fuel tank, there was very little room for luggage.

HD · WD · 34

ON THE TRACK ON THE 1955 MILLE MIGLIA

Meanwhile, something that looked like a Gullwing was making waves again in motor sport. It was the 300SLR of 1955, which with its straight-eight actually owed more to the Mercedes W196 Grand Prix car. It won the Targa Florio, and, in the hands of Stirling Moss, the 1955 Mille Miglia.

The 300SL re-established Mercedes' position at the pinnacle of sporting excellence. Yet it had a wider appeal, for wherever the glitterati gathered there also seemed to be a 300SL nearby, often drawing more media attention than the stars themselves. A youthful King Hussein of Jordan owned one, along with Stirling Moss, British comedian Tony Hancock, and numerous film stars.

But the story did not end there, for in 1969 gull wings appeared again on a Mercedes; but the rotary-engined C111 was a research project that was never seriously contemplated for production.

But the 300SL Gullwing was about to enter a new life. Max Hoffman was so convinced of the 300SL's appeal that he was willing to back up his word with a large order, if Mercedes would build them. The road-going 300SL was clearly based on the racer, with the addition of luxury refinements. Hoffman's hunch was right, for over half of the 1400 Gullwings built from 1954 to 1957 went straight to American customers. As Gullwing production wound down in 1957, a roadster version was introduced, which lasted until 1963.

AFE
USPENSION
wing-axle rear
uspension was
amed to provide
atural
ndersteer.

OPTIONAL THIRD
The SL was essentially a two-seater, although a third, sideways-facing rear seat was available as a (rare) optional extra.

MERCEDES 280SL

The most distinctive design feature of t 280SL is the so-called pagoda-roof removable hardtop. It is said to hav evolved from the need to provide relatively deep windows for a n balanced side-view of the car without at the same tim making it look top-heav from the front or rear. T layout also provided a remarkably efficient of keeping rain aw

TRADE
So-called
are unm
tradema
conceale
indicato

CHRO
The fi
bumpe
central
enough
Britis
the qu
as else
was f

300SL ROADSTER

As Gullwing production wound down, Mercedes introduced the 300SL Roadster, which from 1957 to 1963 sold 1,858, compared to the Gullwing's 1,400. From 1955 to 1963 the 190SL Roadster served as the "poor man's" 300SL.

ALL GULLWINGS WERE ONLY AVAILABLE IN LEFT-HAND DRIVE

ONE BONNET BULGE WAS FOR AIR INTAKES, THE OTHER FOR AESTHETIC BALANCE

MOST OF THE BODY WAS MADE OF STEEL, BUT BONNET, BOOT LID AND DOORS WERE ALLOY

HD·WD·34

MERCEDES 2

THE MERCEDES 280SL has
In 1963, the new SLs too
mantle of the ageing 190
in Mercedes parlance, th
original 230SL, through t
to the 280SL. The most re
modern they look, for with their uncluttered
good looks, it is hard to believe that the la
1971. Underneath the timelessly elegant s
were based closely on the earlier Fintail sa
the decidedly unsporting recirculating-ba

Yet it is the looks that mark this Merc ou
the enduring design, with its distinctive so-
is down to Frenchman Paul Bracq. Some
dismiss it as a woman's car and it is certai
hairy-chested of sporting Mercs. But this
Merc is a beautifully built boulevardier th
a sense of supreme self satisfaction on a

US-MARKET
HAD A MILD
CAMSHAFT

BRAKES ARE
POWERFULLY
SERVO-ASSISTED

ENGINE
The six-cylinder overhead-
camshaft engine saw a process of
steady development starting in July,
1963 with the 2281cc, 150 bhp,
230SL. In December 1966 came
the 2496cc 250SL, with the same
power but slightly more torque,
and from January 1968 to March
1971 the final 2778cc, 170 bhp
280SL shown here.

CITY SLICKER
*With standard power-assisted
steering and a turning circle of less
than 10 m (33 ft), the SL
handled city streets with aplomb.*

MG *TC Midget*

EVEN WHEN IT WAS NEW, the MG TC was not
new. The TC, introduced in September 1945,
displayed a direct lineage back to its pre-war
forbears. If you were a little short on soul, you
might even have called it old fashioned. Yet it
was a trail-blazer, not in terms of performance,
but in opening up new export markets. Popular myth
has it that American GIs stationed in England cottoned on to these
quaint sporting devices and when they got home were eager to take
a little piece of England with them.

Whatever the reality, it was the first in a long line of MG export
successes. The average American family car of the time could drag
a TC off the line, but there was simply nothing remotely like this
TC tiddler coming out of Detroit. It had a cramped cockpit, harsh
ride, and lacked creature comforts, but when the road got twisty
the TC could show you its tail and leave soft-sprung sofa-cars
lumbering in its wake. Yet it was challenging to drive, and all the
more rewarding when you got it right. Mastering an
MG was a thrill in its own right, for in a TC you did
not need to joust with other jalopies; the TC and
its rorty exhaust note was enough to give you
hours of solo driving enjoyment.

ENGINE
Ease of accessibility and maintenance was
another of the TC's attractions. The XPAG
engine was first used on some TB Midgets
in 1939, then became standard MG wear
until replaced by a 1500cc version in 1955.

POWER BOOST
*Though not a factory option, Shorrock
superchargers were often fitted.*

ALTHOUGH OVER
2,000 WERE SOLD
IN AMERICA,
ALL TCS WERE
RIGHT-HAND
DRIVE

RACERS' FAVOURITE
*The TC was a popular race car,
especially in the US, where it
launched many careers and one
world champion, Phil Hill.*

COCKPIT
*Roomier than earlier Midgets,
the TC cockpit was still
cramped by comparison with
less sporting contemporaries.*

DASHBOARD
Big Jaeger dials were in true British
sporting tradition; the driver got the
rev-counter, while the speedo was in
front of the passenger. The close-up
(right) shows the warning light that
came on if you exceeded Britain's 48
km/h (30 mph) urban speed limit.

FBT 112

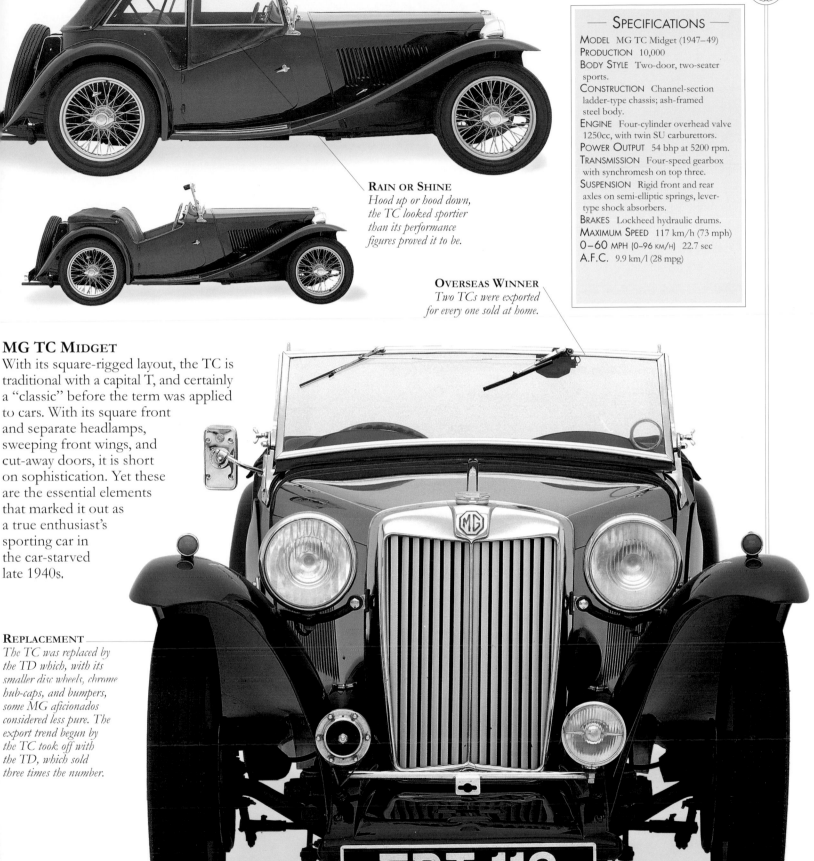

RAIN OR SHINE
*Hood up or hood down,
the TC looked sportier
than its performance
figures proved it to be.*

— SPECIFICATIONS —

MODEL MG TC Midget (1947–49)
PRODUCTION 10,000
BODY STYLE Two-door, two-seater
  sports.
CONSTRUCTION Channel-section
  ladder-type chassis; ash-framed
  steel body.
ENGINE Four-cylinder overhead valve
  1250cc, with twin SU carburettors.
POWER OUTPUT 54 bhp at 5200 rpm.
TRANSMISSION Four-speed gearbox
  with synchromesh on top three.
SUSPENSION Rigid front and rear
  axles on semi-elliptic springs, lever-
  type shock absorbers.
BRAKES Lockheed hydraulic drums.
MAXIMUM SPEED 117 km/h (73 mph)
0–60 MPH (0–96 KM/H) 22.7 sec
A.F.C. 9.9 km/l (28 mpg)

OVERSEAS WINNER
*Two TCs were exported
for every one sold at home.*

MG TC MIDGET

With its square-rigged layout, the TC is
traditional with a capital T, and certainly
a "classic" before the term was applied
to cars. With its square front
and separate headlamps,
sweeping front wings, and
cut-away doors, it is short
on sophistication. Yet these
are the essential elements
that marked it out as
a true enthusiast's
sporting car in
the car-starved
late 1940s.

REPLACEMENT
*The TC was replaced by
the TD which, with its
smaller disc wheels, chrome
hub-caps, and bumpers,
some MG aficionados
considered less pure. The
export trend begun by
the TC took off with
the TD, which sold
three times the number.*

FBT 112

MGA

LAUNCHED IN SEPTEMBER 1955, the MGA was the first of the modern sporting MGs. The chassis, engine, and gearbox were all new, as was the smooth, Le Mans-inspired bodywork. Compared to its predecessor – the TF, which still sported old-fashioned running boards – the MGA was positively futuristic. Buyers thought so too, and being cheaper than its nearest rivals, the Triumph TR3 and Austin Healey 100, helped MG sell 13,000 cars in the first year of production. The company's small factory at Abingdon, near Oxford, managed to export a staggering 81,000 MGAs to America. The car also earned an enviable reputation in competition, with the Twin Cam being the most powerful of the MGA engines.

SPECIFICATIONS

MODEL MGA (1955–62)
PRODUCTION 101,081
BODY STYLES Two-door sports coupé.
CONSTRUCTION Steel.
ENGINE Four-cylinder 1489cc, 1588cc, 1622cc (Twin Cam).
POWER OUTPUT 72 bhp, 80 bhp, 85 bhp.
TRANSMISSION Four-speed manual.
SUSPENSION *Front:* Independent. *Rear:* Leaf-spring.
BRAKES Rear drums, front discs. All discs on De Luxe and Twin Cam.
MAXIMUM SPEED 161 km/h (100 mph), 181 km/h (113 mph) Twin Cam.
0–60 MPH (0–96 KM/H) 15 sec (13.3 sec, Twin Cam)
0–100 MPH (0–161 KM/H) 47 sec (41 sec, Twin Cam)
A.F.C. 7–8.8 km/l (20–25 mpg)

LIMITED SPACE
The boot is deceptively shallow and filled by the spare wheel.

HORN BUTTON IS LOCATED IN THE CENTRE OF THE DASHBOARD AND CAN BE WORKED BY EITHER DRIVER OR PASSENGER

DASHBOARD
The simple dashboard has no glove compartment, but the MG badge and centre grille are for a radio and speaker. Passengers have a map-reading light, but little else.

NO HANDLES
The uncluttered design means no door handles – doors are opened by pulling a cable reached from inside the car.

WHEELS
Perforated steel wheels are standard.

HAND-FINISHED
Although the MGA's steel panels were hand-pressed, bodies were finished by hand and no two are quite the same.

ENGINE
The tough B-Series, push-rod engine goes well and lasts forever. A heater unit in front of the bulkhead was an optional extra.

VENTILATION
The chromed, shroud-panel vents at the front are for engine bay ventilation.

MGA
The slippery, wind-cheating shape of the MGA was created for racing at Le Mans – an early prototype achieved 223 km/h (116 mph). Production MGAs were very similar and the smooth bonnet and sloping wings aid both top speed and fuel consumption.

STARTING HANDLE
Hole is for a starting handle.

BSK 215

MGB

WIDELY ADMIRED FOR its uncomplicated nature, timeless good looks, and brisk performance, the MGB caused a sensation back in 1962. The now famous advertising slogan "Your mother wouldn't like it" was quite wrong. She would have wholeheartedly approved of the MGB's reliability, practicality, and good sense.

In 1965 came the even more practical tin-top MGB GT. These were the halcyon days of the MGB – chrome bumpers, leather seats, and wire wheels. In 1974, in pursuit of modernity and American safety regulations (the MGB's main market), the factory burdened the B with ungainly rubber bumpers, a higher ride height, and garish striped nylon seats, making the car slow, ugly, and unpredictable at the limit. Yet the B went on to become the best-selling single model sports car ever, finding 512,000 grateful owners throughout the world.

SPECIFICATIONS

MODEL MGB Tourer (1962–1980)
PRODUCTION 512,243
BODY STYLE Steel front-engined two seater with aluminium bonnet.
CONSTRUCTION One piece monocoque bodyshell.
ENGINE Four-cylinder/1798cc.
POWER OUTPUT 92 bhp at 5400 rpm.
TRANSMISSION Four-speed with overdrive.
SUSPENSION *Front:* Independent coil; *Rear:* Half-elliptic leaf springs.
BRAKES Lockheed discs front, drums rear.
MAXIMUM SPEED 171 km/h (106 mph)
0–60 MPH (0–96 KM/H) 12.2 sec
0–100 MPH (0–161 KM/H) 37 sec
A.F.C. 8.8 km/l (25 mpg)

AGELESS DESIGN
The MGB's shape was a miracle of compact packaging. The one-piece steel monocoque bodyshell was strong and roomy.

MIRROR SUPPORT
The line down the centre of the windscreen is a mirror support rod.

DASHBOARD
This is vintage traditionalism at its best. Leather seats, crackle black metal fascia, nautical-sized steering wheel, and minor controls are strewn about the dash like boulders with scant thought for ergonomics. The radio speaker is almost Art Deco.

EBW 45B

ADDITIONAL HOOD
To supplement the hood, a glass-fibre detachable hardtop was an option in 1962.

HOOD
Early cars had a "packaway" hood made from ICI Everflex.

BONNET
Bonnet is made out of lightweight aluminium.

SUSPENSION
Front suspension was coil spring with wishbones, and dated back to the MG TF of the 1950s.

MGB TOURER

All MGBs had the simple 1798cc B-series four-cylinder engine with origins going back to 1947. This Tourer's period charm is enhanced by the rare Iris Blue paintwork and seldom seen pressed-steel wheels – most examples were fitted with optional spoked wire wheels.

MORGAN *Plus Four*

IT IS REMARKABLE THAT THEY still make them, but there is many a gent with a cloth cap and corduroys who is grateful that they do. Derived from the first four-wheeled Morgans of 1936, this is the car that buoyed Morgan on after the war while many of the old mainstays of the British motor industry wilted around it. Tweedier than a Scottish moor on the first day of the grouse shooting season, it is as quintessentially English as a car can be. It was a hit in America and other foreign parts and it has also remained the backbone of the idiosyncratic Malvern-based company, which refuses to move with the times. Outdated and outmoded it may be, but there is still a very long waiting list to purchase a Morgan. First introduced in 1951, the Plus Four, with a series of Standard Vanguard and Triumph TR engines, laid the foundations for the modern miracle of the very old-fashioned Morgan Motor Company.

LIKE ALL FOUR-WHEELED MORGANS, THE PLUS FOUR HAD A TWO-PIECE BONNET WITH A PIANO HINGE IN THE MIDDLE

OTHER MODELS

Today, the company builds just two cars: the four-cylinder Ford Zetec-engined Plus Four, with a top speed of 179 km/h (111 mph), and the Plus Eight.

MORGAN PLUS EIGHT
The 3.5-litre Rover V8-engined Plus Eight is slower today, at 195 km/h (121 mph), than it was 20 years ago, but accelerates to 60 mph (96 km/h) in just 6.1 seconds.

ENGINE
The later Triumph TR3A 2138cc engine, as here, gave increased torque. The 2138cc engine was available in the TR3A from summer 1957. The earlier Triumph 1991cc engine was still available for those wishing to compete in sub- two-litre classes.

INTERIOR
From 1958, all Plus Fours had a slightly wider cockpit with a new fascia, identifiable by the cubbyhole on the passenger's side. Speedometer, switches, warning lights, and minor gauges were grouped in a central panel on the dash.

"SUICIDE" DOORS
The earlier two-seat drophead coupé retained rear-hinged "suicide" doors with framed, sliding windows, but the sleeker two- and four-seat sports models had front-hinged doors with removable sidescreens.

ON THE RACK
Morgans have limited luggage capacity, so many owners fitted external racks.

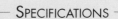

LIGHT WORK
Headlights are big, bold affairs set in pods on the front wings, but sidelights are about as visible as a pair of glow-worms.

REAR ILLUMINATION
Rear lights have never been a Morgan strong point. Amber indicators are a good 15 cm (6 in) inboard of the stop/tail lamps, and partially obscured by the luggage rack.

SPECIFICATIONS

MODEL Morgan Plus Four (1951–69)
PRODUCTION 3,737
BODY STYLES Two- and four-seater sports convertible.
CONSTRUCTION Steel chassis, ash frame, steel and alloy outer panels.
ENGINE 2088cc overhead-valve in-line four (Vanguard); 1991cc or 2138cc overhead-valve in-line four (TR).
POWER OUTPUT 105 bhp at 4700 rpm (2138cc TR engine).
TRANSMISSION Four-speed manual.
SUSPENSION *Front:* Sliding stub axles, coil springs, and telescopic dampers. *Rear:* Live axle, semi-elliptic leaf springs, and lever-arm dampers.
BRAKES Drums front and rear; front discs standard from 1960.
MAXIMUM SPEED 161 km/h (100 mph)
0–60 MPH (0–96 KM/H) 12 sec
A.F.C. 7–7.8 km/l (20–22 mpg)

MORGAN PLUS FOUR

The second-generation Plus Four was the first of what are generally considered the "modern-looking" Morgans – if that is the right expression for a basic design which, still in production today, dates back to 1936. Major distinguishing features are the cowled radiator grille and, from 1959, a wider body (as here) to provide more elbow room for driver and passenger.

BONNET
The dramatically tapering bonnet meant limited engine access.

WHERE'S THE CATCH?
Traditional latches – two for each bonnet half – are among the most tactile features of the Plus Four.

MIRROR POSITION
Doors were the only sensible places for exterior rear-view mirrors; the tops of the front wings were miles away.

TRADITIONAL ASH FRAME

The current four-cylinder Morgan is built in exactly the same manner as most of its predecessors. The chassis is made from "Z"-section steel members, and on it sits a 94- or 114-piece wooden framework (two- and four-seat cars, respectively) clothed in a mixture of steel and aluminium panels.

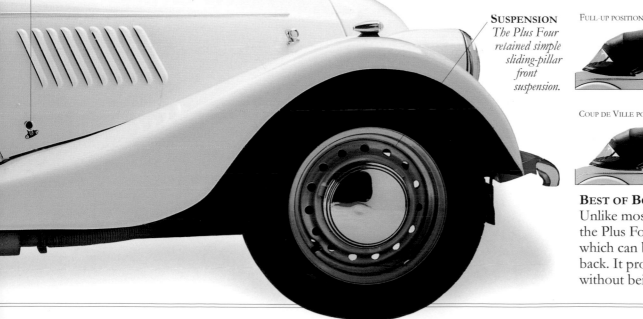

SUSPENSION
The Plus Four retained simple sliding-pillar front suspension.

FULL-UP POSITION

COUP DE VILLE POSITION

BEST OF BOTH WORLDS

Unlike most convertible cars, the Plus Four has a hood which can be partially folded back. It provides fresh air without being too draughty.

MORRIS MINOR MM *Convertible*

THE MORRIS MINOR is a motoring milestone. As Britain's first million seller it became a "people's car", staple transport for everyone from midwives to builders' merchants. Designed by Alec Issigonis, the genius who later went on to pen the Austin Mini *(see pages 40–41)*, the new Series MM Morris Minor of 1948 featured the then novel unitary chassis-body construction. The 918cc side-valve engine of the MM was rather more antique, a hang-over from the pre-war Morris 8.

Its handling and ride comfort more than made up for the lack of power. With independent front suspension and crisp rack-and-pinion steering it embarrassed its rivals and even tempted the young Stirling Moss into high-speed cornering antics that lost him his licence for a month. Of all the 1.5 million Minors the most prized are the now rare Series MM convertibles. Rag-tops remained part of the Minor model line-up until 1969, two years from the end of all Minor production. So desirable are these open tourers that in recent years there has been a trade in rogue rag-tops, chopped saloons masquerading as original factory convertibles.

INDICATORS
With no door pillars above waist height, semaphore indicators were mounted lower down on the tourers; flashers eventually replaced semaphores in 1961.

RAG-TOP RARITY
Convertibles represent only a small proportion of Minor production. Between 1963 and 1969 only 3,500 soft-tops were produced compared with 119,000 two-door saloons.

CHOICE OF MODELS
At its launch the Minor was available as a two-door saloon and as a convertible (Tourer). Four-door, estate, van, and pick-up completed the range.

ORIGINAL MM TOURER HAD SIDE CURTAINS, REPLACED BY GLASS REAR WINDOWS IN 1952

MORRIS BEAM COUNTERS DICTATED OLD-FASHIONED LIVE-AXLE AND LEAF SPRINGS AT REAR

BODY WIDTH
At 155 cm (61 in) the production car was 10 cm (4 in) wider than the prototype.

DASHBOARD
This simple early dashboard was never really updated, but the speedo was later moved to the central console.

SPECIFICATIONS
MODEL Morris Minor (1948–71)
PRODUCTION 1,620,000
BODY STYLES Two- and four-door saloon, two-door convertible (Tourer), estate (Traveller), van, and pick-up.
CONSTRUCTION Unitary body/chassis; steel.
ENGINE Straight-four, 918cc, 803cc, 948cc, and 1098cc.
POWER OUTPUT 28 bhp (918cc); 48 bhp (1098cc).
TRANSMISSION Four-speed manual.
SUSPENSION Torsion bar independent front suspension; live-axle leaf-spring rear.
BRAKES Drums all round.
MAXIMUM SPEED 100–121 km/h (62–75 mph)
0–60 MPH (0–96 KM/H) 50+ sec for 918cc, 24 sec for 1098cc.
A.F.C. 12.7–15.2 km/l (36–43 mpg)

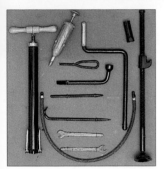

TOOLED UP
A complete original toolkit is a real rarity, a prize companion piece for any owner.

THE SPRUNG-SPOKE STEERING WHEEL IS TRADITIONAL, BUT RACK-AND-PINION STEERING GIVES A CRISP, LIGHT FEEL

MINOR MOTORS
The original 918cc side-valve engine was replaced progressively in 1952 and 1953 by the Austin A-series 803cc overhead valve engine, then by the A-series 948cc, and finally the 1098cc.

UNDER-BONNET SPACE AND EASY ENGINE ACCESS MAKE THE MINOR A DIY FAVOURITE

EVEN ON CROSS-PLY TYRES THE ORIGINAL MINOR WON PRAISE FOR ITS HANDLING; ONE JOURNALIST DESCRIBED IT AS "ONE OF THE FASTEST SLOW CARS IN EXISTENCE"

— BRITAIN'S FIRST MILLION SELLER —

The Morris Minor owes much of its success to the singular vision of one shy man, Alex Issigonis, the Greek-born son of an itinerant marine engineer.

UNDER THE PATRONAGE of Morris vice-chairman Sir Miles Thomas, the young and talented Alex Issigonis, already a respected suspension engineer, was entrusted with the task of developing a small new Morris.

Prototypes of the car that was to become the Morris Minor had already been built in 1943. Back then it was to be called the Mosquito, but the name was abandoned in the run-up to its launch as several other companies claimed rights to the name. Issigonis had wanted a flat-four water-cooled engine and his rear suspension was also compromised, but the car that made its debut at Britain's first post-war motor show, in London in 1948, was still very much his in concept, design, and execution – he had even penned the door handles. The Jaguar XK120 *(see pages 134–35)* was the show-stopper, the car that everyone wanted, but the Morris Minor was the car ordinary people needed. Unusually for a small utility car, its merits were appreciated quite early on, even though

WORLDWIDE MINOR EXPORTS, FROM 1950s SALES BROCHURE

MORRIS
Minor MM
Convertible

MINOR WATERSHED
The split windscreen was replaced by a curved screen in 1956.

BOTH FRONT AND REAR WINGS ARE EASILY REPLACED, BOLT-ON ITEMS

LGO 786

THE FILLET IN THE BUMPER IS ANOTHER SIGN OF THE WIDENING OF THE BODY

The Millionth Minor Rolls off the Production Line

Morris boss Lord Nuffield dismissed the car as a "poached egg".

But there was no stopping the Minor. After its official launch as a two-door saloon and convertible Tourer, a four-door saloon, van, pick-up, and Traveller estate followed, so that in one guise or another the Minor met the needs of every ordinary motorist.

On 22 December 1960, the millionth Minor was made, spawning a limited edition of 349 Minor Millions, painted a sudden lilac and badged "Minor 1000000" on the rear. As the Minor's fortune's dimmed through the Sixties until its eventual demise in 1971, another Issigonis design, the Mini (see pages 40–41), was on the ascendant. The Mini eventually outstripped the Minor's 1,620,000 total to become Britain's best-seller ever, but the Minor will always be remembered as Britain's first million seller and its first "people's car".

Extract from a 1950s French Sales Brochure – "The Best Little Car in the World"

LA PETITE VOITURE LA PLUS AVANTAGEUSE DU MONDE

"Low Lights"

In 1950, the headlights on all Minors were moved to the top of the wings. Earlier models such as the car featured here are now dubbed "low lights".

Starter Handle
Most Minor engines are willing starters, but all models to the end of production came with a starter handle in the tool kit.

Symbols of an ox and a ford represent Morris's home town of Oxford

LGO 786

Issigonis was originally a suspension engineer and independent front suspension is a credit to his genius

Original slimline bumpers later acquired over-riders as the model was updated

NSU *Ro80*

ALONG WITH THE Citroën DS *(see pages 72–75)*, the NSU Ro80 was ten years ahead of itself. Beneath that striking, wind-cheating shape was an audacious twin-rotary engine, front-wheel drive, disc brakes, and a semi-automatic clutchless gearbox. In 1967, the Ro80 won the acclaimed "Car of the Year" award and went on to be hailed by many as "Car of the Decade". Technical pre-eminence aside, it also handled like a kart. But NSU's brave new Wankel power unit was flawed and, due to acute rotor tip wear, would expire after only 24–32,000 km (15–20,000 miles). NSU honoured their warranty claims until they bled white and eventually Audi/VW took over, axing the Ro80 in 1977.

INTERIOR
Power steering was by ZF. Dashboard was a paragon of fuss-free Teutonic efficiency which would later be mirrored by Mercedes and BMW. With no transmission tunnel or propshaft, plenty of headroom, and a long wheelbase, rear passengers found the Ro80 thoroughly accommodating.

TO AVOID OVER-REVVING THE ENGINE, A WARNING BUZZER WOULD SOUND OVER 7,000 RPM

ENGINE HAD TWO SPARK PLUGS PER ROTOR AND BREATHED THROUGH SOLEX TWO-STAGE CARBURETTORS

ENGINE
Designed by Felix Wankel, the brilliant twin-rotary engine was equivalent to a two-litre reciprocating piston unit. Drive was through a torque converter with a Fichel & Sachs electro-pneumatic servo to a three-speed NSU gearbox.

ENGINE POSITION
Engine was mounted on four progressive-acting rubbers with telescopic dampers on each side of the gearbox casing.

CORNERING
The Ro80's stability, roadholding, ride, steering, and dynamic balance were exceptional, and far superior to most sports and GT cars.

NSU Ro80
In 1967, the Ro80 looked like a vision of the future with its low centre of gravity, huge glass area, and sleek aerodynamics. The high rear end, widely imitated a decade later, held a huge, deep boot.

LIGHTS
Hella headlamps give fine night-driving light.

BRAKES
ATE Dunlop with twin circuits and inboard discs at the front.

WHEELS
Stylish five-spoke alloys were optional equipment.

— SPECIFICATIONS —
MODEL NSU Ro80 (1967–77)
PRODUCTION 37,204
BODY STYLE Front-engine five-seater saloon.
CONSTRUCTION Integral chassis with pressed steel monocoque body.
ENGINE Two-rotor Wankel, 1990cc.
POWER OUTPUT 113.5 bhp at 5500 rpm.
TRANSMISSION Three-speed semi-automatic.
SUSPENSION Independent all round.
BRAKES Four wheel discs.
MAXIMUM SPEED 180 km/h (112 mph)
0–60 MPH (0–96 KM/H) 11.9 sec
0–100 MPH (0–161 KM/H) 25 sec
A.F.C. 7 km/l (20 mpg)

PANHARD *PL17 Tigre*

PANHARD WAS ONE of the world's oldest names in car manufacturing, dating back to 1872. But by 1955 they had lost their upmarket image and had to be rescued by Citroën, who eventually bought them out completely in 1965. The Dyna, produced after the war in response to a need for a small, practical and economical machine, had an aluminium alloy frame, bulkhead, and horizontally opposed, air-cooled, twin-cylinder engine.

In 1954, the Dyna became front-wheel drive, with a bulbous but streamlined new body. The 848cc flat-twin engine was a gem and in post-1961 Tigre guise pushed out 60 bhp; this gave 145 km/h (90 mph), enough to win a Monte Carlo Rally. Advertised as "the car that makes sense", the PL17 was light, quick, miserly on fuel, and years ahead of its time.

EFFICIENT DESIGN
Simple design meant fewer moving parts, more power, and more miles to the gallon.

DESIGN
Front-wheel drive ensured stability and safety, with class-leading space for an 848cc car.

ENGINE
The engine design dates back to 1940. Cylinders were cast integral with their heads in light alloy, cooling fins and cast-iron liners. Heads had hemispherical combustion chambers and valve-gearing incorporating torsion bars. Carburettor was Zenith 38 NDIX twin-choke.

STEERING
The steering was rack-and-pinion, with only two turns lock-to-lock and large Bendix hydraulic brakes.

PANHARD PL17 TIGRE
With its aerodynamically shaped body, Panhard claimed the lowest drag coefficient of any production car in 1956. Emphasis was on weight-saving and, despite its quirky Gallic looks, the PL17 was a triumph of efficiency.

INTERIOR
The unusual interior had bizarre oval-shaped pedals, column change, and an unsuccessful pastiche of American styling themes.

SPECIFICATIONS

MODEL Panhard PL17 Tigre (1961–64).
PRODUCTION 130,000 (all models).
BODY STYLE Four-door, four-seater sports saloon.
CONSTRUCTION Separate chassis with steel and aluminium body.
ENGINE 848cc twin horizontally-opposed air-cooled.
POWER OUTPUT 60 bhp at 5800 rpm.
TRANSMISSION Front-wheel drive four-speed manual.
SUSPENSION Independent front with twin transverse leaf, torsion bar rear.
BRAKES Four-wheel drums.
MAXIMUM SPEED 145 km/h (90 mph)
0–60 MPH (0–96 KM/H) 23.1 sec
A.F.C. 13.5 km/l (38 mpg)

PEUGEOT 203

COMPARED TO THE SCORES of upright post-war saloons that looked like church pews, Peugeot's 203 was a breath of fresh air. As well as being one of the French car maker's most successful products, the 203's monocoque body and revolutionary engine set it apart. In its day, the 1290cc ohv power plant was state-of-the-art, with an aluminium cylinder head and hemispherical combustion chambers, said to be the inspiration for the famous Chrysler "Hemi" unit. With a range that included two- and four-door cabriolets, a family estate, and a two-door coupé, the French really took to the 203, loving its tough mechanicals, willing progress, and supple ride. By its demise in 1960, the 203 had broken records for Peugeot, with nearly 700,000 sold.

PEUGEOT 203 AT THE MONTE CARLO RALLY
In the Fifties there were plenty of firms who could give the 203 more urge. Many were tuned and campaigned by privateers in rallies like the Monte Carlo.

TRAFFICATOR
The 203's trafficators were operated by a vacuum from the inlet manifold.

INTERIOR
With post-war steel in short supply, aluminium was used to good effect in the under-dash handbrake and column gear change. The handsome fastback body gave plenty of cabin room.

ROOMY
Clever use of space meant 203 was capacious.

PEUGEOT'S LION BADGE DATES BACK TO 1906, WHEN ROBERT PEUGEOT STARTED UP HIS OWN COMPANY CALLED LION-PEUGEOT

PAINTWORK
A high gloss finish was achieved with several coats of synthetic lacquer.

ENGINE
The 49 bhp ohv pushrod engine was the 203's most advanced feature. With wet liners, low compression ratio, and alloy head, it was smooth, free-revving and long-lasting. The four-speed gearbox is really a three with overdrive. The basic design was still used in the 1980s for Peugeot's 1971cc 505 model.

OAA 950

PEUGEOT 203 CABRIOLET

The 203 Cabriolet turned out as a 2+2 but was originally planned to have a dicky seat. Colours were cheerful pastels instead of dull greys and blacks.

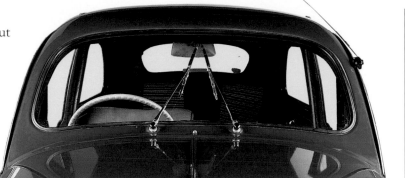

SPECIFICATIONS

MODEL Peugeot 203 (1948–60)
PRODUCTION 685,828
BODY STYLES Two-door coupé, two- or four-door convertible, family estate.
CONSTRUCTION All-steel monocoque rigid one-piece body shell.
ENGINE Four-cylinder OHV 1290cc.
POWER OUTPUT 42–49 bhp at 3500 rpm.
TRANSMISSION Four-speed column change with surmultiplié overdrive.
SUSPENSION Transverse leaf independent front, coil spring rear with Panhard rod.
BRAKES Drums all round.
MAXIMUM SPEED 117 km/h (73 mph)
0–60 MPH (0–96 KM/H) 20 sec
A.F.C. 7–12.4 km/l (20–35 mpg)

WINDSCREEN WIPERS

"Clap hand" windscreen wipers may look a period piece, but the motor was so robust that it was still in use 43 years later on the tailgate wiper of the 504 model.

BUDGET INTERIOR

Interior was built to a budget with rubber mats, metal dash, and cloth seat facings.

SMART DESIGN

The bonnet swings up on counterbalanced springs and the front grille comes away by undoing a butterfly nut.

STYLING

These stylish sweeping curves were influenced by the 1946 Chevrolet.

FUEL FILLER

This was concealed under a flush-fitting flap – unheard of in 1948.

PEUGEOT 203

Widely acclaimed at the 1948 Paris Motor Show, the 203's slippery shape was wind-tunnel tested in model form and claimed to have a rather optimistic drag coefficient of just 0.36 – lower than a modern Porsche 911 *(see pages 194–95)*. Quality touches abound, such as the exterior brightwork in stainless steel and integral mounting points for a roof rack.

BOOT

A vast boot with a low-loading sill made the 203 ideal family transport.

OAA 950

PLYMOUTH *Barracuda*

BACK IN 1964, WHEN Ford's Mustang *(see pages 120–23)* gave its name to a new breed of sporty compact, Chrysler was alongside in the starting gate with its own "pony car", the Plymouth Barracuda, launched for the 1965 model year. Admittedly, Chrysler had hastily revised its Valiant tooling to reach the starting gate in the pony-car stakes, but there is no doubt the Barracuda was a worthy contender. Over the years it grew in stature, and in 1970 really came of age with a complete redesign that was altogether more purposeful-looking. The Barracuda never matched the Mustangs and Camaros *(see pages 66–67)* in sales terms, but attracted a loyal band of followers with its clean, lean looks. It was a brief flowering though, for the Barracuda's fate was sealed when insurance companies took exception to muscle cars and government emission laws started to strangle the performance; the fuel crisis of 1973-74 finished it off once and for all.

INTERIOR
Many ordinary buyers were attracted by Barracuda successes on the NASCAR stock-car circuit and once they had tried out the cockpit, appreciated the "race-bred" features. These included a three-spoke woodrim steering wheel, 150 mph (241 km/h) speedo, and high-backed bucket seats with headrests.

STREAMLINING
Attention to aerodynamics included retractable aerial, streamlined door mirrors, and hidden windscreen wipers.

WIDE DOORS
The huge doors give access to low front-seating and make rear entry manageable.

GO-FASTER PINS
External bonnet pins are a racing-style accessory.

HEMI OPTION
One engine option was the famous Chrysler Hemi, so named for its hemispherical combustion chambers.

OVERHEAD VIEW
From the top the Barracuda could be a different car; compared to its slim and lean side aspect the top view is almost completely rectangular.

SLOPING TAIL
The first Barracudas had a glass-filled roof sloping gently back to the tail. The hardtop option, introduced as part of the 1970 redesign, became more popular.

SHARED SHELL
The Barracuda shared the same bodyshell as another Chrysler pony car, the Dodge Challenger.

PLYMOUTH BARRACUDA

The Plymouth Barracuda range was developed from the Valiant to become Chrysler's prime pony car contender. With its rivals, the 'Cuda shared the then-popular two-door coupé styling on a short-wheelbase chassis. The second-generation cars built, from 1970 to 1974, are favoured by many devotees. This is a top-of-the-range Cuda 440, with the biggest (7.2-litre) engine and special bodywork package. Power and handling options made Barracudas great performers.

NAME ORIGINS
The name came from Plymouth Rock, where the first white settlers landed.

ENGINE
Engine options ranged from "small" six to V8 of seven litres plus. The air cleaner for the triple carbs protruded through the bonnet, and could be seen vibrating; hence the term "shaker hood" for this type of bonnet *(below)*.

PONTIAC *Trans-Am*

THE BIG-HEARTED Pontiac Trans-Am was born in those heady days when America's "big three" (Ford, General Motors, and Chrysler) built bold-as-brass, brawny machines. GM's Pontiac Division, under the dynamic John Z. DeLorean, adopted a sporting image across its whole range in this era. The first Pontiac "muscle car" was the 1964 GTO *(see pages 190–91),* followed in 1967 by the Firebird "pony car". Pontiac raced this in the Trans-Am championship and before long a higher-performance version was put on sale, with go-faster stripes, boot spoiler, and sports cockpit. But the classic Trans-Am was much more, with a stiffened chassis and better brakes to cope with the 350 bhp engine. By the mid-1970s, though, the fuel crisis and American emission laws turned it from a roaring lion into a tame pussy-cat.

HOLLYWOOD STAR
The Trans-Am was a Hollywood favourite, a four-wheeled film star in its own right. One of its biggest roles was in *Smokey and the Bandit*, in which it upstaged Burt Reynolds. The Firebird, on which the Trans-Am was based, was made famous in the television detective series, *The Rockford Files.*

INTERIOR
Leather-rimmed steering wheel, floor-shift, milled dash-panel, and bucket seats make the Trans-Am cockpit about as sporting as that of any American car – even if the seats are vinyl-trimmed.

PONTIAC CALLED THIS INSTRUMENT PACKAGE ITS "RALLY CLUSTER"; IT WAS OPTIONAL ON SOME OTHER PONTIACS

BIG V8s (400 OR 455CID) PROVIDED THE TRANS-AM POWER

AROUND 350 BHP WAS AVAILABLE FROM THE VARIOUS ENGINE OPTIONS, BUT 1973 EMISSION LAWS TAMED THE BEAST

FRONTAL FEATURE
All post-1964 Pontiacs were quickly identifiable from the front by the divided air intake. The 1969–73 "bull-nose" Trans-Am was more attractive front-on than some of its successors, which almost became cartoon pastiches of the original. Early Trans-Ams all came with white paintwork and blue flashes.

PARKING LIGHTS
Front parking lights were a distinguishing feature of the very first Trans-Ams, as the early base Firebird models had none.

TRANS AM

D L R 305 MASSACHUS

PONTIAC TRANS-AM

Clean Trans-Am styling was welcomed by at least some sectors of the American market as a departure from the finned and chromed monsters which still made up the bulk of Detroit production at the time. Family resemblance to other GM "pony cars" of the time, such as the Chevrolet Camaro *(see pages 66–67)* and Pontiac's own Firebird, is clear, sharing their chic Coke-bottle shape.

DEBUT
The first Trans-Ams appeared in 1969, two years after the Firebird.

FIREBIRD
The logo was based on Native American firebird legend; it is often affectionately called "chicken" or even "dead eagle".

FISHER BODYWORK
Fisher was the coachbuilding division of GM; the logo appeared on top-line models.

BULL-NOSE
Post-1973 models were given a more sloping front end.

RACING MIRRORS
Streamlined mirrors were another tell-tale Trans-Am feature.

HIDDEN WIPERS
The Trans-Am's concealed windscreen wipers aided aerodynamic efficiency and enhanced the uncluttered appearance of the whole package.

HARD TOP
Although convertible Firebirds were freely available at the time, only eight rag-top Trans-Am versions were built, all in the first year of production.

LUGGAGE SPACE
Small by U.S. standards, but bigger than most European cars.

REAR VIEW
Another advantage over many European sporting cars was adequate rear visibility.

PONTIAC

TRANS AM

TRANS AM

3055 D
DLR
MASSACHUSETTS

PONTIAC *GTO*

Speak softly and carry a GTO

THE CAR THAT STARTED the whole muscle-car movement was really down to a piece of corporate defiance. When General Motors clamped down on performance cars, Pontiac chief engineer John Z. DeLorean skirted the edict by simple "hot-rod" methods, placing the biggest engine available into their medium-sized Tempest Le Mans range. The GTO immediately hit home, especially in the youth market, and it was the first to offer near-race performance and roadholding in a full-sized car. Americans queued to buy: 207,000 chose the GTO option in the first three years. From the original option package, the GTO was elevated to a separate Tempest model in 1966, and became a model in its own right in 1968. It withered back into the Le Mans range in 1972, but in the course of its joyride, the GTO had created a uniquely American expression of performance motoring.

IMAGES OF ADVERTISING
In this 1966 advertisment, the GTO was described as "A Pontiac in a sabre-toothed tiger skin". Whatever it meant, the GTO upheld Pontiac's recent strong following in the youth market.

INTERIOR
The interior looks more like a speed boat than a car. The Tempest was a six-seater with front bench; Tempest Le Mans, on which the GTO was based, was a five-seater with separate front seats.

WALNUT GRAIN DASH

WIPER MOVE
For the 1968 facelift, disappearing wipers tidied up the scuttle area.

POWER TOP
Apart from the first few, all GTO convertibles came with power-operated top.

GTO NICKNAME
The GTO very quickly earned the nickname of "Goat", as it was agile for its size.

HARD FACTS
In some years pillarless hard-top coupés outsold convertibles by nearly ten to one.

TYRE CHOICE
For many production years, GTO buyers could choose between red-line or white-wall-stripe tyres.

CAPACIOUS
Bowling-alley rear deck enclosed capacious boot.

HEADLIGHTS
Twin lights were horizontal in 1964, then vertical for 1966–67, before reverting to side-by-side format in line with GM design trends.

PONTIAC GTO

While the GTO was by no means a giant in American terms, at a little over 5.18 m (17 ft) it was a step up in size from the "pony cars" of the period. With routine annual updates, GTO spotters can identify model years with ease. The car featured here is from 1966; the grille, different from preceding and following year models, is one giveaway. The slab sides of 1965 now have hip-kink or "Coke-bottle" treatment. After various facelifts, an all-new design appeared for 1970. From 1969 to 1971, the ultimate GTO was the "The Judge", with all top GTO options as standard. They are rare too – only 11,000 were built.

POWER BULGE
Hood scoop in various guises easily distinguished the GTO from the Tempest Le Mans.

SPECIFICATIONS

MODEL Pontiac GTO (1964–1971)
PRODUCTION 497,122
BODY STYLES Two-door, five-seat coupé, hardtop, or convertible.
CONSTRUCTION Semi-unit chassis/body.
ENGINE V8; 326–455cid.
POWER OUTPUT 250–280 bhp at 4700 rpm (326cid); 325 bhp at 4800 rpm (389cid); 335–350 bhp at 5000 rpm (400cid); 360 bhp at 5000 rpm (455cid).
TRANSMISSION Three- or four-speed manual; two-speed automatic.
SUSPENSION *Front:* independent, coil springs. *Rear:* live axle, coil springs, upper and lower trailing arm links.
BRAKES Drums all round, front discs from 1968.
MAXIMUM SPEED 217 km/h (135 mph)
0–60 MPH (0–96 KM/H) 6.6 sec
0–100 MPH (0–161 KM/H) 14.9 sec
A.F.C. 2.8–4.2 km/l (8–12 mpg)

GRAN TURISMO
The GTO name, ("Gran Turismo Omologato"), was hijacked by GM from Ferrari.

ENGINE
GTO engines were always the most powerful in the Pontiac range. This 1966 car has that year's standard GTO 389cid V8 (6.4-litre), pumping out 335 bhp.

PORSCHE *356B*

VOLKSWAGEN BEETLE designer Ferdinand Porsche may have given the world the "people's car", but it was his son Ferry who, with long-time associate Karl Rabe, created the 356. These days a Porsche stands for precision, performance, purity, and perfection, and the 356 is the first chapter in that story. Well not quite. The 356 was so-named because it was actually the 356th project from the Porsche design office since it was set up in 1930. It was also the first car to bear the Porsche name. Post-war expediency forced a make-do reliance on Beetle underpinnings, but the 356 is much more than a Bug in butterfly's clothes. Its rear-engined layout and design descends directly from the father car, but in the athletic son the genes are mutated into a true sporting machine. A pert, nimble, tail-happy treat, the pretty 356 is the foundation stone of a proud sporting tradition.

TRACK RECORD
Here Porsches are seen retro racing at Palm Springs, USA in 1990. The first Porsche 356s distinguished themselves almost immediately with a 1951 Le Mans class win and a placing of 20th overall. Since then, Porsche have always been associated with performance, boasting an enviable track and rally victory tally.

SPLIT-SCREEN DECEIT
On convertibles, the rear-view mirror is attached to a slim chrome bar that gives a deceptive split-screen appearance from the front.

1949 PORSCHE 356
This original incarnation of the 356 has slimmer wheels, split screen, lower bumpers, and is a more bulbous shape.

REDESIGN
On the 356B, headlamps and bumpers moved higher up the wing.

INTERIOR
The interior is delightfully functional, unfussy, un-faddish, and, because of that, enduringly fashionable. Below the padded dash are the classic green-on-black instruments. Seats are wide and flat, and the large, almost vertical, steering wheel has a light feel. Passenger gets a grab handle.

TRANSMISSION LOCK WAS A USEFUL SECURITY FITMENT AVAILABLE ON LATER CARS

SLICK CHANGES
The lever is long, but the patented Porsche baulk-ring synchromesh gives smooth changes with quick and positive engagement.

DYU 40C

EXTRA LUGGAGE
With limited luggage accommodation in the front, the rear rack provides useful extra luggage space.

ACCESS COVER
Not a covered jacking point but an access cover to allow you to retrieve the torsion bar.

BRAKES
Drum brakes gave way to all-round discs with the 356C in 1963.

PORSCHE 356B SUPER 90

The first Porsche 356 was a triumph of creative expediency and inspired engineering, taking basic VW Beetle elements to create a new breed of sports car. Aficionados adore the earliest cars, often affectionately dubbed "jelly moulds", and like a jelly settling on a plate, the shape settled and spread out over the years to become flatter and sleeker.

EXHAUSTS
On the 356B, twin exhausts exit on each side through bumper over-riders.

ENGINE

The rear-engined layout was determined by reliance on VW Beetle mechanicals and running gear. The flat-four engine, with its so-called "boxer" layout of horizontally opposed cylinders, is not pure Beetle, but a progressive development. Engines grew from 1086cc, producing 40 bhp, to 1996cc in the final versions. This is the 1582cc engine of the 1962 356B.

─ SPECIFICATIONS ─

MODEL Porsche 356B (1959–63)
PRODUCTION 30,963
BODY STYLES Two-plus-two fixed-head coupé, cabriolet, and Speedster.
CONSTRUCTION Unitary steel body with integral pressed-steel platform chassis.
ENGINE Air-cooled, horizontally opposed flat four 1582cc & twin carbs.
POWER OUTPUT 90 bhp at 5500 rpm (Super 90).
TRANSMISSION Four-speed manual, all synchromesh, rear-wheel drive.
SUSPENSION *Front*: independent, trailing arms with transverse torsion bars and anti-roll bar. *Rear*: independent, swing half-axles, radius arms, and transverse torsion bars. Telescopic shocks.
BRAKES Hydraulic drums all round.
MAXIMUM SPEED 177 km/h (110 mph)
0–60 MPH (0–96 KM/H) 10 sec
A.F.C. 10.6–12.5 km/l (30–35 mpg)

PORSCHE *Carrera 911 RS*

AN INSTANT LEGEND, the Carrera RS became the classic 911, and is hailed as one of the ultimate road cars of all time. With lighter body panels and stripped out interior trim, the RS is simply a featherweight racer. The classic, flat-six engine was bored out to 2.7 litres and boasted uprated fuel injection and forged flat-top pistons – modifications that helped to push out a sparkling 210 bhp.

Porsche had no problem selling all the RSs it could make, and a total of 1,580 were built and sold in just 12 months. Standard 911s were often criticised for tail-happy handling, but the Carrera RS is a supremely balanced machine. Its race-bred responses offer the last word in sensory gratification. With one of the best engines ever made, an outstanding chassis, and 243 km/h (150 mph) top speed, the RS can rub bumpers with the world's finest. Collectors and Porsche buffs consider this the pre-eminent 911, with prices reflecting its cult-like status, The RS is the original air-cooled screamer.

INTERIOR
Touring or road versions of the RS had creature comforts like sunroof, electric windows, and radio cassette. Large central rev counter and "dog-leg" gear shift are RS hallmarks. Leather seats and steering wheel are non-standard later additions.

RACING 911
The RS outclassed everything else on the track, winning the Daytona 24-hours in 1973 and beating heavyweights like the Ferrari 365 GTB/4.

ENGINE
The bored-out, air-cooled 2.7-litre "Boxermotor" produces huge reserves of power. Externally, it is identifiable only by extra cylinder cooling fins. Internally, things are very different from the stock 911 unit.

WINDSCREEN
Steeply raked screen helps the 911's wind-cheating shape.

GoldStar

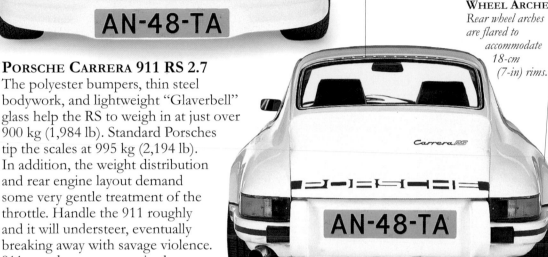

LIGHTS
Classic slanted headlights betray 911's VW Beetle origins.

VENTILATION
Cockpit ventilation is through tiny louvres above the rear window.

WHEEL ARCHES
Rear wheel arches are flared to accommodate 18-cm (7-in) rims.

PORSCHE CARRERA 911 RS 2.7

The polyester bumpers, thin steel bodywork, and lightweight "Glaverbell" glass help the RS to weigh in at just over 900 kg (1,984 lb). Standard Porsches tip the scales at 995 kg (2,194 lb). In addition, the weight distribution and rear engine layout demand some very gentle treatment of the throttle. Handle the 911 roughly and it will understeer, eventually breaking away with savage violence. 911s need great respect in the wet.

INTERIOR
Racing RSs do not even have headlining, sun visors, or sound-proofing.

REAR SPOILER
The RS has a glass-fibre Burzel rear spoiler, fitted to reduce tail-end lift at speed. This boosted the RS's maximum speed by 3 km/h (2 mph).

SPECIFICATIONS

MODEL Porsche Carrera 911 RS (1972–73)
PRODUCTION 1,580
BODY STYLES Two door, two seater coupé.
CONSTRUCTION Thin-gauge steel panels.
ENGINE Flat-six, 2687cc.
POWER OUTPUT 210 bhp at 5100 rpm.
TRANSMISSION Close-ratio, five-speed manual.
SUSPENSION Front and rear torsion bar.
BRAKES Ventilated discs front and rear, with aluminium calipers.
MAXIMUM SPEED 243 km/h (150 mph)
0–60 MPH (0–96 KM/H) 5.6 sec
0–100 MPH (0–161 KM/H) 12.8 sec
A.F.C. 8.1 km/l (23 mpg)

TARGA STAMP
The 911 Targa had a lift-out roof panel and built-in roll bar. But enthusiasts preferred the Beetle-backed lines of the closed 911.

RENAULT-*Alpine A110*

THE RENAULT-ALPINE A110 may be diminutive in its proportions but it has a massive and deserved reputation, particularly in its native France. Although wearing the Renault badge, this pocket rocket is a testimony to the single-minded dedication of one man – Jean Redélé, a passionate motor sport enthusiast and son of a Dieppe Renault agent. As he took over his father's garage he began to modify Renault products for competition, then develop his own machines based on Renault engines and mechanicals. The A110, with its glass-fibre body and backbone chassis, was the culmination of his effort, and from its launch in 1963 went on to rack up a massive list of victories in the world's toughest rallies. On the public roads, it had all the appeal of a thinly disguised racer, as nimble as a mountain goat, with sparkling performance and just about the most fun you could have this side of a Lancia Stratos *(see pages 152–53).*

SAFETY CUT-OUT
External cut-out switches are a competition requirement, allowing outsiders to switch off the engine to prevent fire in an accident.

INTERIOR
Instrument layout is typical of sporting cars of the period, and the stubby gear-lever is handily placed for ease of operation. Getting in and out was not easy though, because of the low roof-line and high sills. Examples built for road rather than race use lacked the racing seats but were better trimmed and were still fun cars to drive.

ALPINE ACTION
The Alpine was most at home in rally conditions and won everything on the world stage, including a staggering 1–2–3 in the 1971 Monte Carlo Rally. The picture shows our featured car on the way to winning the Millers Oils RAC Rally Britannia in November, 1994.

COMPACT SIZE
It is a compact little package just 1.16 m (44.5 in) high, 1.5 m (60 in) wide, and 3.85 m (151.5 in) in length.

MILLERS OILS
RAC International Historic Rally of Great Britain

104

RALLY CAR REGISTER New Crown CARTOONS & ILLUSTRATIONS CLASSIC Boost

LEFT HOOKERS
Sadly for British enthusiasts, the Alpine A110 was only available in left-hand drive.

ENGINE
Myriad engine options mirrored Renault's offerings but, in Alpine tune – by Gordini or Mignotet – really flew. First models used Dauphine engines, progressing through R8 and R16 to R12. This 1967 car sports the 1442cc unit. Engines were slung behind the rear axle, with drive taken to the gearbox in front of the axle.

RENAULT-ALPINE A110 BERLINETTE

Squat, nimble and slightly splay-footed on its wide tyres, the Alpine looks purposeful from any angle. Climb into that tight cockpit and you soon feel part of the car; start it up and there is a delicious barrage of noise. On the move, the sting in the Alpine's tail is exhilarating as it buzzes behind you like an angry insect. The steering is light too, and the grip limpet-like, but when it does let go that tail wags the dog in a big way. Its singular appearance remained intact through its production life, with only detail changes to the trim, which these days is hard to find.

NAME
Cars were known at first as Alpine-Renaults, then became Renault-Alpines as Renault influence grew.

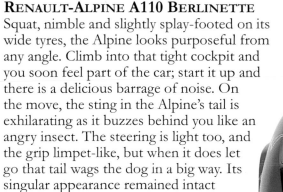

BOOT AJAR
Competition versions had engine covers fixed slightly open to aid cooling.

SPECIFICATIONS

MODEL Renault-Alpine A110 Berlinette (1963–77)

PRODUCTION 8,203

BODY STYLE Two-seater sports coupé.

CONSTRUCTION Glass-fibre body integral with tubular steel backbone chassis.

ENGINE Various four-cylinders of 956 to 1796cc.

POWER OUTPUT 51–66 bhp (956cc) to 170 bhp (1796cc)

TRANSMISSION Four- and five-speed manual, rear-wheel drive.

SUSPENSION Coil springs all round. *Front:* Upper/lower control arms. *Rear:* Trailing radius arms & swing-axles.

BRAKES Four-wheel discs.

MAXIMUM SPEED 212 km/h (132 mph), 1595cc.

0–60 MPH (0–96 KM/H) 8.7 sec (1255cc), 10 sec (1442cc)

A.F.C. 7.6 km/l (27 mpg) (1296cc)

ROLLS-ROYCE *Silver Cloud*

IN 1965, £5,500 BOUGHT a seven-bedroomed house, 11 Austin Minis, eight Triumph Heralds, or a Rolls-Royce Silver Cloud. The Rolls that everybody remembers was the ultimate conveyance of landed gentry and captains of industry. But, by the early Sixties, Britain's social fabric was shifting. Princess Margaret announced she was to marry a divorcee and aristocrats were so short of old money that they had to sell their crumbling country houses to celebrities and entrepreneurs. Against such social revolution the Cloud was a resplendent anachronism.

Each Cloud took three months to build, weighed two tonnes, and had 12 coats of paint. The body sat on a mighty chassis and drum brakes were preferred because discs made a vulgar squealing noise. Beneath the bonnet slumbered straight-six or V8 engines, whose power output was never declared, but merely described as "sufficient". The Silver Cloud stands as a splendid monument to an old order of breeding and privilege.

GEAR SELECTOR
All Clouds were automatic, using a four-speed GM Hydra-Matic box which R.R. used under licence, but made themselves.

DASHBOARD
A haven of peace in a troubled world, the Silver Cloud's magnificent interior was a veritable throne room, with only the finest walnut, hide, and Wilton carpeting.

WIDE REAR THREE-QUARTER PANEL WAS DESIGNED SO REAR OCCUPANTS COULD BE OBSCURED FROM PRYING EYES

ROLLS CLAIMED THEIR CHROME PLATING WAS THICKER THAN ON ANY OTHER CAR IN THE WORLD

LEATHER COMFORT

The rear compartment might have looked accommodating, but Austin's little 1100 actually had more legroom.

QUALITY TOOLS

Every Cloud had a complete tool kit. So obsessed was Rolls-Royce with integrity that they tested every tool to destruction.

STANDARD WALNUT PICNIC TABLES WERE IDEAL FOR CHAMPAGNE AND CAVIAR PICNICS

EVERYTHING ABOUT THE CLOUD'S STYLING WAS ANTIQUE, LOOKING MORE LIKE A PIECE OF ARCHITECTURE THAN A MOTOR CAR

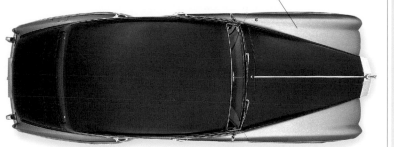

ENGINE

Cloud IIs and IIIs – aimed at the American market – had a 6230cc five-bearing V8 power unit, squeezed into a cramped engine bay. Cloud Is had a straight-six, 4.9-litre engine that could trace its origins back to before the Second World War.

BODYWORK

Standard steel bodies were made by the Pressed Steel Co. of Oxford, England, with the doors, bonnet, and boot lid hand-finished in aluminium to save weight.

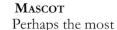

SPECIFICATIONS

MODEL Rolls-Royce Silver Cloud III (1962–65)
PRODUCTION 2,044 Standard Steel
BODY STYLE Five-seater, four-door saloon.
CONSTRUCTION Girder chassis with pressed-steel body.
ENGINE 6230cc five-bearing V8.
POWER OUTPUT 220 bhp (estimate)
TRANSMISSION Four-speed automatic.
SUSPENSION Independent front with coils and wishbones, rear leaf springs and hydraulic dampers.
BRAKES Front and rear drums with mechanical servo.
MAXIMUM SPEED 187 km/h (116 mph)
0–60 MPH (0–96 KM/H) 10.8 sec
0–100 MPH (0–161 KM/H) 34.2 sec
A.F.C. 4.4 km/l (12.3 mpg)

MASCOT

Perhaps the most famous car mascot in the world, the Spirit of Ecstasy graced a German silver patrician radiator shell that took several men five hours to polish.

THE FRONT WINGS LOOKED LIKE THEY WERE SEPARATE FROM THE REST OF THE BODY

DEEPLY RESISTANT TO CHANGE, ROLLS-ROYCE MADE THE CLOUD'S BONNET OPEN SIDEWAYS IN THE BEST PRE-WAR TRADITION

MASCOT WAS ATTACHED BY A SPRING AND WIRE TO DETER SOUVENIR-HUNTERS

—THE NOUVEAU ROLLER—

Launched in 1955, styled like the Albert Memorial, with stone-age mechanicals, the Silver Cloud was old before its time.

THE CLOUD I had a venerable straight-six 4.9-litre engine (conceived as early as 1938), heavy separate chassis, drum brakes, and no power steering. Its post-war engineering survived until the end of the decade, when Rolls were forced to pay lip service to modernity and exchange their antediluvian six for a V8 and make power steering standard. Cloud IIs ran until 1962, when the car enjoyed its first major facelift — a lowered bonnet line and radiator shell,

plus the fitment of voguish twin headlamps as a sop to the all-important American market. But, for those who thought the Cloud's imposing architecture a bit flamboyant, there was the more discreet Bentley S-Series. At £100 less than the Cloud, it was identical apart from the round-shouldered radiator, hub-caps, and badging. But even the Bentley's self-conscious restraint could not

ADVERTISEMENT FOR 1965 ROLLS-ROYCE SILVER CLOUD

ROLLS-ROYCE
Silver Cloud

DOORS WERE SECURED BY THE HIGHEST QUALITY YALE LOCKS

MAX HEADROOM
The roof line was high in the best limousine tradition. Rear passengers had enough room to wear top hats.

ROMAN NUMERALS WERE CHOSEN FOR THE CLOUD III SCRIPT TO LEND AN AIR OF DIGNITY

EEL 800C

GB

Silver Cloud
III

protect it from a changing world.
Previously, Royces had been driven by chauffeurs, but the Cloud was one of the first Rollers to be driven by owners. In the early Sixties, a British film called *Man at the Top* was released, featuring a new breed of thrusting executive at the wheel of a Regal Red Cloud III. The film showed him driving the car himself, filling it up with petrol, even breaking down and picking up hitchhikers. At roughly the same time, John Lennon decided to give his Rolls-Royce Phantom a psychedelic paint job. Both these events triggered a huge change in

JOHN LENNON AND HIS PSYCHEDELIC R.R. PHANTOM

public perception of the Silver Cloud. It instantly slipped a rung on the social ladder, and it was new rather than inherited money that now prised Rolls-Royces from showrooms.
By the late Sixties the Cloud, looking like a prodigious antique, fell rapidly from grace and could be bought from

bomb-site car dealers for a couple of thousand pounds. In the Seventies, many met with a low-rent end, stripped of their haughty Edwardian dignity, whitewashed, ribboned, and harnessed into service as wedding workhorses.

NEW IMPROVED

When the Cloud II was unveiled in 1962, one magazine saw the changes as "more power, more passenger space, better lighting and easier steering".

ON THE VERY LAST CLOUDS, THE REAR-VIEW MIRROR-MOUNTING WAS MOVED FROM THE DASHBOARD TO THE ROOF LINING

TURN INDICATORS WERE MOVED FROM THE FOGLAMP TO THE FRONT WING ON THE CLOUD III

150-WATT 14-CM (5¼-IN) LUCAS DOUBLE HEADLAMPS WERE NECESSITATED BY ONEROUS NORTH AMERICAN SAFETY REQUIREMENTS

EEL 800C

SAAB 99 Turbo

EVERY DECADE OR SO, one car comes along that overhauls accepted wisdom. In 1978, the British motoring magazine *Autocar* wrote, "this car was so unpredictably thrilling that the adrenalin started to course again, even in our hardened arteries". They had just road-tested a Saab 99 Turbo. Saab took all other car manufacturers by surprise when they announced the world's first turbocharged family car, which promptly went on to be the first "blown" car to win a World Championship rally.

Developed from the fuel-injected EMS model, the Turbo had Bosch K-Jetronic fuel injection, a strengthened gearbox, and a Garrett turbocharger. A hundred prototypes were built, and between them they covered 4.8 million kilometres (2.9 million miles) before Saab were happy with their prodigy. Although it was expensive, there was nothing to equal its urge. Rare, esoteric, and historically significant, the mould-breaking 99 Turbo is an undisputed card-carrying classic.

ENGINE
The five-bearing, chain-driven single overhead cam engine was an 1985cc eight-valve, water-cooled, four cylinder unit, with low compression pistons and altered cam timing. The result was 145 bhp and 196 km/h (122 mph).

RALLY BREAKTHROUGH
Stig Blomqvist won the 1977 Swedish Rally and the next year gave the 99 Turbo some serious exposure. He made a thunderous run down Esgair Dafydd in Wales on the first televised rally sprint – with a punctured front tyre.

BODYSHELL
Shell is stiff and light, and a full four-seater. It is remarkably durable too, with factory underseal and cavity wax-injection.

RARE TWO-DOOR
Hatchback three-door versions are the most common 99 Turbo incarnation. The booted, faster and lighter two-door cars are much rarer, with only 1,000 made.

WHEN THE TURBO-BOOST GAUGE NEEDLE SWEPT
UP ITS ARC, ALL HELL WOULD BREAK LOOSE

SPECIFICATIONS

MODEL Saab 99 Turbo (1978–80)
PRODUCTION 10,607
BODY STYLES Two/three/five-door, four-seater sports saloon.
CONSTRUCTION Monocoque steel bodyshell.
ENGINE 1985cc four-cylinder turbo.
POWER OUTPUT 145 bhp at 5000 rpm.
TRANSMISSION Front-wheel drive four/five-speed manual with auto option.
SUSPENSION Independent front double wishbone and coil springs, rear beam axle, coil springs, and Bilstein shock absorbers.
BRAKES Four-wheel servo discs.
MAXIMUM SPEED 196 km/h (122 mph)
0–60 MPH (0–96 KM/H) 8.2 sec
0–100 MPH (0–161 KM/H) 19.8 sec
A.F.C. 9.3 km/l (26 mpg)

INTERIOR
Seventies interior looks a mite tacky now, with red velour seats and imitation wood. Buyers did get a leather steering wheel and heated driver's seat.

STYLING
Never as visually threatening as the Audi Quattro (see pages 32–35), the 99 is pleasantly rounded but unremarkable.

SAAB 99 TURBO

The car appeared at the 1978 Frankfurt Show as a three-door EMS. The body has a certain business-like presence, helped by specially made Inca alloys designed to mimic the shape of turbocharger blades, standard front and rear spoilers, and a sliding steel sunroof. Colours were chosen to be deliberately assertive – only red and black. The chassis was exemplary, with taut, high-speed steering, four-wheel discs, minimal understeer, and incredible levels of grip. Between 65 km/h (40 mph) and 161 km/h (100 mph) it accelerated faster than any other four-seater of its day.

TURBOCHARGER
The turbo is reliable, but its Achilles' heel is a couple of seconds lag on hard acceleration.

HANDLING
99 Turbos were poised. Crisp turn-in came from front-wheel drive, with prodigious adhesion courtesy of 195/60 Pirelli P6s.

COMMON PARTS
Turbo shared most parts with the Saab 99 EMS Saloon. But camshaft valves and pistons were uprated for performance and durability.

SUSPENSION
Independent front suspension was the usual wishbone and coil spring set-up, with a dead beam-axle at the rear.

SIMCA *Aronde Plein Ciel*

BY APING AMERICAN FIFTIES' styling trends and regular face-lifts, Simca metamorphosed from a company building Fiats under licence into France's top privately owned car maker. And the Aronde was the car that turned the tide. Brainchild of Henri-Théodore Pigozzi, the comely Aronde was the first popular French car to have post-war transatlantic lines. Over a 12-year lifespan, 1.3 million Arondes were sold, and by 1955 Simca had overtaken both Peugeot and Citroën. With bodywork by Facel of Facel Vega fame *(see pages 94–97)*, the Aronde was an affordable *haute couture* confection based on run-of-the-mill mechanicals. 1958 saw a complete American-influenced re-style, with engine names such as "Flash Special". Even so, the Aronde is a quaint hybrid that stands as a testament to the penetrating influence of Fifties' Detroit design.

OTHER MODELS
Plein Ciel Coupé and Ocean Convertible were rebodied Arondes, available up until 1963, when the range disappeared in favour of the 1300 and 1500 models.

SIMCA OCEAN
The 1957 Ocean bears a deliberate resemblance to the Ford Thunderbird (see pages 116–17).

DASHBOARD
The Aronde's interior is pure Pontiac pastiche, with no less than six different types of plastic used – the cabin is nothing less than a riot of two-tone synthetic.

THE ARONDE NAME
A delicate, bird-like thing, Aronde is French for swallow.

ENGINE
"Flash Special" had a four-cylinder, 57 bhp push-rod engine bored out to 1288cc, with a Solex carb. Four-speed manual box had obligatory American-style column change.

WHEEL EMBELLISHMENT
Full-width polished chrome hub-caps and wheel trims were an American fad, embraced by European imitators.

WHAT'S IN A NAME?
Plein Ciel ("open air") motif accords with the airy cockpit and generous glass area.

Plein Ciel

SPECIFICATIONS

MODEL Simca Aronde Plein Ciel
(1957–62)

PRODUCTION 170,070 (Facel-bodied
Arondes)

BODY STYLES Cabriolet or fixed head
sports coupé.

CONSTRUCTION Steel body over
separate steel chassis frame.

ENGINE 1288cc four-cylinder push-rod.

POWER OUTPUT 57 bhp at 4800 rpm
("Flash Special").

TRANSMISSION Four-speed manual.

SUSPENSION *Front:* Independent by
coil springs and wishbones.
Rear: Half-elliptic leaf springs.

BRAKES Four-wheel drums.

MAXIMUM SPEED 140 km/h (87 mph)

0–60 MPH (0–96 KM/H) 15.6 sec

A.F.C. 9.9 km/l (28 mpg)

SIMCA ARONDE PLEIN CIEL

The Facel connection is unmistakable; compare the steep wrap-around screen and bubble-like cockpit with the Facel Vega HK500. The finned rear, flowing script on the front wings, liberal use of chrome, and raked rear lights would not look out of place on a 1957 Chevrolet. The moustache-like, chip-cutter grille and recessed sidelamps lend the Aronde an air of class and quality.

HANDLING
The Aronde handled as well as it looked but, because it did not have a blancmange-like ride, the French motoring press disapproved. Despite conventional underpinnings, it felt sporting with positive, if servoless, brakes, and a firmly tied-down chassis.

COLOUR
The Aronde was available in 22 different duotone colour schemes.

SEATING
Despite a sloping rear roof line, the Aronde was just about a four-seater.

REFINEMENTS
"Flash Special" engine had punchier low-range torque, stronger crankshaft and big-end journals, plus an improved lubrication system.

LUGGAGE CAPACITY
The elongated rear meant that the boot was surprisingly ample, even though the high sill meant loading baggage required some serious effort.

MODERNISM
Flush-fitting, lockable petrol filler-flap was surprisingly avant-garde for 1958.

SUNBEAM *Tiger*

THERE WAS NOTHING NEW about popping an American V8 into a pert English chassis. After all, that is exactly what Carroll Shelby did with the AC Ace to create the awesome Cobra *(see pages 22–23)*. When Rootes in Britain decided to do the same with their Sunbeam Alpine, they also commissioned Shelby to produce a prototype and although Rootes already had close links with Chrysler, the American once again opted for a Ford V8. To cope with the 4.2-litre V8, the Alpine's chassis and suspension were beefed up to create the fearsome Tiger late in 1964. In 1967, the Tiger II arrived with an even bigger 4.7-litre Ford V8, but this was a brief swansong as Chrysler took control of Rootes and were not going to sanction a car powered by rivals Ford. Often dubbed "the poor man's Cobra", the Tiger is still a lot of fun to grab by the tail.

SPECIFICATIONS

MODEL Sunbeam Tiger (1964–67)
PRODUCTION Mk1, 1964–67, 6,496; MkII, 571.
BODY STYLE Two-plus-two roadster.
CONSTRUCTION Steel monocoque.
ENGINE Ford V8 4261cc or 4727cc (260 or 289cid).
POWER OUTPUT 164 bhp at 4400 rpm (4261cc), 200 bhp at 4400 rpm (4727cc)
TRANSMISSION Four-speed manual.
SUSPENSION Coil springs and wishbones at front, rigid axle on semi-elliptic leaf springs at rear.
BRAKES Servo-assisted front discs, rear drums.
MAXIMUM SPEED 188 km/h (117 mph) (4261cc), 201 km/h (125 mph) (4727cc)
0–60 MPH (0–96 KM/H) 9 sec (4261cc), 7.5 sec (4727cc).
A.F.C. 7 km/l (20 mpg)

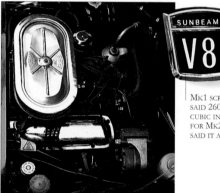

MK1 SCRIPT SAID 260 FOR CUBIC INCHES; FOR MK2, V8 SAID IT ALL

ADAPTED ALPINE
Alpine chassis and suspension had to be beefed up to cope with the weight and power of the V8. Modifications included heavy-duty back axle, sturdier suspension, and chassis stiffening.

STEERING
The Tiger's steering system was rack-and-pinion, as normal Alpine recirculating-ball gear would not fit with the V8 engine. Wood-rim steering wheel was a standard Tiger fitting.

HOT HOUSE
Tigers often suffered overheating, which was not surprising as the Alpine engine bay originally accommodated a 1494cc four-cylinder engine.

RACE BONNET
Race and rally Tigers had improved air-flow with slightly raised bonnet.

ENGINE
The first Tigers used 4.2-litre Ford V8 engines, replaced later – as shown here – by a 4727cc version, the famous 289, but not in the same state of tune as those fitted to the Shelby Cobras.

SUNBEAM TIGER
The MkII Tiger had an egg-crate grille to distinguish it from the Alpine. Earlier cars were less easy to tell apart: a chrome strip along the Tiger's side was the giveaway, together with discreet badging.

OPC 53E

TOYOTA *2000GT*

TOYOTA's 2000GT is more than a "might have been" – it is a "should have been". A pretty coupé with equipment and performance to match its good looks, it pre-dated the rival Datsun 240Z *(see pages 84–87)*, which was a worldwide sales success. The Toyota failed to reach much more than 300 sales partly because of low capacity at its Yamaha factory, but even more because the car was launched before Japan was geared to export. That left only a domestic market, largely uneducated in the finer qualities of sporting cars, to make what they could of the offering. As a design exercise, the 2000GT proved that the Japanese motor industry had reached the stage where its products rivalled the best in the world. It is just a pity not more people were able to appreciate this fine car at first hand.

FASHIONABLE THREE-SPOKE WOOD-RIM WHEEL LINKED TO PRECISE RACK-AND-PINION STEERING

SPEEDO SHOWED AN OPTIMISTIC 250 KM/H (160 MPH)

SHORT-THROW WOODEN-TOP GEAR-LEVER OPERATED A FIVE-SPEED, ALL-SYNCHRO BOX

INTERIOR
The 2000GT's snug cockpit featured a walnut-veneer instrument panel, sporty wheel, stubby gear-lever, form-fitting seats, and deep footwells. The eight-track stereo is a nice period touch.

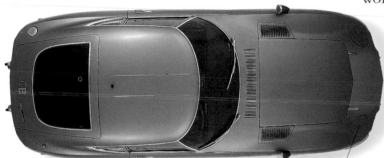

TOYOTA 2000GT
The design of the Toyota 2000 GT is based on an earlier prototype penned by Albrecht Goertz, creator of the BMW 507 and Datsun 240Z. When Nissan rejected the design, it was offered to Toyota and evolved into the 2000 GT.

LIGHTING
Unusual combination of high-tech pop-up and fixed headlights gives the front a fussy look.

YAMAHA ENGINE
The engine was a triple-carb six-cylinder Yamaha, which provided 150 bhp. A competition version boosted output to 200 bhp.

TOPLESS STAR
A modified convertible starred with Sean Connery in the James Bond film, You Only Live Twice.

SIDE BOXES
Panel on the right conceals the battery; on the left is the air cleaner. This arrangement enabled bonnet to be kept low.

SPECIFICATIONS

MODEL Toyota 2000GT (1966–70)
PRODUCTION 337
BODY STYLE Two-door sports coupé.
CONSTRUCTION Steel body on backbone frame.
ENGINE Yamaha inline DOHC six, 1988cc.
POWER OUTPUT 150 bhp at 6600 rpm.
TRANSMISSION Five-speed manual.
SUSPENSION Fully independent by coil springs and wishbones all round.
BRAKES Hydraulically operated discs all round.
MAXIMUM SPEED 206 km/h (128 mph)
0–60 MPH (0–96 KM/H) 10.5 sec
0–100 MPH (0–161 KM/H) 24 sec
A.F.C. 11 km/l (31 mpg)

TRIUMPH *TR2*

IF EVER THERE WAS A SPORTS CAR that epitomized the British bulldog spirit it must be the Triumph TR2. It is as true Brit as a car can be, born in the golden age of British sports cars, but aimed at the lucrative American market, where the Jaguar XK120 *(see pages 134–35)* had already scored a hit. At the 1952 Earl's Court Motor Show in London, the Healey 100 had been transformed overnight into the Austin-Healey, but the "Triumph Sports" prototype's debut at the same show was less auspicious. It was a brave attempt to create an inexpensive sports car from a company with no recent track record in this market segment.

With its dumpy *derriere*, the prototype was no oil painting; as for handling, incoming chief tester Ken Richardson described it as a "bloody deathtrap". An all-new chassis, revised rear, and other modifications saw Standard-Triumph's new TR2 emerge into a winner at the Geneva Motor Show in March, 1953. No conventional beauty certainly, but a bluff-fronted car that was a worthy best-of-breed contender in the budget sports car arena, and the cornerstone of a stout sporting tradition.

OTHER MODELS

The TR2 began a fine tradition of sporting TRs that was only eventually let down by the controversially styled, wedge-shaped TR7 of the 1970s.

TRIUMPH TR3
The TR3 was the first development, with more power and front disc-brakes on later cars. External door handles and lift-off hardtop were options.

TRIUMPH TR3A
The most obvious difference from the TR3 was the full-width grille. The TR3A was produced from 1957–61.

ENGINE

Legend says that the TR2 engine came from a Ferguson tractor – in fact it was developed from a Standard Vanguard engine, as was the tractor's. The twin-carb TR2 version was reduced to just under two litres.

LIKE THE AUSTIN-HEALEY'S, THE TR CHASSIS RUNS UNDER THE AXLE AT THE REAR

STOCK DESIGN

There is nothing revolutionary in the design of the pressed-steel chassis; a simple ladder with X-shaped bracing. It was a transformation, though, from the prototype's original chassis.

SPORTING PROWESS

The car featured on these pages was a "works" competition car, pictured here with its race driver Ken Richardson.

FOR RACING

The TR2 came with small holes drilled in the scuttle to fit aero-screens for racing.

THE TR2 CHASSIS WAS PRAISED FOR ITS TAUTNESS AND FINE ROAD MANNERS

TRIUMPH TR2

The design, by Walter Belgrove, was a far cry from the razor-edged Triumph Renown and Mayflower saloons that he had previously styled. If not beautiful, the TR2 has chunky good looks with a bluff, honest demeanour. Unusual recessed grille perhaps presents a slightly grumpy disposition, but the low front helped the car to top 161 km/h (100 mph). Fittings were spartan – you did not even get external door-handles.

INTERIOR
Stubby gear lever and full instrumentation gave TR a true sports car feel; steering wheel was large, but the low door accommodates vintage "elbows out" driving style.

WINDSCREEN
It looks flat, but the windscreen actually has a slight curve; this prevents it from bowing at speed, which is what the prototype's flat screen did.

LOW-CUT DOORS
You could reach out over the doors and touch the road. External door handles only arrived with the TR3A of 1957.

LUGGAGE SPACE
The prototype had a stubby tail with exposed spare wheel; the production model had a real opening boot and locker below for spare wheel.

OVC 276

— SPECIFICATIONS —

MODEL Triumph TR2 (1953–55)
PRODUCTION 8,628
BODY STYLE Two-door, two-seater sports car.
CONSTRUCTION Pressed-steel chassis with separate steel body.
ENGINE Four-cylinder, overhead valve, 1991cc, twin SU carburettors.
POWER OUTPUT 90 bhp at 4800 rpm.
TRANSMISSION Four-speed manual with Laycock overdrive option, initially on top gear only, then on top three (1955).
SUSPENSION Coil-spring and wishbone at front, live rear axle with semi-elliptic leaf springs.
BRAKES Lockheed hydraulic, drums.
MAXIMUM SPEED 169 km/h (105 mph)
0–60 MPH (0–96 KM/H) 12 sec
A.F.C. 10.6+ km/l (30+ mpg)

OVC 276

SPORTY TRIUMPH
The Triumph sporting tradition was firmly established when TR2s came first and second in the 1954 R.A.C. Rally.

WHEEL CHOICE
The first TR2s came with pressed-steel disc wheels, complete with chromium hub-caps, but most customers preferred the option of wire wheels, considered much sportier.

TRIUMPH *TR6*

To MOST TR TRADITIONALISTS this is where the TR tale ended, the final flourishing of the theme before the TR7 betrayed an outstanding tradition. In the mid-Sixties, the TR range was on a roll and the TR6 continued the upward momentum, outselling all earlier offerings. Crisply styled, with chisel-chin good looks and carrying over the 2.5-litre six-cylinder engine of the TR5, the TR6 in early fuel-injected form heaved you along with 150 galloping horses. This was as hairy chested as the TR got, and a handful too, with some critics carping that, like the big Healeys, its power outstripped its poise. But that just made it more fun to drive.

OTHER MODELS

The TR6 was a natural progression from the original TR2; the body evolved from the TR4/5, the 2.5-litre six-cylinder engine from the TR5.

TRIUMPH TR4
The TR4 of 1961 was the first TR to carry all-new Michelotti-styled bodywork, updated by Karmann into the Triumph TR6.

TRIUMPH TR5
In 1967 the TR5 became the first of the six-cylinder TRs, its 2.5-litre engine going on to power the TR6.

ENGINE

The first engines, as on this 1972 car, produced 150 bhp, but public pressure for something more well-mannered resulted in a 125 bhp version in 1973.

AMERICAN VERSIONS HAD CARBS RATHER THAN FUEL INJECTION AS HERE

INTERIOR

The interior is still traditional but more refined than earlier TRs. Yet with its big dials, wooden fascia, and short-throw gear knob, its character is still truly sporting.

EASY ACCESS

Big, wide-opening doors gave easy access to the TR6, a far cry from the tiny doors of the TR2 and 3.

FAT WHEELS
Wider wheels were a TR6 feature, as was the anti-roll bar at the front.

POWER DROP
Revised injection metering and reprofiled camshaft reduced power from 1973; US carburettor versions were more sluggish (and thirstier) still, but sold many more.

SALES FIGURES
British sales stopped in February 1975, but continued in the US until July 1976. Ten times as many TR6s were exported as remained in Britain.

TRIUMPH TR6
There is an obvious difference between the TR4/5 and the later TR6, restyled by Karmann; sharper, cleaner lines not only looked more modern, but also gave more luggage space. The chopped off tail was an aerodynamic aid. One-piece hardtop was available as an option, and more practical than the two-piece seen on earlier models. The TR6's good looks, and a long production run, made this model the biggest selling of all TR models.

SPECIFICATIONS
MODEL Triumph TR6 (1969–76)
PRODUCTION 94,619
BODY STYLE Two-seat convertible.
CONSTRUCTION Ladder-type chassis with integral steel body.
ENGINE In-line six-cylinder, 2498cc, fuel-injection (carburettors in US).
POWER OUTPUT 152 bhp at 5500 rpm (1969–1973), 125 bhp at 5250 rpm (1973–1975), 104 bhp at 4500 rpm (US).
TRANSMISSION Manual four-speed with optional overdrive on third and top.
SUSPENSION Independent by coil springs all round; wishbones at front, swing-axles & semi-trailing arms at rear.
BRAKES *Front:* discs; *Rear:* drums.
MAXIMUM SPEED 191 km/h (119 mph, 150 bhp), 172 km/h (107 mph, US)
0–60 MPH (0–96 KM/H) 8.2 sec (150 bhp); 9.0 (125 bhp); 10.6 (104 bhp).
0–100 MPH (0–161 KM/H) 29 sec
A.F.C. 8.8 km/l (25 mpg)

ROOMY INTERIOR
The cockpit was more spacious than earlier TRs, providing excellent driving position from comfortable seats.

ENGINE NOISE
Deep-throated burble is still a TR6 come-on.

MERGER
The TR6 was launched just after the 1968 merger of Leyland and BMC.

VOLKSWAGEN *Beetle Karmann*

BEETLE PURISTS MAY WAX LYRICAL about the first-of-breed purity of the original split-rear-screen Bugs and the oval window versions of 1953 to 1957, but there is one Beetle that everybody wants – the Karmann-built Cabriolet. Its development followed that of the saloons through a bewildering series of modifications, but it always stood apart. With its hood retracted into a bulging bustle, this Beetle was not only cheerful, but chic too, a classless cruiser at home equally on Beverly Hills boulevards, Cannes, and the Kings Road. The final incarnation of the Karmann convertible represents the ultimate development of the Beetle theme, with the peppiest engine and improved suspension and handling. This model is from the final year of manufacture, the most refined Bug of all, but still true to its original concept. It's strange to think that once, long ago, the disarming unburstable Bug was a vehicle of fascist propaganda, branded with the slogan of the Hitler Youth, "Strength through Joy". Today, its strength has given joy to millions of motorists as the undisputed people's car.

— OTHER MODELS —
The Beetle has been subjected to a bewildering 78,000-plus modifications through its production life, but has somehow managed to retain its essential character.

VW BEETLE SALOON
This 1131cc Beetle from 1947 shows how the myriad of modifications amount to minor detailing only.

DASHBOARD
The Beetle is still bare, its dash dominated by the one minimal instrument; on this model the speedo incorporates a fuel gauge. It also has a padded dash, replacing the original metal

FOUR-SPOKE STEERING WHEEL IS NOT AS CLASSIC AS EARLIER THIN-RIMMED TWO- AND THREE-SPOKED WHEELS

CURVED "PANORAMIC" WINDSCREEN REPLACED FLAT SCREEN IN 1972

PRODUCTION PLANS
Before Karmann chopped the lid off the Bug, there had been plans for a Beetle-based roadster which in some ways foreshadowed later custom Bugs. The prototypes inspired coachbuilders Joseph Hebmüller & Sons to build a short-lived roadster, but just 696 were built before a factory fire scuppered the project. That left the way for the four-seater Karmann convertible.

ORIGINAL 40-CM (16-IN) WHEELS WERE REDUCED TO 38 CM (15 IN) IN 1952. FRONT DISC BRAKES WERE INTRODUCED IN 1966

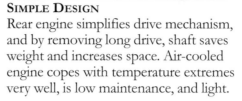

SIMPLE DESIGN
Rear engine simplifies drive mechanism, and by removing long drive, shaft saves weight and increases space. Air-cooled engine copes with temperature extremes very well, is low maintenance, and light.

THE WORLD RECORD FOR A BEETLE ENGINE SWAP IS JUST OVER THREE MINUTES

ENGINE
You can always tell that a Beetle is on its way before it comes into sight thanks to the distinctive buzzing of the air-cooled, horizontally opposed four-cylinder engine. Its capacity grew from 1131cc to 1584cc and the engines have a deserved reputation as robust, rev-happy units.

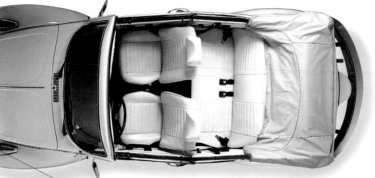

FIRST CARS HAD SEMAPHORES; THEN INDICATORS WERE WING-MOUNTED, AND IN SOME CASES PLACED WITHIN FRONT BUMPERS

SPECIFICATIONS
MODEL VW Beetle Karmann Cabriolet (1972–1980)
PRODUCTION 331,847 (all Karmann Cabriolets from 1949 to 1980).
BODY STYLE Four-seater cabriolet.
CONSTRUCTION Steel-bodied, separate chassis/body.
ENGINE Rear-mounted, air-cooled flat four, 1584cc.
POWER OUTPUT 50 bhp at 4000 rpm.
TRANSMISSION Four-speed manual.
SUSPENSION *Front:* Independent MacPherson strut; *Rear:* Independent trailing arm and twin torsion bars.
BRAKES *Front:* disc; *Rear:* drums.
MAXIMUM SPEED 133 km/h (82.4 mph)
0–60 MPH (0–96 KM/H) 18 sec
A.F.C. 8.5–10.6 km/l (24–30 mpg)

ONE-MODEL POLICY
The one-model policy that VW adopted in its early years was successful while Beetle sales soared, but by 1967 Fiat had overtaken VW as Europe's biggest car manufacturer. VW's new models had failed to displace the Beetle and it was not until 1974 that the Golf and Polo revived the company's fortunes.

ON ALL CABRIOLETS THE ENGINE BREATHES THROUGH SLATS ON THE ENGINE COVER

THE WORLD BEATER

The VW Beetle is one bug they can't find a cure for. Hitler's vision of a "people's car" has become just that and more — the world car to beat all other contenders.

PRODUCED CONTINUOUSLY from 1945, every Beetle that rolls off the remaining Mexican and Brazilian production lines sets a new production record that is unlikely ever to be beaten. With production running as high as 1,000 a day, the Beetle is a 21-million-plus world-beater.

But the Beetle had a long and painful birth. In the early 1930s, Herr Hitler's vision for mass motoring began to take shape when he entrusted Dr Ferdinand Porsche with the project.

1935 TATRA 77

Both Hitler and Porsche were influenced by the fabulous streamlined Czechoslovakian Tatras. Hitler, a keen motoring enthusiast, had ridden in Tatras on political tours of Czechoslovakia. He had often dined with Tatra designer Hans Ledwinka and after one of these dinner-table conversations is reported to have remarked to Porsche, "This is the car for my roads". On Ledwinka, Porsche was reported as saying, "Well, sometimes I looked over his shoulder and

VOLKSWAGEN
Beetle Karmann

FRESH AIR
With the hood raised, the Karmann cabriolet is a bit claustrophobic, but it comes into its own as a timeless top-down cruiser that is still a full four-seater.

CABRIOLETS LIKE THIS CALIFORNIAN-REGISTERED CAR ARE A MAINSTAY OF SURFING CULTURE THE WORLD OVER

KARMANN

COACHBUILDER
As well as the Beetle convertible, Karmann also built the Type 1 VW Karmann-Ghia, a two-seater based on Beetle running gear.

MANY LATER DESIGN CHANGES LIKE THESE "ELEPHANT FOOTPRINT" REAR LIGHT CLUSTERS WERE DRIVEN BY US REGULATIONS

CALIFORNIA
1RWL494

sometimes he looked over mine". There is also no doubt that the Beetle bore a marked resemblance to earlier Tatras, both in shape and concept. In fact, after the war a large out-of-court settlement was made to Tatra. Although the Tatra influenced the Beetle, it served as a departure point for a unique car, developed by Porsche and his team into a machine-age artifact. Some 630 or so Beetles had been made before hostilities disrupted production. Back then, Beetles were propaganda wagons too, named KdF-Wagen, after the slogan of the Hitler Youth, "*Kraft durch Freude*", which

HITLER AND
FERDINAND PORSCHE

means strength through joy. When production resumed in 1945 the Beetle, now a more friendly Volkswagen, gathered an irresistible momentum, notching up 10,000 sales

in 1946, 100,000 by 1950 and a million by 1955. In 1972, it overtook the Model T Ford's production record of 15 million. Today, the amazing story of the world's most popular car is not yet over.

BEETLE PRODUCTION LINE

STATE OF PLAY
Although the Beetle is still in production, Karmann stopped making the elegant cabriolet in 1980. In 1994, combined daily Mexican-Brazilian Beetle production exceeded 1,000 on a good day.

REAR VISION WITH THE HOOD RAISED IS NOT MUCH BETTER THAN ON EARLY SPLIT-SCREEN AND OVAL-WINDOWED MODELS

FROM 1967, THICKER SO-CALLED EUROPA BUMPERS WERE FITTED

VOLKSWAGEN *GOLF GTi*

EVERY DECADE OR SO a really great car comes along. In the Seventies it was the Golf. Like the Beetle before it *(see pages 212–15)*, the Golf was designed to make deep inroads into world markets, yet while the Beetle evolved into the perfect consumer product, the Golf was designed and planned that way. The idea of a "hot" Golf was not part of the grand plan. It came about almost accidentally, the brainchild of a group of enthusiastic Volkswagen engineers who worked evenings and weekends, impressing VW's board so much that the Golf GTi became an official project in May 1975.

Despite its extreme youth, the GTi is as much of a classic as any Ferrari. Its claim to fame is that it spawned a traffic jam of imitators and brought an affordable cocktail of performance, handling, and reliability to the mass-market buyer. Few other cars have penetrated the suburban psyche as deeply as the original Golf GTi, and fewer still have had greatness thrust upon them at such an early age.

INTERIOR
With its dark headlining and trim, the cockpit may be Teutonically austere, but features like the golfball-shaped gear lever add a touch of humour.

ALLOYS
Much admired cross-spoke BBS alloy wheels were both a factory-fitted and after-market option.

SIMPLE FRONT DESIGN
Factory spec Golfs were understated, with just a GTi badge and a thin red stripe around the grille. Owners who wanted to show off would bolt on bodykits, front spoilers, and twin headlamp kits.

REAR VIEW
The Giugiaro-designed Mk I Golf was neat, roomy and compact, admirably predicting the then burgeoning Seventies craze for hatchbacks.

> ### SPECIFICATIONS
>
> **MODEL** *Volkswagen Golf GTi Mk 1 (1976–83)*
> **PRODUCTION** 400,000
> **BODY STYLE** Three-door five-seater hatchback.
> **CONSTRUCTION** All steel/monocoque body.
> **ENGINE** Four-cylinder 1588cc/1781cc.
> **POWER OUTPUT** 110–112 bhp at 6100 rpm.
> **TRANSMISSION** Four- or five-speed manual.
> **SUSPENSION** *Front:* Independent; *Rear:* Semi-independent trailing arm.
> **BRAKES** *Front:* disc; *Rear:* drum.
> **MAXIMUM SPEED** 179 km/h (111 mph)
> **0–60** MPH (0–96 KM/H) 8.7 sec
> **0–100** MPH (0–161 KM/H) 18.2 sec
> **A.F.C.** 10.3 km/l (29 mpg)

VOLKSWAGEN GOLF GTi

GTi suspension was lower and firmer than the standard Golf, with wider tyres and wheels. Front disc brakes were ventilated along with a larger servo, but keeping standard drum brakes at the rear was a big mistake – early Golfs were very disinclined to stop.

WIPERS
Driver's windscreen wiper had a small aerodynamic wing. The faster you went, the more wind pressure pushed the wiper down onto the screen.

ENGINE
Capable of 240,000 km (150,000 miles) in its stride, the 1588cc four-cylinder power unit breathed through Bosch K-Jetronic fuel injection, pushing out 110 bhp. Later cars were blessed with a five-speed gearbox and even more willing 1781cc engines.

ENGINE SUCCESS
Initially, only 5,000 GTis were to be built for racing homologation, but the silky smooth engine and poised handling meant that sales went berserk.

SPOILER
Standard Golfs had a miniature front spoiler. This larger aftermarket BBS add-on makes the car look lower and meaner.

VOLVO *P1800*

THERE HAS NEVER BEEN a Volvo like the P1800, for this was a one-time flight of fancy by the sober Swedes, who already had a reputation for building sensible saloons. As a sports car the P1800 certainly looked stunning, every sensuous curve and lean line suggesting athletic prowess. But under that sharp exterior were most of the mechanicals of the Volvo Amazon, a worthy workhorse saloon. Consequently, the P1800 was no road-burner; it just about had the edge on the MGB *(see page 175)*, but only in a straight line. Another competitor, the E-Type Jag *(see pages 140–43)*, was launched in 1961, the same year as the P1800 and at almost the same price, but there the comparison ends. The P1800 did have style, though, and its other virtues were pure Volvo – strength, durability, and reliability. These combined to create something quite singular in the sporting idiom – a practical sports car.

LUGGAGE
As you would expect, the sensible sports car has a decent-sized boot, although the spare wheel lies flat on the boot floor and takes up space.

INTERIOR
The instrumentation has a real flight-deck feel; revs, oil pressure, and oil temperature are all displayed on a well laid-out dash. Although you are sitting low to the floor, the leather seats are comfortable.

SUPPORTING ROLE
The P1800 is eternally typecast as the "Saint Volvo" after appearing alongside Roger Moore in the long running television series, *The Saint*. The producers actually wanted to use the "sexiest car of 1961", the E-Type Jag; Jaguar declined and Volvo leapt at the chance. Roger Moore drove a P1800 off screen for many years.

JENSEN'S SIGNATURE
Early cars like this were built in Britain by Jensen, identified by Volvo badge on rear pillar.

STEERING
Big, upright vertical wheel looks sporty, with twin spokes seemingly drilled for lightness.

COW HORNS
Attractive cow-horn bumpers became simpler, straight affairs in 1964.

TWO-PLUS-TWO COUPÉ
Space for two toddlers only in the back, or one adult sitting sideways; rear seat folds down flat to increase load capacity.

VOLVO P1800

Official Volvo history credits the award-winning design of the P1800 to Frua of Italy, but it is not as simple as that. In 1957 Volvo approached Ghia to style a two-plus-two coupé and the assignment fell to chief designer Pietro Frua. However, he walked out halfway through, set up his own studio in Turin, and tendered his own proposals; the chosen design was actually penned by young Swede Pelle Petterson, then a trainee at Ghia. The Italian influences are obvious in the final form.

SPECIFICATIONS

MODEL Volvo P1800 (1961–73)
PRODUCTION 47,707 (all models)
BODY STYLES Two-plus-two fixed-head coupé; sports estate (P1800ES).
CONSTRUCTION Unitary steel body/chassis.
ENGINE 1778cc straight four, overhead valves; 1985cc from 1968–73.
POWER OUTPUT 100 bhp at 5,500 rpm (P1800); 124 bhp at 6,000 rpm (P1800E, P1800 ES).
TRANSMISSION Four-speed manual with overdrive/optional automatic.
SUSPENSION *Front:* independent coil-sprung with wishbones. *Rear:* rigid axle, coil-sprung, Panhard rod.
BRAKES Front discs, rear drums.
MAXIMUM SPEED 169 km/h (105 mph, P1800); 185 km/h (P1800 E/ES)
0–60 MPH (0–96 KM/H) 9.7–13.2 sec
0–100 MPH (0–161 KM/H) 31.4–53 sec
A.F.C. 7–10 km/l (20–25 mpg)

ROBUST ENGINE
Early cars had 1778cc four-cylinder units with twin SU carbs, as shown here; the 1985cc unit came later, followed by electronic fuel injection.

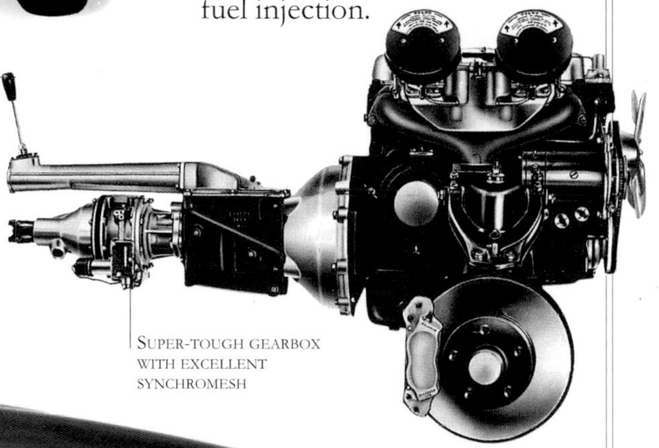

SHORT, STUBBY LEVER GAVE POSITIVE, SHARP CHANGES THAT FELT TRULY SPORTING

SAFETY MEASURES
The P1800 had a padded dash and seatbelts of Volvo's own design.

WHEELS
Stylised fake spokes identify this as an early P1800.

SUPER-TOUGH GEARBOX WITH EXCELLENT SYNCHROMESH

THE INNOVATORS

From ground-breaking design to heroic failure, the following figures have all played their part in the development of some of the classic cars included in this book.

COLIN CHAPMAN *(1928–1982)*
Son of a publican, engineering graduate Colin Chapman founded the Norfolk Lotus company which produced glass-fibre pocket rockets like the trend-setting Sixties Elite and Elan. Lotus won the World Championship and Constructors Championship twice running.

ANDRÉ CITROËN *(1878–1935)*
Known as the French Mr. Ford, André Citroën started producing silent-meshing chevron-toothed gear wheels and went on to build the legendary 2CV, Traction Avant and DS. An innovator rather than an accountant, his company was taken over by Michelin in 1934 and he died a year later.

ENZO FERRARI *(1898–1988)*
Known as *Il Commendatore*, Enzo Ferrari gave his name to one of the most emotive cars in the world. As well as making brilliant cars, he could pick brilliant racing drivers, like Ascari, Fangio

JOHN DELOREAN *(1925–)*
John Zachary DeLorean headed a business empire funded by $500 million of other people's money. His Belfast-built gullwing stainless steel sports car failed along with his company, leaving a paper trail of skulduggery. He was indicted for a $24 million cocaine sting and, after a 63 day hearing, was acquitted.

HARLEY EARL *(1893–1969)*
Harley Earl penned the Cadillac Eldorado, Chevrolet Corvette and Buick Skylark and gave the American car its chromium pomp and ceremony. As General Motors' Chief of Design, he was responsible for the shape of 50 million cars. Few men have had such an influence on man-made objects.

HARRY FERGUSON *(1884–1960)*
Eccentric, irascible and rude, Ferguson built ploughs and tractors and sued Ford for $9¼ million for infringement of patents. His greatest achievement was the incorporation of his four-wheel drive system into the Jensen FF, the world's first successful production four-wheel drive car.

and Lauda. A silver-haired recluse in dark glasses, Ferrari was as passionate and charismatic as the cars he made.

DANTE GIACOSA *(1905–)*
One of Italy's most outstanding designers, Giacosa helped establish Fiat as an Italian national institution. Obsessed with the economies of scale, he came up with the Topolino of 1936, the 600 of 1955 and the 500 of 1957, the first really small cars to be properly refined and the first to be free of the savage compromises of size and usability.

DONALD HEALEY *(1898–1988)*
Donald Healey, a smart-suited bon viveur, designed the rally-winning Austin Healey in his attic at home. The Healey-Austin alliance spawned one of the most successful and charismatic British sports cars of the Fifties and Sixties. After designing the Jensen-Healey, he went into retirement and died in the late Eighties.

LEE IACOCCA *(1924–)*
Originator of the Ford Thunderbird, Iacocca was a marketing genius. He saw a huge vacuum in the American youth market of the Sixties and promptly plugged it with one of the most perfectly conceived consumer products ever, the Pony Mustang.

SIR ALEC ISSIGONIS *(1906–1988)*
Alexander Issigonis, a charming, eloquent and artistic man, conceived the million-selling Morris Minor and that miracle of automotive packaging, the Mini. His basic design philosophy was always

HARLEY EARL ALONGSIDE A PROTOTYPE.

stiff structure, independent suspension, low weight and high torque. He was knighted in 1969.

SIR WILLIAM LYONS *(1901–1985)*
An elder statesman of the British motor industry, Sir William Lyons was an inspirational engineer who single-handedly masterminded the Jaguar phenomenon. From SS100 through XK120, E-Type and XJ6, Lyons was the creator of one of the most admired marques in the world which won Le Mans five years in a row.

HEINZ NORDHOFF *(1899–1968)*
An ex-Opel executive, Nordhoff took over the war-ravaged Wolfsburg Volkswagen factory in 1948. Under his direction the Volkswagen Beetle became the largest-selling single motor car in the world with an estimated quarter of a million people earning their living directly from VW.

FERDINAND PORSCHE *(1875–1952)*
Son of a tinsmith, Porsche was the most versatile car engineer in history, working for Mercedes, Volkswagen, Auto Union and Cisitalia as well as designing the World War II Tiger tank. Despite creating the Beetle, one of the most famous cars in the world, his association with Hitler caused him to be imprisoned for two years by the Allies after the war.

CARROLL SHELBY *(1925–)*
A smooth-talking Texan chicken farmer and race driver, Shelby was responsible for the wild AC Cobra and Shelby Mustang. A firm believer that there was no substitute for cubic inches, he was a seminal figure in the Sixties' American muscle car movement.

INDEX

ACKNOWLEDGMENTS

**DORLING KINDERSLEY WOULD LIKE TO THANK
THE FOLLOWING:**
Helen Stallion for picture research; Mick Hurrell for setting
the editorial ball in motion; Maryann Rogers of production for
overseeing the book in its early stages; Colette Ho for
additional design assistance; Ken McMahon of Pelican
Graphics for a superb electronic retouching job; Gerard
Maclaughlan, Cangy Venables, Tracie Lee, Sharon Lucas and
Annabel Morgan for additional editorial assistance; Daniel
McCarthy for additional DTP assistance; Clive Webster and
Miriam Sharland for additional picture research; Kilian and
Alistair Konig of Konig Car Transport for vehicle
transportation and invaluable help in sourcing cars; Steve at
Trident Recovery; Jenny Glanville at Plough Studios; Ashley
Straw for assisting Matthew Ward; Garry Ombler, Andy
Brown and Sarah Ashun for assisting Andy Crawford; George
Solomonides for help with sourcing images; Antony Pozner at
Hendon Way Motors for helpful advice and supply of nine cars;
Phillip Bush at Readers Digest, Australia for supervising the
supply of the Holden; Derek Fisher; Bill Medcalf; Terry
Newbury; John Orsler; Paul Osborn; Ben Pardon; Derek
Pearson; Peter Rutt; Ian Smith; John Stark; Richard
Stephenson; Kevin O' Rourke of Moto-technique; Rob Wells;
Colin Murphy; Bill McGarth; Ian Shipp; Jeff Moyes of AFN
Ltd; Rosie Good of the TR Owners Club; Bob and Ricky from
D.J. Motors; Acorn Studios PLC; Straight Eight Ltd; Action
Vehicles of Shepperton Film Studios and John Weeks of
Europlate for number plate assistance; and Peter Maloney for
compiling the index.

DORLING KINDERSLEY WOULD LIKE TO THANK THE FOLLOWING FOR ALLOWING THEIR CARS TO BE PHOTOGRAPHED:

Page 20 courtesy of Anthony Morpeth; p. 22 A J Pozner (Hendon Way Motors); p. 24 Louis Davidson; p. 26 Richard Norris; p. 28 Brian Smail; p. 30 Desmond J Smail; p. 32 David and Jon Maughan; p. 36 restored and owned by Julian Aubanel; p. 38 courtesy of Austin-Healey Associates Ltd, Beech Cottage, North Looe, Reigate Road, Ewell, Surrey, KT17 3DH; p. 40 Tom Turkington (Hendon Way Motors); p. 42 courtesy of Mr Willem van Aalst; p. 46 A J Pozner (Hendon Way Motors); p. 50 Terence P J Halliday; p. 52 L & C BMW Tunbridge Wells; p. 54 "57th Heaven" Steve West's 1957 Buick Roadmaster; p. 56 Stewart Homan, Dream Cars; p. 58 Garry Darby, American 50's Car Hire; p. 62 Benjamin Pollard of the Classic Corvette Club UK (vehicle preparation courtesy of Corvette specialists D.A.R.T Services, Kent, UK); p. 66 car owned and restored by Bill Leonard; p. 68 on loan from Le Tout Petit Musée/Nick Thompson, director Sussex 2CV Ltd; p. 70, 72 courtesy Classic Restorations; p. 76 Derek E J Fisher; p. 78 Daimler SP 250 owned by Claude Kearley; p. 82 Steve Gamage; p. 84 Kevin Kay; p. 88 D Howarth; p. 90 Lewis Strong; p. 92 Neil Crozier; p. 94 owned and supplied by Straight Eight Ltd (London); p. 104, 106, 108 A J Pozner (Hendon Way Motors); p. 105 Dr Ismond Rosen; p. 110 by kind permission of J A M Meyer; p. 112 Janet & Roger Westcott; p. 114 Stu Segal; p. 116 Teddy Turner Collection; p. 118 Stewart Homan, Dream Cars; p. 120 Max & Beverly Floyd; p. 124 Bell & Colvill PLC, Epsom Road, West Horsley, Surrey KT24 6DG, UK; p. 128 Gordon Keeble by kind permission of Charles Giles; p. 132 David Selby; p. 134 Jeff Hine; p. 136 c/o Hendon Way Motors; p. 140 owner Phil Hester; p. 144 John F Edwins; p. 146 privately owned; p. 148 A R J Dyas; p. 150 courtesy of Ian Fraser, restoration Omicron Engineering, Norwich; p. 152 courtesy of Martin Cliff; p. 154 Geoff Tompkins; p. 158 owner Phillip Collier, rebuild by Daytune; p. 160 Alexander Fyshe; p. 162 Edwin J Faulkner; p. 164 Irene Turner; p. 170 Mrs Joan Williams; p. 172 courtesy of Chris Alderson; p. 174 John Venables; p. 175 John Watson, Abingdon-on-Thames; p. 176 Martin Garvey; p. 178 E.J. Warrilow saved this car from the scrapyard in 1974; restored by the owner in 1990, maintaining all original panels and mechanics; winner of many concourse trophies; p. 182 NSU Ro80 1972 David Hall; p. 183 Panhard PL17 owned by Anthony T C Bond, Oxfordshire, editor of "Panoramique" (Panhard Club newsletter); p. 184 Nick O'Hara; p. 186 Alan Tansley; p. 188 owner Roger Wait, Backwell, Bristol; p. 190 courtesy of Peter Rutt; p. 192 owner Mr P G K Lloyd; p. 194 c/o Hendon Way Motors; p. 196 Richard Tyzack's historic rally Alpine; p. 198 owned by Ian Shanks of Northamptonshire; p. 202 David C Baughan; p. 204 Julie A Lambert (formerly Julie A Goldbert); p. 206 Peter Matthews; p. 207 Lord Raynham of Norfolk; p. 208 E A W Holden; p. 210 Brian Burgess; p. 212 Nick Hughes & Tim Smith; p. 216 Roy E Craig; p. 218 Kevin Price, Volvo Enthusiasts' Club.

PHOTOGRAPHIC CREDITS

t= top b= bottom c=centre l= left r=right a= above

All photography by Andy Crawford and Matthew Ward except:
Linton Gardiner: pp. 64–65, 114–115
National Motor Museum: pp. 11t, 13b, 167c, b
Nick Goodall: pp. 15br, 22cr, 38c, 79tl, tr, 118r, 128t, 132t, 135tc, 166tl, tr, 167t, cr, 168cr, 180t, 181tr, 185c, 190tr, 195cr, 206cr, 208cr, 222–23, 224
Clive Kane: 130–31

PICTURE CREDITS

AC Cars: 8t. Adams Picture Library: 56tr. Advertising Archives: 8b; 54cl; 118tr; 135tr; 200tr, b; 223t. Aerospace Publishing: 3; 48tl, tr, cl, cr; 48–49; 49tl, cl, cr; 76tr, cr; 76–77; 77tl, tr, cl, crb; 90tl, tr, cl, cr; 90–91; 91t, cr, crb, 94cl, cr; 94–95; 95t, cl, cr, crb; 96c, b; 97b; 102t, cl, crb; 103tl, tr, c, b; 138t, 138tl, ca, cb; 138–139; 139tr, cl, cr; 145t, cra, clb, crb, b; 148c; 148tr; 148–149; 149tl, tr, cl, cr; 166cl; 167cla, crb; 168b; 169b; 207cl, cr, b. Allsport: 2; 123tr; Allsport/Mike Pavell: 192tr. Art Directors: 137cb. Autosport Photographic 35tr; Doug Baird: 40cl, b. Bell & Colvill 125tl; BMW : 50tr; 52tr. British Film Institute: Back to the Future/Copyright © by Universal City Studios, Inc.Courtesy of MCA Publishing Rights, a Division of MCA Inc. All Rights Reserved, 88tr Neill Bruce: 9t; 20bl; 26cr; 30tr; 44t; 66tr; 70tl; 79t; 106tr; 107crb; 110tr; 142tl; 176tr; 208t; 224b. Neill Bruce/Peter Roberts Collection 14t; 37br; 38cr; 45t; 60c; 61tl, c; 70tl; 80t; 86t; 87tl; 168tl; 169tl, tr; 215tr. Classic and Sportscar: 141clb; 155c. Ford Motor Company: 114cb; 127tr. General Motors/Pontiac Division: 190tr. Gordon Keeble Cars: 128t. Ronald Grant Archive: The Living Daylights/Danjaq 31cr; Pink Cadillac/Malpaso 59cl; Bullit/Warner Brothers Pictures 92tr; Smokey and the Bandit/Raspar 188tr. Haymarket Publishing: 12c; 28tr; 94tr. David Hendley: 177cr. Eddy Holden: 208clb. Hulton Deutsch Collection: 81t; 97t; 215tl; 220tr. Jaguar Cars: 143cr. LAT Photographic: 126tr. Ludvigsen Library: 42c; 85tr; 123tc; 140ct; 202c; 214t. Mathewson Bull: 213tr. Mercedes Benz: 166tl, tr; 167t, cr; 168cr; 222b. Don Morley: 35tl; 87tr; 162tr. National Motor Museum/Motoring Picture Library: 9b; 22tr; 26tr; 47c; 50cr; 58tr; 62bl; 64bl; 70tr; 73tl, crb; 79cl; 80c; 81c, 96t, 98tr, cr; 99cra; 101tl; 104cra; 113cr; 114bl; 121ct; 122tr; 123tl; 126c; 136cl; 139tl; 152tr; 156t; 166–167; 167cl; 181tl; 182cra; 184tr; 192cr; 194ca; 204tr; 210tr, cra. Peugeot: 185ca; 221b; Phillip Porter: 142tr. Popperfoto :124cl. Quadrant Picture Library: 10t; 11b; 12t; 17b; 18b; 26cl; 34t; 62tr; 74t; 75t; 76cl; 91cl; 112tr; 127c; 140tr; 143tl; 157tl, tr; 182 cla; 198tr, cr; 208cra; 212tl, tr. Readers Digest: 130tl, tr, ct, cl, cr; 131tl, tc, ca, cb, b. Rex Features: 100t; 101tr; 168tr; 201tr. Triumph: 15br; 208crb. Richard Tyzack: 196c. Volvo UK Ltd: 218cr; 219cb. Matthew Ward: 10b; 12b.

NOTE

Every effort has been made to trace the copyright holders. Dorling Kindersley apologizes for any unintentional omissions and would be pleased, in such cases, to add an acknowledgment in future editions.